Working in
Higher Education

D0266933

SRHE and Open University Press Imprint
General Editor: Heather Eggins

Working in Higher Education

Edited by
Rob Cuthbert

The Society for Research into Higher Education
& Open University Press

Published by SRHE and
Open University Press
Celtic Court
22 Ballmoor
Buckingham
MK18 1XW

and 1900 Frost Road, Suite 101
Bristol, PA 19007, USA

First Published 1996

Copyright © The editor and contributors 1996

All rights reserved. Except for the quotation of short passages for the purposes
of criticism and review, no part of this publication may be reproduced, stored
in a retrieval system, or transmitted, in any form or by any means, electronic,
mechanical, photocopying, recording or otherwise, without prior permission
of the publisher or a licence from the Copyright Licensing Agency Limited.
Details of such licences (for reprographic reproduction) may be obtained from
the Copyright Licensing Agency Ltd of 90 Tottenham Court Road, London,
W1P 9HE.

A catalogue record of this book is available from the British Library

ISBN 0 335 19721 3 (pb)   0 335 19722 1 (hb)

Library of Congress Cataloging-in-Publication Data

Working in higher education / edited by Rob Cuthbert.
     p.   cm.
   Includes bibliographical references and index.
   ISBN 0–335–19722–1 (hdb)   ISBN 0–335–19721–3 (pbk)
   1. College teaching—Great Britain.   2. Education, Higher—Great
Britain.   I. Cuthbert, Robert E.
LB2331.W64   1996
378.1′25—dc20   96–25915
                                                              CIP

Typeset by Graphicraft Typesetters Limited, Hong Kong
Printed in Great Britain by St Edmundsbury Press Ltd, Bury St Edmunds, Suffolk

Contents

Acknowledgements

The editor of a book drawing on many disciplines must acknowledge the truth of Herbert Simon's proposition that almost anything in the world can be discovered after four or five telephone calls; if the first person doesn't know, then he or she can nevertheless give you the name of someone who knows more, and so on. So it was in compiling this book, and I am grateful to the many who received my telephone calls, reframed my questions and redirected my enquiries.

Heather Eggins and Oliver Fulton of SRHE provided the advice and support needed at an early stage. John Skelton at Open University Press gave wise counsel throughout. I was fortunate that Jennifer Bone, Chair of SRHE's Research and Development Committee, was also a colleague readily able to advise as the book took shape, and the SRHE's 1996 Conference Committee chaired by Derek Winslow was a valuable sounding board.

Judith Stewart demonstrated the truth of Chapter 7's arguments by providing imaginative, enthusiastic, professional librarian support.

Peggy Tovey typed and retyped, converted many formats to one, rescued corrupted disk files, chased tardy contributors, became fluent in Open University Press house style and probably read more of the book in draft more often than anyone should ever have wished.

Finally, when seeking authors it is always wise to give the job to someone who is already fully occupied. I am grateful to all the contributors for so willingly agreeing to add to their many other commitments to 'working in higher education'.

Rob Cuthbert

Notes on Contributors

Michael Bradford is Head of Department of Geography at the University of Manchester. He was Dean for Undergraduate Studies in the Faculty of Arts for four years (1992–6). His research concentrates on the geography of education and urban policy evaluation. He has written texts for first-year university and A level, and he is the chair of examiners for a new A level syllabus. He was the higher education representative for geography on the Slimming of the National Curriculum.

Sheila Corrall is Librarian of the University of Reading. She has worked in public, national and academic libraries as an information specialist, manager and consultant, specializing in strategic planning, service quality and human resource management. She has served on many national committees and working parties of government and professional bodies. Her publications include *Strategic Planning for Library and Information Services*.

Rob Cuthbert is Assistant Vice Chancellor at the University of the West of England, Bristol. He has worked as an academic and as a manager in old and new universities, colleges of further education and higher education, local and national government, and as an education management consultant in Europe, North America, Africa and China. His books include *Going Corporate*, the handbook for managers in new HE and FE corporations.

Sara Delamont is Reader in Sociology at the University of Wales, College of Cardiff, where she has worked since 1976. She is the author of *Knowledgeable Women*, *Appetites and Identities* and *Fighting Familiarity*, and was the first woman President of the British Educational Research Association in 1984.

Oliver Fulton is Professor of Higher Education at Lancaster University, where he works in the Centre for the Study of Education and Training. In his work for the Society for Research into Higher Education he has held several offices, including Chair of the Society in 1996–7. His research interests centre on the adaptation of higher education institutions and their staff to changing external demands, including projects on access to higher education, vocationalizing higher education (enterprise and work-based learning), how universities cope with uncertainty in government policy and an international survey of the academic profession.

Frank Hartle is a Director of Hay Management Consultants, where he leads the performance management expertise area. He has worked with public and private clients in Europe, the USA and Africa. He has also worked in secondary schools as a geography teacher and was an education officer in two county councils. He is the author of *How to Re-engineer the Performance Management Process* and *The Performance Management Guide for Schools* (with the National Association of Head Teachers), and contributed to *Competency-based Human Resource Management* (with Alain Mitrani, Murray Dalziel and David Fitt).

Ron Johnston is Professor of Geography at the University of Bristol, where he specializes in political and electoral geography. He was previously Vice Chancellor of the University of Essex and Pro Vice Chancellor for Academic Affairs at the University of Sheffield. Before his appointment as Professor of Geography at the University of Sheffield in 1974 he held posts at Monash University, the University of Canterbury and the University of Toronto. His books include *Geography and Geographers, Anglo-American Human Geography since 1945, Nature, State and Economy, The Political Economy of Environmental Problems* and (with P. J. Taylor and M. J. Watts) *Geographies of Global Change: Remapping the World in the Late Twentieth Century.*

Ewart Keep is a senior research fellow in the Industrial Relations Research Unit, Warwick Business School. He has published work on UK training policy, training for the unemployed and for the low-paid, personnel management systems for the teaching profession and personnel management in higher education.

Ray Lester is Director of Information Systems at the London Business School. He has worked in universities and in industry as an information scientist, systems analyst, librarian and manager, specializing in electronic information and networked services. He has lectured and written on many aspects of strategy and policy in academic library and information services, and is the author of *Information Sources in Finance and Banking.*

Ian McNay has a degree in English, which he tries to use whenever possible. The first 25 years of his professional life seemed to be organized round committee meetings, first as a relatively silent administrator, later as a less silent academic member. That experience was based in Scotland, England, Belgium and Spain, and he has worked around the world. He is now giving up committees and, as displacement therapeutic activity, heads the Centre for Higher Education Management at Anglia Polytechnic University where he leads research and organizes bespoke development workshops on topics which include Decision-making and Committee Skills.

Helen Murlis is a leading reward specialist and Head of Central Government/Agency consulting at Hay Management Consultants. Her experience has included reward strategy reviews for many major clients in both the public and private sectors, as well as providing detailed advice on remuneration and performance management issues from the shopfloor to the boardroom. She has also acted as expert adviser to the OECD on reward strategy development. With Michael Armstrong, she is co-author of *Reward Management*, the standard UK text on salary policy development and practice. With Derek Pritchard (another Hay senior director), she is co-author of *Jobs, Roles and People – the New World of Job Evaluation*. Between 1992 and 1994 she was IPM Vice President – Pay and Employment Conditions.

Brian Ramsden is the Chief Executive of the Higher Education Statistics Agency. Before embarking on the establishment of the agency in 1993, he was for many years an administrator in UK universities, and developed an interest in and concern about the availability of consistent and objective management information about higher education in the UK. He was a member of the Joint Performance Indicators Working Group established by the Higher Education Funding Councils of the UK, and sits on the steering groups of a number of research projects in the HE sector.

Keith Sisson is Director of the Industrial Relations Research Unit, Warwick Business School. Before entering an academic career, he was Labour Secretary of the Newspaper Publishers' Association. He is the author of *The Management of Collective Bargaining*, and editor of *Personnel Management in Britain* and *Personnel Management: a Comprehensive Guide to Theory and Practice in Britain*.

John Storey is Professor of Human Resource Management at the Open University Business School, and a former member of the Industrial Relations Research Unit at Warwick. He is one of the leading writers on both the theory and practice of human resource management, and his books include *Managing Human Resources and Industrial Relations* (with Keith Sisson), *Developments in the Management of Human Resources* and *Blackwell Cases in Human Resource and Change Management*. He is editor of the *Human Resource Management Journal*.

Marie L. Thorne is a principal lecturer in organizational behaviour at Bristol Business School. Working as a consultant and researcher, she has been involved in a wide range of activities and organizations, including a national pilot programme for senior women managers and a regional programme for NHS clinical directors. Her main interest is in strategic management and the management of cultural change, working primarily with senior managers of professional organizations in both the public and private sectors. Her publications include *Interpersonal Skills for Women Managers* (with Rennie Fritchie), a widely used facilitators' handbook.

Gaby Weiner has been involved in education at a number of levels: as a parent, primary school teacher, researcher, course developer and lecturer in higher education. Currently she is Professor of Educational Research at South Bank University, London. She has published widely, in particular on social justice issues in education, writing and editing a number of books and research reports. Her most recent publications are *Equal Opportunities in Colleges and Universities* (1995, with M. Farish, J. McPake and J. Powney) and *Educational Reforms and Gender Equality in Schools* (1996, with M. Arnot and M. David).

Richard Winter is Professor of Education at Anglia Polytechnic University. He worked for many years in teacher education, developing courses for post-qualifying professional development based on an action research process (described in *Learning from Experience*), and is currently engaged in similar work with nurses and social workers. For five years recently, he worked on the development of a competence-referenced practice-based honours degree, the ASSET Programme, the topic of his recently published book *Professional Competence and Higher Education* (with Maire Maisch).

Introduction

1

Working in Higher Education

Rob Cuthbert

For many people 'work' is something you do after leaving higher education. Students enter 'the world of work', and lecturers may be exhorted to enter the 'real world' or to 'get a proper job'. With the growing pressures on hard-working higher education staff and students worldwide, this odd prejudice is increasingly irritating to those within higher education. However, the implicit restriction on the concept of work is even compounded by many already working in higher education. Consider, for example, the preconceptions which led Brennan *et al.* (1995) to call their European survey of links between universities and the wider employment community *Higher Education and Work*.

Work, says *Chambers Dictionary* (1993), is 'physical or mental effort directed towards making or achieving something'. On this definition students, because they are most numerous, do most of the work in higher education, but this book is not about them. On student work, see Haselgrove's (1994) *The Student Experience*, a book which is in some respects a sister volume to this one. In a complementary way, *Working in Higher Education* addresses the staff experience in and of higher education. It offers a set of chapters aiming to inform, stimulate and encourage new ways of looking at the phenomenon of working in higher education. For purposes of definition, then, we must return to *Chambers*, which goes on to define work as 'employment'. With the increasing fluidity of higher education (HE) employment modes and patterns, not all staff are employees, and not all those employed in higher education are staff. Nevertheless, the concepts of staff and employment perhaps suffice to identify an intelligible theme for the process of enquiry which this book attempts.

How should we try to comprehend 'working in HE'? Some ways of understanding are familiar, perhaps even unduly familiar. Staff development, for example, is not so much well trodden ground as completely trampled underfoot, so that one can sometimes look in vain for the green shoots of new meaning in 'new' writing from this perspective. Themes and perspectives in the higher education literature, such as quality and equal opportunities, despite their enduring weight and significance, also some-times offer a relatively low return on the effort needed to keep up to date.

At the same time, some perspectives remain surprisingly undeveloped, or pursued only by a brave handful of pioneers, who open up a territory not yet colonized by a significant community of academic settlers. Consider, for example, the work of Becher (1981, 1989) and Evans (1988, 1993) on disciplinary and academic cultures, offering new theoretical directions that are still largely underdeveloped.

Other perspectives exhibit the imperialistic ambitions of disciplinary perspectives everywhere, in asserting their superior explanatory power or assuming a breadth which they cannot justify. Smyth's (1995) treatment of academic work, for example, aims 'to bring the issue of academic work out of the closet and to subject it to the kind of discussion, analysis and debate it so desperately deserves' (Smyth, 1995: 1–2). However, the pre-dominance of a Braverman-inspired labour process perspective in that analysis, while justified by the book's subtitle – *The Changing Labour Process in Higher Education* – denies the rather bolder claims of its preamble.

Thus, when we consider the staff experience of working in higher edu-cation, we confront a mixture of unduly familiar and unduly strange per-spectives, which combine to tell us less than they claim, and less than we should know. Multiple perspectives clamour for attention. Synthesis would be reductionist, illusory or overweeningly ambitious – and out of keeping with a postmodern multivocality. But that should not be an excuse for lack of an attempt to make sense. So this introduction offers a map, or a set of maps, to help the reader navigate through the book and around the phe-nomenon of working in higher education from a variety of perspectives.

Disciplinary perspectives on working in higher education

To illuminate the staff experience of working in HE, which perspectives are most useful? This was the question I faced as editor when beginning to construct this volume. My answers are reflected in the book's contents, but they are to a considerable extent a contestable personal choice. My choice was driven by one major consideration. Mindful of the perils of the unduly familiar, noted above, I aimed especially to include relatively novel ways of thinking about working in HE. In some cases I invited leading exponents within particular disciplines to apply their disciplinary understanding to the HE context, with the intent of casting light from a new direction, thus creat-ing new highlights – and new shadows – in the HE landscape. In others I sought contributors who would go beyond what their discipline had pre-viously offered to an understanding of HE, perhaps by focusing it on rela-tively new problems, or using it to analyse future possibilities. Another kind of contribution came from leading professionals and practitioners, who applied their professional or managerial expertise to particular aspects of

HE work. The book in total therefore aims to illustrate, without of course exhausting, the enormous variety of ways in which we can meaningfully interpret working in HE, to encourage further research, study and debate.

A glance at the disciplines embraced by any large university is enough to show how narrowly selective the study of higher education has been in its perspectives. It may perhaps be true that the physical sciences can make a more limited contribution to our understanding of working in HE than the social sciences. However, we should beware of easy generalizations. The built environment in which higher education work proceeds is no doubt a specialist study among those who teach and research in civil engineering, construction, town planning and surveying, and emergent disciplines such as urban design and facilities management. Town planners have perhaps done most to bring their discipline's insights to the wider attention of those in HE, as exemplified in the Committee of Vice Chancellors and Principals' (CVCP, 1994) public discussions of links between universities and their communities. Yet still relatively little of their specialist knowledge becomes visible outside the disciplines; for example, the annual conferences and publications of the Society for Research into Higher Education have rarely if ever broached such topics as a subject for study. At the same time, the built environment metaphors of the 'Ivy League' and the 'redbrick' university are commonplace, offering intriguing pointers to an undeveloped seam of potential insight into the workings of higher education.

In similar vein, there is much that could be known more widely about the visual environment for work in HE, and the designed world it inhabits. Again, specialist studies within the disciplines of art and design have rarely breached the boundaries of the community of researchers into higher education. Since that community is made up primarily of social scientists, we might perhaps begin to excuse them, were it not for the fact that even within the ranks of the social sciences some are notable by their absence in, or their relative lack of contribution to, our understandings of HE.

In general, the phenomenon of working in higher education demands a multidisciplinary approach for its illumination. We need to select from a wide range of, in particular, social science perspectives, not least because many of the salient issues in HE, like most real world problems, do not fall neatly into one disciplinary category. Consider, for example, modularization and semesterization, and the questions they pose in terms of epistemology, psychology/learning theory, sociology/social interaction, political science/ organizational politics, economics/resource allocation and so on – as Billing's (1996) case study shows. There is, of course, nothing new in the call for a multidisciplinary perspective. Clark's (1984) explicit aim to assemble a variety of disciplinary perspectives on HE drew on history, politics, economics, organizational theory, sociology, culture, science and policy studies. However, there remain apparently large gaps in the response of the HE research community to this evocation of the possibilities.

From among the social science perspectives available to interpret working in HE, I will briefly consider the potential contributions of geography, history, politics/political science, sociology, economics, anthropology, psychology, organization theory and management, especially human resource management. These are a personal choice of the disciplines with much to offer the study of working in HE.

Geography has been particularly neglected as a source of understanding of HE phenomena. While much has been written about the distribution of HE institutions, the multicampus university, distance learning and other overtly geographical phenomena, very little has actually been written by geographers within their own disciplinary perspective. Yet the discipline might have a great deal to say about, for example: when, how and why distance learning succeeds; the driving forces behind the mid-1990s rash of 'new new university' initiatives in places, such as Swindon, Cornwall, Lincoln and the Scottish Highlands, without a major higher education institution; the limits of workability of multicampus universities and regional networks of higher and further education institutions; and so on.

History has been less neglected, but remains under-exploited in research into HE. Institutional histories, for example, could inform a wider audience than the institution itself. Locke's (1978) history of Woolwich Polytechnic showed, in its elaboration of the thesis of 'academic drift', how historical perspective can contribute to a wider understanding of HE policy and institutional development in changing the nature of working in HE. Biography and social history might offer similarly rich insight, but Gronn's (1983) call for educational administration to adopt extended biography as a fruitful source of new understanding has, it seems, been largely ignored. At a wider level, careful historical studies, such as that by Sharp (1987) of the creation in England of a local authority sector of HE, have been relatively rare. There seems little doubt that the study of the history of higher education could offer more than it has so far delivered to illuminate working in HE.

Politics and political science are altogether better represented in the study of HE (see, for example, Kogan, 1984; Johnson, 1994). The question of how order and control are maintained in HE institutions and systems, and issues of academic democracy, academic freedom and governance, are well represented in writing and thinking about the experience of working in higher education. Marketization, commoditization and other concepts born in a Thatcherite age, and increasingly deployed to interpret HE contexts, either spring from or may be well illuminated by a predominantly political perspective.

Similarly, sociology has always been well represented in writings about higher education. The sociology of the professions, the literature on social mobility and status, the study of credentialism and competences, labour process analyses and others within a sociological frame of reference have made significant contributions to our understanding. However, classic studies such as Halsey and Trow's (1971) survey of British academics have exerted perhaps too much continuing influence on thinking about the nature and structure of the academic profession and its work, despite Halsey's (1982, 1987) later work. Clark (1987a, b), who has also made a massive contribution to analysis of the academic profession, observed of North America that 'the greatest paradox of academic work in modern America is that most professors teach most of the time, and large proportions of them teach all the time, but teaching is not the activity most rewarded by the academic profession nor most valued by the system at large' (Clark, 1987a: 98–9). Halsey's European perspective on the same phenomenon described the evolution of higher education in terms of phases, first priestly, then aristocratic, through professional, to democratic. His patrician conclusion was: 'We need universities for the scholarly few and higher education, pluralistically funded, for everyone' (Halsey, 1987: 341). The academic world has changed, and the sociologists have interpreted those changes, but academics' perceptions of their world, and the world's perception of academics, struggle to keep up.

Rice (1992) has suggested a way forward by developing a model recognizing distinctive types of scholarship of teaching, practice, discovery and integration. However, in putting forward his broader model of scholarship, Rice also recognizes 'that what is being proposed challenges a hierarchical arrangement of monumental proportions – a status system that is firmly fixed in the consciousness of the present faculty and the academy's organizational policies and practices' (Rice, 1992: 126). Nevertheless, models such as this are urgently needed to illuminate emergent phenomena, such as the accelerating differentiation of work roles in the new HE.

In similar vein, Abbott's (1993) review of the literature of the sociology of work argues that structural analysis, which is, he says, less common than studies at an individual level, too often treats structural phenomena as static aggregates rather than dynamic and emergent. In a conclusion which this book echoes and responds to, Abbott says: 'By far the most exciting study of culture and work concerns the imagining of work itself ... It is absolutely certain that analysis of the culture of work will be one of work and occupations' major future topics' (Abbott, 1993: 203).

This view supports the choice of anthropology as a key discipline for enhancing the understanding of working in HE. The 'imagining' of work is a task to which anthropologists are well suited, disposed as they are to interpret cultures by examining behaviour and meaning. Becher (1989) and others have shown the way towards analysis of disciplinary cultures, but much remains to be done. For example, it is too readily asserted or taken for granted that academic disciplines are in effect worldwide organizations, independent of national culture. However, Hofstede (1991) has developed a characterization of national cultures and traced their impact on the cultures of organizations within the national cultural milieu. However strong the disciplinary culture may be, there is much work to be done in exploring the impact of national culture on the nation's HE institutions and their work.

What workers in higher education do has changed and continues to change rapidly; consequently there have been many changes in the workforce, both in terms of the participation by different groups and in terms of differentiation of roles and functions. It would be unwise to assume that what work means to the people who do it has not changed too. Anthropology could make a major contribution to our understanding of these changes, as later chapters in the book demonstrate.

Economists could also cast fresh light on the same phenomenon of differentiation of work roles, via analysis of the changing production function in HE. Staff might likewise benefit from a much wider appreciation and recognition of the massive increases in productivity which have been achieved during the 1980s and 1990s. However, the discipline of economics has always been well represented in the HE literature, as Williams (1984) exemplifies. The time may be ripe for some old themes to be revisited in the modern context, such as the links between investment in higher education and economic growth and employment. Such studies might appear at first to offer little to an understanding of working in higher education, but if conceived as micro- rather than macro-economic studies, addressing local and regional economic contexts as much as national ones, then they offer potential for illuminating and reconstruing both the work and the work contexts of many HE staff.

For example, impact studies such as that by Taylor (1990) identify and analyse the major importance of universities as an element in the local economy. Pratt (1987) has shown how economic analysis can inform our understanding of institutional responses to resource constraint and the use of performance indicators. I have argued elsewhere (Cuthbert, 1987) that an economic perspective on organization and management could transform our understanding of the concept of efficiency, and shows that the efficiency of markets as a form of regulation is contingent on the norms prevailing and the information available in the organization. Mackintosh *et al.* (1994: 339) use an economic perspective to explore the 'dilemmas' in managing higher education institutions as 'hybrids . . . organizations which both provide tax-supported services and rely on income from the commercial market.' The ability of an economic perspective to illuminate HE work contexts remains substantially under-exploited.

Psychology offers similarly rich possibilities. The potential of the discipline for understanding and analysing the consequences of the appraisal and performance management movement has probably not yet been realized. Concepts such as motivation, job satisfaction, reward and career are also now beginning to reappear in topical guise in studies of stress in academic life such as Fisher (1994) and Bradley and Eachus (1995). Clearly, psychology as a focus of enquiry can play a leading part in helping to illuminate the staff experience.

The familiar role of organization theory in studies of HE has already been alluded to, but it also offers relatively new (to HE) perspectives, such as organizational culture. However, in research into HE, cultural studies have tended to be true to the anthropological origins of the concept, exploring the deep structures of HE as professional subcultures rather than the managerial manipulability of corporate culture as a variable, to use Smircich's (1983) distinction between culture as a perspective on and a property of organizations. Notwithstanding the limitations of the managerial view of corporate culture, there is room for cultural studies of HE organizations both within and beyond the managerial paradigm, to complement the work of Becher (1989) on disciplinary cultures, Evans (1988, 1993) on disciplinary communities and Clark (1987a, b) on academic life and the academic profession.

In contrast, the literature on management in higher education is broad, if not always deep. The managerial perspective has almost certainly been over-represented in studies of the experience of working in higher education. In North America, an academic perspective on management, the start of its golden age perhaps signalled by Rourke and Brooks's (1966) declaration of *The Managerial Revolution in Higher Education*, has been sustained and sustainable because of the widespread existence of formal postgraduate programmes of study, and thus bodies of scholars, of HE management. In contrast, the more pragmatic British approach was heralded rather later by Fielden and Lockwood's (1973) handbook, *Planning and Management in Universities: a Study of British Universities*. That more pragmatic tradition has in turn been sustained by the momentum of political and institutional change without a critical mass of scholars and students of HE management *per se* to develop a broad-based academic commentary.

However, the steady growth of scholarship and formal programmes of study in this field in the UK has in the 1990s begun to fuel expansion of the horizons of the British literature. In particular, human resource management is 'a term . . . in increasing use in respect of higher education management across Europe' (Partington, 1994: 1). Warner and Crosthwaite's (1995) collection could justifiably claim to be the first British volume devoted to a human resource management perspective on higher education, albeit still largely within the pragmatic tradition that emphasizes practitioner accounts rather than original discipline-based inquiry. Kogan *et al.* (1994) might claim rather higher academic ground in the same territory, while vigorously rejecting any 'managerialist' label. Equivalent firsts, drawing on such disciplines as marketing, operations management, industrial relations or even accounting to analyse HE contexts, have yet to appear.

This brief *tour d'horizon* shows both the range of contributions to the study of working in higher education and the unexplored potential of many disciplines to take this study further. These disciplinary perspectives are the first set of maps to aid navigation around the multifaceted theme of working in higher education. To them will be added a simple set of categories, derived from a rudimentary systems perspective which aims to support understanding without unduly distorting it. The categories provide headings for the book's main sections: 'The workers', 'The work' and 'The work context'.

The structure of the book

To make the territory of the book rather more accessible, it is divided into three parts, like Gaul, but without making in this division any Gallic claims to exactness in terms of clear boundaries, mutual exclusivity of the parts or otherwise. The three parts deal with 'The workers', 'The work' and 'The work context'. These are foci for attention, intended to help organize thinking and understanding, but not purporting to create watertight analytical compartments.

In the remainder of this introduction a consideration of these three foci will be interwoven with an appreciation of the disciplinary perspectives discussed above, to explain the selection of particular topics and treatments in the book's main chapters. It will also aim to account for, if not justify, some of the more notable omissions.

The workers

Thinking about the workers in higher education prompts a series of initial questions, in particular who works in HE, and why? This immediately leads to demographic questions: how many; how old; what balance between the sexes; what mix of ethnicity? Such questions would ideally consider all categories of staff, but data about support staff are patchy and in many cases non-existent; here there is another fruitful field for further research.

In the early 1990s a recognition of the shortcomings of available data about British higher education led to the creation of a new national Higher Education Statistics Agency (HESA), which itself was forced to confront these demographic questions in developing its own statistical database about staff in higher education. In Chapter 2, 'Academic staff: information and data', Brian Ramsden, Chief Executive of the new agency, examines what we may hope to know about academic staff in HE and how such knowledge can be achieved, with reference to the HESA experience of developing a new kind of database. He explains why HESA too was driven to begin by developing data on academic staff, and considers the limitations of the information thus available, alongside the first analysis of the data gathered by HESA.

The new availability of this database to researchers into higher education, thanks to explicit planning by HESA and the Society for Research into Higher Education, offers a rich source of reliable and consistent information about workers in British HE. More broadly, the HESA experience, and the choices made in constructing its database, may also illuminate study in other national systems. The Carnegie Commission has sponsored a major international survey of academic work and the academic profession, and the emerging findings of that survey are considered further in Chapters 12 and 13, described below.

Following close behind the establishment of a staffing database come questions about motivation, contracts and rewards, whether psychological, legal, financial or social. These questions are represented here by two chapters. In the first, Ewart Keep, John Storey and Keith Sisson, three leading academics in human resource management, turn the attention of their discipline on higher education. Chapter 3, 'Managing the employment relationship in higher education: quo vadis?', explores the different ways in which people are engaged as workers in HE, recent trends and their implications. Drawing on best practice in human resource management in a range of public and private sector contexts, the authors develop a powerful critique of management in higher education for its neglect of human resources management knowledge and its failure to adopt a sufficiently well informed and strategic approach to the management of higher education's most important resource.

This failure is perhaps all the more surprising in the light of the trade unions' articulation of the case for a different approach, which Keep, Storey and Sisson identify. The fact that there is no shortage of public expressions of such trade union views is part of the explanation for not including a trade union perspective among the chapters of the book: the primary aim here is to stimulate new thinking rather than to provide a platform for the rehearsal of already familiar arguments. Furthermore, Smyth's (1995) *Academic Work* offers extensive coverage of HE work seen from the point of view of the worker, and many chapters in this book also draw on such perspectives.

Turning to the question of individual motivation and reward, a perspective from outside HE is provided by Helen Murlis and Frank Hartle of Hay Management Consultants, known individually and corporately for their distinctive competence in the field of reward systems and managing performance. Their analysis in Chapter 4, 'Does it pay to work in universities?', draws on trends in reward systems in both public and private sectors and how they affect HE. They address explicitly the need to consider both the economic and the psychological contract, and how to balance intrinsic and extrinsic rewards through financial and non-financial rewards. Coupled with a review of how jobs, roles and performance criteria are changing, this leads to identification of critical issues for the development of pay policy and how universities need to develop 'pay literacy' to promote effective working.

A dynamic rather than static approach to these questions leads into consideration of career patterns and trajectories. For the relatively narrow literature on career, the field of higher education seems to have been largely a no-go area, save for the occasional foray by personnel officers (e.g. Palmer, 1989). One explanation is offered by Keep and Sisson (1992: 75): 'the notion of career in higher education, in the sense that it exists in other organizations that manage their individual employees' development and progression, is almost totally lacking.' Alternatively, we might suppose that alternative approaches, such as the study of the academic profession, have appeared to offer more to illuminate the working experience of staff who, until relatively late in the twentieth century, tended to develop without moving between organizations, or even between jobs. However, as times changed so the need emerged for a more dynamic modelling of changes in individual work experiences over time. Some of this has come with exhaustive research and debate about equality of opportunity, or the lack of it, in higher education employment. The growth of attention to equal opportunities in

HE (see, for example, Bagilhole, 1993; Farish *et al.*, 1995) has been such that the topic features in this book as a recurrent theme rather than as a separate chapter heading.

Human resource management might also have delivered new ideas about career, but that perspective has already been extensively mined in earlier chapters. Balance demands a different perspective, one which begins as much from a worker's as a manager's perspective, and aims to examine the experience of the majority, rather than to misrepresent the experience of a few as the norm defining 'career'. In this spirit, Gaby Weiner asks in Chapter 5, 'Which of us has a brilliant career? Notes from a higher education survivor'. She examines the concept of career, and how it reflects both personal choice and structural constraint. A broad view of all kinds of workers in higher education inevitably raises questions about equal opportunity, the different balance between men and women in different kinds of work in higher education and the disproportionate representation of ethnic minorities in lower-paid and lower-status work roles. Weiner's analysis connects these questions with the changing nature of academic work, and sets the scene for later chapters, where this becomes a central focus. In conclusion, she writes autobiographically about her own experience of working in higher education, showing the power of personal account in making academic analysis come to life.

Ideas about career are closely connected with ideas and issues about staff development. The central importance of developing higher education's key asset, its staff, means that the literature on staff development is voluminous. This explains, though it will not justify for every reader, the editorial decision not to include a chapter dedicated explicitly and primarily to staff development in this volume. For recent surveys of the field, see Zuber-Skerritt (1992) and Brew (1995).

In remarkable contrast to the proliferation of work on the development of the workers, there have been relatively few academics who have sought to examine their own work, and even fewer the work of their colleagues in support services, as a topic of study. Such study is overdue not least because old ideas about academic work persist and co-exist with contrasting work experiences, as McInnis (1992: 12) argues: 'Perhaps it is time to reassess the appropriateness for all academics of the "dominant fiction" of the academic as the cosmopolitan research scientist, and introduce – not revive – a broader image of scholar for the profession.'

The work

Smyth (1995: 1) makes the point that academic work is surprisingly undeveloped as a field of enquiry. Blau's (1973) magisterial if rather dry sociological/organizational analysis remained too solitary for too long as an attempt to address explicitly the nature of academic work, as a literature search rapidly confirms. Furthermore, much of the work in higher education is not academic work, and is not done by academics. There is more to working in higher education than what lecturers, readers, researchers and professors do.

While the work of leaders and managers has also received considerable attention – see, for example, Middlehurst (1993) – there has been relatively little attention paid in the literature to the increasingly diverse contributions of staff who work as librarians, information scientists and technologists, teaching and research assistants, demonstrators, instructors, technicians, course managers, departmental administrators, accountants, surveyors, personnel officers, porters, cleaners, kitchen assistants and in a host of other administrative, professional, technical, clerical and manual roles.

For a better understanding of the phenomenon of working in higher education we should therefore ask: what is the nature of the work and how is it accomplished? What is the range of work roles which staff occupy? What trends can we identify in how the spectrum of roles is changing? How is the balance changing between: permanent and temporary contracts; normative and calculative rewards; academic and support roles; cosmopolitan and local orientations; and so on?

Academic work is unusual, though not unique, as an activity explicitly seeking to generate new understandings and new knowledge. Teaching and facilitating learning is inherently open-ended, albeit apparently increasingly circumscribed by the demands of accountability, quality assurance and student consumerism. Research is by definition a process of enquiry without predictable outcomes. Academic institutions are also unusual as organizations in being wholly devoted to such open-ended pursuits, which begins to justify an emphasis on academic work as the prime focus of study. Certainly, narrow objectives-based approaches to understanding university operation (e.g. Norris, 1978) may capture little of the real substance of work in HE, while in contrast more open-minded studies of university organization have spawned distinctive theories, such as the garbage can model of organizational choice (Cohen *et al.*, 1972) and the organized anarchy model of organization and management, stressing the importance of handling ambiguity in academic leadership (Cohen and March, 1974).

The work of teaching and promoting learning has, of course, been exhaustively studied and analysed. While there have been times in the development of the literature when one has felt lost in a desert of curriculum theory, nevertheless the centrality of teaching and learning means that curriculum change is always a contemporary issue. With recent reviews such as that of Barnett (1992), there is no need for repetition in this book, which aims instead to analyse some recent trends, especially in the new universities in England, which point towards possible major shifts in the work of teaching and learning.

Leading this investigation, Richard Winter writes in Chapter 6 of 'New liberty, new discipline: academic work in the new higher education'. His chapter considers three important phenomena in academic work: modularization, competence-based curricula and the accreditation of work-based learning. He explores ideas about order and control in academic work organizations, aiming to go beyond both the closed ideological interpretations of a narrow labour process view and Barnett's (1990) attempt to develop a new conception of liberal education. Locating universities in the debate about 'modern' organizations and identifying epistemological shifts, he urges an optimistic view of the possibilities for new academic formats. These, while imposing new forms of control and new discipline – in more than one sense – also create new liberties for academic workers to maintain a critical stance as the defining feature and fundamental duty in their work.

For Winter, then, reports of the death of academic freedom have been greatly exaggerated. Where Fielden (1975) once claimed to discern the 'decline of the professor, and the rise of the registrar', it might now be more appropriate to speak of 'the redefinition of the professor, and the rise of the professionals'. The growing role of librarians, information scientists and computing services, and the differentiation and specialization of tasks in delivering modular learning programmes, are in many colleges and universities redefining and highlighting the role of 'lecturers' as designers, guides and assessors, as much as deliverers, of increasingly individualized and student-centred learning programmes.

These changes are the focus of study for Sheila Corrall and Ray Lester in Chapter 7, 'Professors and professionals: on changing boundaries'. They explore the changing boundaries of responsibility for different areas of work in universities, and the professionalization and specialization of support services. Written by two senior library/information professionals, the chapter identifies critical issues in the provision and resourcing of academic support services. The authors address a series of key questions facing HE institutions and offer their views on the way forward, in response to the impact of information technology on patterns of academic work and service delivery, the blurring of work boundaries and convergence of operations, and the changing customer base.

The key questions they identify include the following. What is the contribution traditionally sought from and offered by 'professional' library, information and computing services? How is the electronic imperative changing the mix of 'professional' inputs needed? What is the impact of different institutional missions and subject mixes? Are merged library and computing services inevitable and/or desirable? How critical are these services to institutional success?

In conclusion, the chapter considers whether there can be a generic model to which all HE institutions' information services should aspire, to what extent information services should assume a proactive role in setting institutional objectives and priorities, and how institutions can determine appropriate levels of resource allocation in relation to competing demands.

Corrall and Lester's authoritative account of trends in learning support shows how the individualization of increasingly student-centred learning programmes evokes complex institutional responses, not least the rapid differentiation and specialization of work roles. These potentially far-reaching changes emerged in English higher education as it finally completed its transition, in Trow's (1992) terms, from an elite to a mass system, with participation by 30 per cent or so of 18-year-olds, and began to contemplate the next stage of development towards 50 per cent participation in a universal system. The inevitable resource pressures accompanying such expansion have accelerated the innovation in teaching and learning which might otherwise not have achieved such momentum.

In an apparent paradox, the massive 'efficiency gains' which have been achieved in the expansion of the English HE system in the 1980s and 1990s have been accompanied by an explosion of pressure for increased accountability and more and different quality control, assurance and audit, in a movement which has in fact been experienced worldwide. The paradox is easily dissolved by a recognition that increasing resource pressures and growing societal commitment to higher education inevitably bring new external pressures for accountability. Nevertheless, the growth of the 'quality industry' has been perceived by HE staff as adding significantly to the pressure under which they work. Tierney and Rhoads (1995: 108) argue that the accountability movement has reinforced a culture of assessment, in which 'Assessment, then, might be seen as a tool of control where managers exert more authority, and academic labour becomes deskilled and less powerful.' If McInnis (1992: 10) is right to argue that 'self-regulation in daily work practices stands out – regardless of teaching or research orientation – as the most distinctive feature of academic work and one of the most attractive aspects of the job', then it follows that increased external control and accountability directly diminishes what academics most value. However, the book will explore this proposition rather than take it for granted. It will perhaps take some time before the opportunities, as well as the costs, of the quality movement become clearer. Given the burgeoning literature on quality, this book has avoided the temptation to add to it with a chapter dedicated to that theme. There was perhaps a stronger case for including – though space precluded it – an explicit treatment of ethics in higher education, both because of the changes in work roles and participation patterns, and because of the as yet uncharted effects of increasing pressure of work in HE.

Pressures are felt equally strongly in the research and teaching domains, although they may manifest themselves in different ways. The open-endedness of research enquiry brings with it particular pressures of time management. Ron Johnston addresses this theme, drawing on his experience both as teacher/researcher and as vice chancellor in Chapter 8, 'Managing how academics manage'.

He identifies the key problem for individual academics as how to carve out and protect the 'quality time' that is crucial if the tasks of teaching and research are to be well done. Their ability to do so is constrained, most of all by the size of the tasks that they are given. It follows that, at institutional level, management of academic activity involves winning and allocating the resources which enable individual staff to manage their own time effectively. In a climate of increasing pressure on resources, and increasing competition for the scarce resources that exist, his chapter recasts and reframes the classic argument that the route to excellence in university performance is through appointing the best people and giving them the right working conditions. Only this, he argues, will enable them to succeed by consistently delivering unpredictable outcomes.

An alternative and equally longstanding view of academics' time management is that it exhibits an excessive concern for process. Caricatures of academic life are as old as universities themselves, as is witnessed by Cornford's (1908) classic elucidation of the rules of academic life, such as the 'Principle of the wedge' – of which any new initiative may be the thin end, and hence is dangerous and should be avoided. Almost a century later, the caricature was alive and well in Laurie Taylor's weekly commentaries in the *Times Higher Education Supplement* on academic life at the University of Poppleton.

In a modern, *a fortiori* a postmodern, collection of writings about work in higher education, it would have been odd to disregard 'what everyone knows' is a defining feature of university work: the committee. Yet a straightforward academic analysis of committees and their role in higher education work would not tempt many readers to devote their 'quality time' to it. The book, therefore, offers something different. Ian McNay rose to the challenge to provide an 'alternative' view of 'Work's committees' in Chapter 9. Informed by sources as diverse as Shattock and Shakespeare, with 'When shall we three meet again?' exposed as simply an Elizabethan agenda item, his chapter offers an irreverent guided tour of committee people, performance and purposes.

Adapting Parkinson's Law, we might argue that in higher education the number of meetings expands to fill the time available. Whether or not as a consequence, for many workers in HE the time available is not confined to the hours spent on campus. Working in HE can pose a strong challenge to the boundary between 'work' and 'home' life, a boundary which many academics regard as at best highly permeable. Such considerations lead inevitably to consideration of the work context.

To lead towards the last major section of the book, Michael Bradford offers an account of 'Geographical transitions' in Chapter 10. His chapter offers a case study of one area of HE work, the changes in geography education. It examines two interfaces: those between secondary and higher education, and between higher education and subsequent graduate employment. In so doing the chapter begins to rectify the under-representation of geographical perspectives in the study of HE *per se*. It also provides a substantive account of one significant area of HE work and how it has changed, with reference to generic concerns, including the changing backgrounds of students entering HE, the impact of the National Curriculum and national subject cores in schools, the pressures for a common core in HE and the changing graduate labour market.

The stage is thus set for an examination of context: where is higher education work accomplished, and how does the context influence the work? These questions are the focus for the next section.

The work context

The discussion so far has tended to emphasize the disciplinary context of higher education work. In shaping context, disciplines are of course highly significant. In the case of academics, for whom ideas are the tools of the trade, it should not be surprising that 'the attitudes, activities and cognitive styles of groups of academics representing a particular discipline are closely bound up with the characteristics and structures of the knowledge domains with which the groups are professionally concerned' (Becher, 1989: 20). The disciplinary context is so significant that it can transcend national cultural boundaries. In Becher's (1989: 22) elegant metaphor, 'disciplines provide a carrier wave on which the signals of distinctive national groups are modulated.'

The argument above was that there is much greater scope for using the idea of culture to enrich the study of higher education. Becher (1994) has shown how this perspective may be applied at every level, from the academic profession as a whole to the subdisciplinary specialism. The starting point for a cultural perspective is to begin to recognize those underlying assumptions, attitudes and values which shape how people make sense of their context. To reinterpret the context of university work, then, we must first identify what it is we take for granted about it. Sara Delamont leads us down this difficult path in Chapter 11, 'Just like the novels? Researching the occupational culture(s) of higher education'.

To make the university context sufficiently strange for us to see how it might be reinterpreted, Delamont begins by drawing on a study of postwar British university fiction, which also identifies a 'familiarity problem': a few Oxbridge plots dominate the genre. The same criticism can be levelled at much educational research, and it is argued that the first task of the social scientist is to make the familiar sufficiently anthropologically strange.

Challenges to the status quo in university fiction have their parallels in five research strategies which Delamont identifies as helping to create strangeness: ethnomethodology; comparative analysis of HE in other societal cultures; a focus on gender; comparison with non-educational settings; and the study of occupational cultures other than lecturers and students. The exploration of these approaches provides a challenging demonstration of how new perspectives can indeed expose the taken-for-granted familiarity of university life and reinterpret its possibilities. The chapter draws to a close by reminding us of postmodernism's challenge to one of the most fundamental familiarities in academic life, the belief that universal, objective truths can be reached by scientific methods. With a nod to academic familiarity, the valediction is a call for more research.

The study of occupational cultures reminds us that all professional groups of HE staff – librarians, accountants, personnel officers and so on – will identify with their profession as well as with their department, organization or other local focus of identity. The university's key staff groups are thus very heavily populated by people whose world of work extends significantly beyond the organizational boundaries. Indeed, the university has often been construed as a loose amalgamation of relatively independent units, 'loosely coupled', in Weick's (1976) famous phrase, or even completely uncoupled in the organizational garbage can (Cohen *et al.*, 1972). These distinctive concepts, derived from research in HE contexts, have, however, had limited appeal for subsequent researchers. Indeed, a literature search suggests that it is only librarians who have found the concept of an organized anarchy of continuing relevance (see, for example, Hughes, 1992; Schwartz, 1994).[1] We might speculate that this is because librarians in particular must confront the operational consequences of loose coupling and organized anarchy as part of their everyday struggle to provide coherent learning support services for a disparate community of scholars, whose reference points may be international rather than interdepartmental.

However, even academics may display a local rather than cosmopolitan orientation, and this will be true *a fortiori* of other groups of HE staff. Such local orientations will not be much illuminated by using discipline or profession as an organizing concept. They might be interpreted in terms of culture at organizational level, but such studies have, in higher education, been relatively few and far between. Rather more common at one time were interpretations starting from concepts of organizational structure and organizational politics, such as Moodie and Eustace's (1974) classic account, *Power and Authority in British Universities*. It is a sign of the times that for a reliable account of more recent developments in terms of university organization one must turn as much to official reports as to the academic literature, with an emphasis on management rather than workers.

Another key distinction in understanding the context of HE work is that between different kinds of HE institution. There has been much examination over many years of the differences between supposedly traditional universities and newer HE institutions with a greater emphasis on applied and vocational programmes, and a different balance between teaching and research (for example, Brosan, 1971; Scott, 1983). In the 1990s, there has been growing recognition of the significance of a third force in HE, which takes different forms in different countries, but everywhere offers a new kind of context for higher education work. Gellert describes

> the emergence, in addition to the formally recognised 'alternative' sectors, of a further 'third sector'. This consists of diverse groups of programmes which are predominantly privately organized and financed, which are often of short duration and narrowly vocational, offered by private institutions and industrial firms ... there is growing evidence

that they are now beginning to cater for a substantial number of qualified secondary school-leavers.

(Gellert, 1991: 15)

In North America, the 'corporate classroom' (Eurich, 1983) has long
been important and recognized. In the UK, there has been a more recent
burgeoning of HE work in this context, but also a rapid expansion of
higher education in the further education sector (HEFCE, 1995a). Thus, to
the well recognized work contexts of old and new universities and colleges
of higher education one must add the corporate classroom in its many
forms, and the further education colleges which increasingly collaborate
with HE institutions to create regional networks of HE opportunities.

Some of the effects of these increasingly important differences are explored through comparative analysis by Oliver Fulton in Chapter 12, 'Which
academic profession are you in?' He draws on data from the Carnegie Commission's international survey to articulate different perspectives on academic
work. In some national systems the distinction between different kinds of
HE institution and HE worker is explicitly recognized, as Clark (1994) has
argued with his distinction between 'professors' (akin to McInnis's (1992)
'cosmopolitan research scientists') and 'teachers'. Fulton examines the ideas
about professionalism which underpin such roles. He suggests that, despite
the diversifying institutional contexts and resource pressures in British
HE, the British academic culture still clings to a unifying notion of what
Clark (1994) calls the 'research-teaching-study nexus'. However, he questions
whether the context can continue to sustain such a unifying value assumption.

Beyond physical contexts we should also recognize another dimension,
which might be labelled the virtual university. The growth of electronic
communication systems such as the Internet and the World Wide Web,
augmenting the longer-established academic networks, has multiplied the
possibilities for academic work to be done at a distance from any HE organization, through networks of academic collaborators who may develop and
deliver teaching or research programmes while rarely meeting in one physical location. In this book, such developments are addressed directly by
Corrall and Lester in Chapter 7, but their impacts on HE culture may also
be illuminated by the analyses of work context offered throughout Chapters
11 and 12.

Finally, in terms of work context, we should consider the time dimension.
When is work accomplished? The taken-for-granted world view of many academics is that work is confined neither to a physical campus location, nor
within office hours. Such thinking was implicit in the negotiations about
the new 'professional' contract for lecturers in the new universities in the
UK in the early 1990s, whereby institutional managers sought to move away
from strict measurement of workload in terms of hours (House and Watson,
1995; Ward, 1995). However, the growing differentiation of roles and functions among staff, discussed above, also imposes new disciplines on academics in terms of when the support services they need will be available.

Many support staff provide services necessarily dependent on their physical presence; many will also have the kind of psychological and employment contract with the university which means that once they are out of site, then their work goes out of mind. A complex modular course timetable can require many hundreds of staff – teachers, administrators, technicians, secretaries, porters, cleaners, catering staff etc. – to do specified kinds of work at specified times, and get it right first time, because resource pressures and schedules will not permit any repeat. Effective delivery depends on complex and tightly scheduled teamwork. The old notion of the academic as always thinking, always working, is not especially helpful in interpreting the meaning of working in these newly complex circumstances.

The implications of this 'new HE' are explored by Winter in Chapter 6, but largely at the levels of the individual, the discipline and the institution. In a final look at context, Marie Thorne and I consider 'Autonomy, bureaucracy and competition: the ABC of control in higher education' in Chapter 13. We draw on the broader experience of reform in the public services to develop a macro-perspective on work context, which addresses issues of structure and control in the national system of HE. The chapter considers major forces for change in HE, the conflicting values which they represent and how those value conflicts are played out in the changing patterns of control in HE. It concludes by offering a framework for interpreting the effects of competing values, and a model for understanding the dynamic interrelationship between the different stakeholders who seek to exercise control over HE work.

Conclusion

The conclusion of the book is also its premise: we need to know more about working in higher education, and we need to work on and in more ways of knowing. Koestler (1964) has argued that humour is in essence a device dependent on reframing the familiar so that it is seen from an unfamiliar angle. In this spirit, the book concludes by asking whether the study of working in HE is itself too limiting as a mode of understanding the staff experience. Chapter 14, 'All work and no play?', points out the lack of attention there has been to ideas about play, fun and humour in interpreting the phenomenon of higher education work. There is indeed always room for more research, and we should enjoy it. I hope you enjoy the book.

Note

1. This is an appropriate point at which to acknowledge the invaluable professional librarian support of Judith Stewart in literature searches and other work underpinning this and later chapters.

Part 1

The Workers

2

Academic Staff: Information and Data

Brian Ramsden

Introduction

The purpose of this chapter is to consider, from a statistical point of view, what we know about staff in higher education (HE) in the United Kingdom, what we do not but should know and what concerns we may have about this important area.

It is well known that staff costs represent more than half of the expenditure in higher education institutions (HEIs); and it is axiomatic that the staff of our universities and colleges are the single most important resource which supports the functions of the sector. It is also well known that social and economic changes in the United Kingdom, deriving both from international trends and from governmental policy directions during the past 16 years, have had major effects on employment practices and on the expectations of individuals in employment. These effects apply in higher education as much as in other areas of employment.

The concerns of the sector about aspects of staffing have tended to be given the most publicity in the area of remuneration, but have extended also to contractual issues, and into areas such as 'deskilling' and retraining as a result of the adoption of new technology, equal opportunities policies and 'restructuring' (which has almost invariably implied the reduction of the number of directly employed staff, usually in response to financial and competitive pressures).

From the point of view of the staff themselves and the communities in which they live, higher education institutions have continued to be seen as major employers, which have been and are attractive, in the eyes of many, because of the nature of the work which they offer, or because of their ethos (either absolutely or by comparison with other local employers), or because of a perceived element of security of employment. However accurate or inaccurate this perception may be, it is indisputable that the staff employment function of higher education institutions is of major economic importance. Some £5 billion per annum is expended by the HEIs on the employment of staff, and this investment contributes significantly to the economy, both directly and indirectly.

Equally importantly, the staff of higher education institutions have close relationships with the industrial, commercial and public sector organizations in the localities which they serve. The contribution of higher education to economic and social development locally and nationally has never been fully documented, and this relationship is one which will repay further study.

Finally, in this introduction, it is important to note the significant changes which have occurred in recent years in the support of students in higher education, and the more flexible methods which institutions have adopted in providing this support. There is now a synergy with other organizations, which, at least at the margins, has changed the nature of the teaching process by bringing into it organizations and individuals who would not in the past have been thought of as participating in higher education. Every time an institution contracts a museum or a professional partnership to participate in supporting the learning process, there is an input which, in the past, might have been one of teacher and student. These interactions are difficult to document through conventional data collection methods, yet their importance must not be overlooked. At the most simple level, it is no longer possible to compute a 'staff : student ratio' by calculating the number of students of an institution or department and dividing into that figure the number of 'staff' employed: for the support of those students in many instances is obtained by a financial transfer of funds between institutions or organizations. This change in emphasis underlines many of the decisions which have been made recently about a new approach to data collection in respect of staff in higher education, which is at the core of this chapter.

The collection of data and provision of information about staff in HE

The 1991 White Paper *Higher Education: a New Framework* (DES, 1991) and the Further and Higher Education Act 1992 included provision for the introduction of more coherent arrangements for the collection of statistical data about higher education than had previously existed. These provisions were consistent with the establishment of a more closely integrated HE sector, with common funding arrangements (although these are administered by different organizations in each part of the UK). Statistical data collection and information provision were operationalized through the establishment of the Higher Education Statistics Agency (HESA), with commitments both to the institutions and to the responsible statutory authorities for higher education, i.e. the government departments and the funding councils, and with the objective of collecting, analysing and disseminating statistical data for the whole of the HE sector throughout the UK, i.e. a group of 182 institutions, funded from the public purse.

Until the provisions of the 1992 Acts were implemented, the higher education institutions were disparate both in their funding arrangements and in the requirements placed on them to provide management information. The various public sector colleges, polytechnics and Scottish central institutions were committed to the provision of data to the relevant government education department, and (in the case of English and Welsh institutions only) to the Polytechnics and Colleges Funding Council, which coordinated the collection of financial and (to a limited extent) staffing data for these. The universities which were funded by the Universities Funding Council submitted data about students, staff and finance to the Universities' Statistical Record (USR), a section of the Universities' Central Council for Admissions. The Open University (in simple volume terms the largest provider of HE teaching in the UK, with over 100,000 part-time students) was not included in these arrangements, except that it provided data about academic and academic-related staff to the USR (although it did not provide student or financial data). In the area of staff records, the situation was unusually complicated by the fact that the 'old' universities had historically prepared an annual individualized staff record for all academic and academic-related staff, whereas the other institutions had not done so – indeed, the concept of 'academic-related' was not one which was meaningful to many of them – and the definition of 'academic' could not be generalized.

The complexity, diversity and lack of coherence in these arrangements led to severe difficulties in constructing meaningful and comparable statistics across the HE sector as a whole. However, there was an underlying further complication, in that the sector had become highly dynamic because of economic and other pressures, which caused some aspects of the previous arrangements to be out of date. These changes included a more flexible approach to staff contracts, which were less easily categorized according to national 'pay bargaining groups': the trend appeared to be away from nationally agreed salary scales and grades for all staff towards more flexible arrangements, including local pay bargaining, performance-related pay and so on. (This trend is still evident, and it follows that a statistical analysis of staff by groups becomes more difficult.) At the same time, some universities and colleges followed the general trend in outsourcing some functions, rather than employing their own workforce. Conventional staff categories therefore became less meaningful. Even in the mainstream area of teaching, it was clear that many institutions were employing staff on a much more flexible basis than hitherto, with a large number of individuals being engaged on a 'casual' or hourly paid basis.

It was in this context that HESA was established, and was required to determine its own data definitions, in order to construct meaningful management information for the sector and for the agency's statutory customers. After much consultation and consideration, the agency concluded that it should collect an individualized record for each member of the *academic staff (i.e. those whose primary employment function was teaching and/or research)* and whose normal employment was for more than 25 per cent of a full-time equivalent member of staff (FTE). The rationale for this decision was that the academic workforce is of central concern to the sector, and that it was of basic importance to collect data about the characteristics of these staff: at the same time, it was felt to be unhelpful to include within an individualized return details of staff whose time commitment was only very limited, and who might be employed simultaneously within several different institutions (especially the specialist colleges), thus complicating statistical data collection. In setting up its data collection arrangements, the agency gave priority to the quality of data to be collected, and it was believed that, by adopting this limited catchment area for staff data collection, quality could be safeguarded.[1] It may be noted in passing that adoption of the definition of 'academic staff' as being those whose primary employment function is teaching and/or research was by consent the only way in which the various different areas of the sector could use broadly similar definitions; the alternative, of linking this definition to terms and conditions of service, was found to be untenable.

At the time of the writing of this chapter, the agency has recently completed the first collection of data about academic staff in HE institutions throughout the UK. Although the detailed analysis of the data has yet to be carried out, it is possible at this stage at least to draw out some broad hypotheses. I shall do so in this chapter.[2]

The data

The data which are being collected about academic staff in higher education are:

1. Employing institution.
2. Campus (where appropriate).
3. Date of birth.
4. Gender.
5. Terms of employment (permanent, temporary etc.).
6. Mode of employment (full-time, part-time etc.).
7. Primary employment function (teaching only, research only or teaching and research).
8. Percentage time academic (in order to assess the time commitment given by academic staff to non-academic activities, e.g. management roles).
9. Proportion of FTE year (in order to observe trends over time in the use of part-time employees).
10. Primary cost centre (i.e. an academic departmental grouping).
11. Nationality.
12. Ethnicity.
13. Disabled status.
14. Date entered current service in current HEI.

15. Highest academic qualification.
16. Academic discipline (of most recent qualification).
17. Professional qualification (if any).
18. Active in 1992 Research Assessment Exercise.
19. Ability to teach through the medium of Welsh (Welsh institutions only).
20. Teaching through the medium of Welsh (Welsh institutions only).
21. Clinical status.
22. NHS joint appointment.
23. Grade structure (if any).
24. Principal source of salary.
25. Proportion of salary charged against general income.
26. Secondary source of salary.
27. Salary point.
28. Current salary.
29. Employment in previous year.
30. Date left.
31. Destination on leaving.

The functions of higher education: teaching and research

We have noted that academic staff are the principal resource in support of the dual functions of teaching and research. This is not new. However, some perceived changes in the nature of staff deployment in higher education have caused HESA to introduce a new dimension in its categorization of staff. In the past, individualized staff data collected from the old universities were categorized as 'teaching and research' staff and 'research only' staff. In establishing HESA's data definitions, it was felt that the new higher education sector required a categorization which allowed for 'teaching only' staff, in the belief that this category was growing in number. Preliminary analysis of the data confirms that there is a significant number of staff whose role is 'teaching only', though these are less numerous than the group of 'research only' staff. The breakdown in the UK as a whole is broadly as shown in Figure 2.1.

We should note at this point that there are some marked regional variations in employment patterns, with a significantly lower proportion of 'teaching only' staff in the workforce in Scotland and Northern Ireland, and a significantly higher proportion (some 17 per cent) in Wales. This feature corresponds with other findings by HESA, which suggest a more traditional pattern of higher education in Scotland and Northern Ireland than in England and, especially, Wales.

We might also note that, on the basis of a preliminary analysis of the data, it appears that whereas the large majority of 'teaching and research' staff are employed on a full-time and permanent basis, very few 'research

Figure 2.1   Academic staff by primary employment function

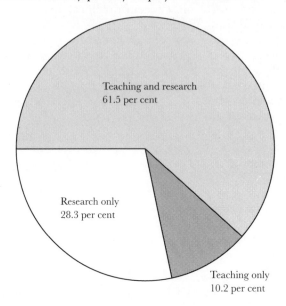

only' staff are employed on permanent contracts, and although 'teaching only' staff are more likely to have permanent contracts, many of them are employed on a part-time basis. It is also, predictably, the case that the average age of 'research only' staff is considerably younger than that of either 'teaching and research' staff or 'teaching only' staff. We might also note that staff who are primarily employed as 'teaching only' and 'research only' are generally remunerated at a lower level than those who undertake both teaching and research.

It will, of course, continue to be the case that the majority of staff in higher education carry out the two roles of teaching and research. At the time of the construction of the academic staff record, institutions were asked whether it would be possible for them to quantify the teaching and research components in their roles: with few exceptions the institutions made clear that they could not. This is axiomatic in many parts of HE, but it is not a view which generates sympathy outside the sector. It is unlikely that any other component part of either the public or the private sector would disclaim knowledge of the attribution of expenditure between its two major activities, given that these have separate sources of income. The argument to support this stance is that the two functions cannot be separated, because they are interrelated; but this in turn begs a question about how and why they are separately funded. Although this perhaps represents an insoluble problem, it is worthy of note that, for the foreseeable future, it will be impossible to derive a clear notion of the amount of time spent by most academic staff on each of the two functions.

Quality, qualifications and specialization

This section investigates some of the special features of the various disciplines represented within higher education. The HESA staff record, as has been noted, records both the discipline within which a member of staff has taken his or her most recent qualification and the 'cost centre', i.e. an academic departmental grouping, within which he or she teaches or undertakes research. It will thus become possible to derive some detailed information about the backgrounds of staff within different departmental areas, including the subject of their qualifications. (What will not, however, fall out from this record is any quantification of 'staff: student ratios', since the total teaching input cannot be identified separately from research, and for other reasons described above.)

On the basis of the data available so far, we can postulate that the major subject differences in the staffing of higher education are:

1. That 'teaching only' staff predominate in certain specialist subjects, e.g. agriculture, languages, the creative arts and education.
2. That, as would be anticipated, 'research only' staff predominate in the sciences and technology.
3. That, again as anticipated, the possession of a doctorate or any higher degree is more common among those who teach or do research in the sciences; overall, 'teaching only' staff are less likely to possess a higher degree than the other categories.
4. That female staff are comparatively few in departments of engineering and physical sciences; but that they predominate in nursing, and are in equilibrium with male staff in departments of education.
5. That staff who do both teaching and research in clinical departments and in departments of science (but less obviously engineering) tend to be more highly paid than those in other disciplines.
6. That, on the basis of preliminary analysis, it appears that staff working in arts and social sciences departments are somewhat older than staff working in scientific and clinical departments (after adjusting for differences in the balance of primary functions).

Equal opportunities: issues of gender and ethnicity

Interest in and concern for issues of equal opportunity in higher education have grown in recent years. In 1993 the Committee of Vice Chancellors and Principals launched the Commission on University Career Opportunity, which shortly afterwards published the results of a survey of universities carried out in December 1993 (CUCO, 1994). That report noted serious limitations in the availability of statistical data about gender and other issues. (For example, it noted that 'around 75% of universities keep statistical records

Figure 2.2   Primary employment function by gender

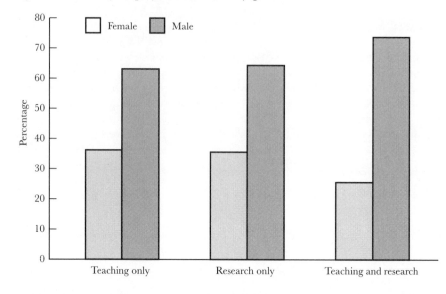

which record gender. For ethnicity, disability and marital status, the figure is much lower.')

The introduction of HESA's staff record has required institutions to make provision for recording ethnicity, disability and gender (there is no intention to collect data about marital status). Within the limitations of the initial data available to date, this chapter will describe some of the emerging information.

Gender

Overall, about 70 per cent of academic staff in universities and colleges are men. There appears to be a predominance of female staff only in the areas of nursing and health and community studies. There are very few women employed in departments of physics, or engineering subjects. These imbalances closely reflect imbalances in the student population by subject area, as reported elsewhere by HESA (1995).

An examination of the available data regarding the primary function of staff reveals that women are more likely to be employed as 'research only' and 'teaching only' staff than as 'teaching and research' staff: Figure 2.2 is self-explanatory.

We observed earlier that those staff who do not undertake a role in both teaching and research tend to have less favourable salaries and conditions of service. Inevitably, therefore, the concentration of women in roles which are limited to 'teaching only' or 'research only' depresses the average earnings of women, as compared with men; and these are depressed further by the fact that they are employed predominantly in those disciplines in which,

Figure 2.3 Percentage of female staff by age band

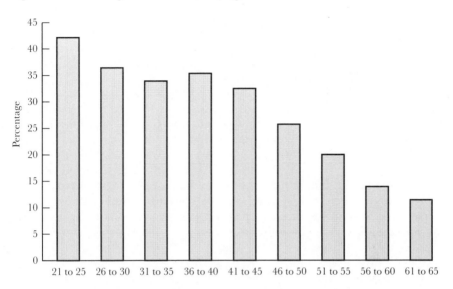

as observed earlier in this chapter, salaries are lower than the average. There are two further factors which have a similar effect. The first is that, on the basis of available data, women are more likely than men to be undertaking work on a part-time basis; the second is that it appears that the average age of female staff is several years lower than that of men. That this may lead to a change over time in some of the preliminary conclusions in this chapter is suggested by Figure 2.3, which shows the percentage of women in various age bands.

Ethnicity

Ethnicity is a field which will always provide only partial data, since there can be no obligation on individuals to disclose their ethnicity. Additional difficulties in the first year of data collection (1994–5) were identified by some institutions, which had not previously collected ethnicity data about their staff; and in one instance, a university indicated that it had a policy that it would not collect data of this kind. In the first year of data collection, therefore, institutions which had not previously collected this item of data were allowed to return a default code ('information not yet sought'). Institutions have, however, been advised that a full return will be required in 1995–6.

Despite these limitations, it appears to be the case that ethnicity data for over 80 per cent of academic staff will be returned. It is premature to begin to draw conclusions or even hypotheses on the basis of the data available so far, except to observe that 'research only' posts appear to be more likely to be occupied by staff from ethnic minority groups. The topic of ethnicity in higher education is one which generates considerable interest, especially among academic researchers, and a series of research datapacks is being constructed by HESA in order to bring the relevant data into the public domain.

Staff movements

A further area of interest and concern with regard to academic staffing has traditionally been the movement of people into and out of employment in higher education. It is perhaps unclear what are or should be the sector's objectives in this area. However, it is reasonable to assume that the sector (and the taxpayer) would wish to see a stable, but not stagnant, body of staff, bringing into higher education relevant transferable skills from other sectors, both public and private, and perhaps from other cultures. Conversely, the issue of 'brain drain' has always been one of considerable public interest. And finally, within society as a whole, it would probably be regarded as desirable that there should be two-way interaction between academic institutions and private industry.

The initial data available through HESA suggest that, with one exception to which we shall return, the sector should not be too concerned about this area. Preliminary findings suggest that there is a modest level of mobility of academic staff, but that this is concentrated within higher education itself, i.e. it consists largely of movements between HEIs in the UK. While there is a small amount of movement of UK staff to overseas institutions, this is more than compensated for by the movement into UK higher education of staff from overseas institutions (and in particular institutions in the USA and the countries of the European Union). There is also a healthy exchange of staff between HEIs and private industry both in the UK and overseas.

The one area of possible concern arising from the data about staff mobility relates to the departure of 'research only' staff. Although it should be emphasized that the figures available at present are initial estimates, it appears, as might be expected given their contractual basis of employment, that the turnover of research staff is higher than that of the other categories of academic staff; and also that a higher proportion are 'not in regular employment' after leaving employment in their institutions. If this is confirmed by further examination of the full data, some more detailed analysis of the characteristics of those staff who are not able to gain further employment may be called for, since it cannot be desirable for the sector to train and develop a core of staff without providing realistic long-term employment opportunities.

Non-academic staff

At the time of writing, HESA has not collected any data about non-academic staff in higher education, although there is an intention to collect limited data about these in the coming year. Any such exercise will be hindered by the different definitions used, for perfectly good reasons, in different parts of the HE sector. This is an area in which 'diversity' is very real, and not susceptible to generalization.

Conclusion

In 1995–6 the higher education sector is putting together an information system about academic staff in higher education which will be a marked improvement on anything which has previously existed in the UK. It is, however, by no means comprehensive. The changes in the delivery of courses in recent years have served to break down many of the traditional barriers in staff employment. Terms and conditions of service have become more flexible, and other categories of staff than 'academic' have become much closer to the teaching process. For the future, the sector will need to consider whether it wishes the concept of the individualized record to be extended to more categories of staff, not least because differentiation of categories has become more difficult. At the same time, issues of accountability for time spent (and therefore resources consumed) will not go away, and it would be unwise to assume that financial pressures both on employers and on staff will diminish.

For the time being, however, the new HESA record will provide data about the academic workforce which was previously unavailable, and it is important that this should be studied thoroughly. The agency has put in place a collaborative arrangement with the Society for Research into Higher Education, which will enable academic researchers to mine the data and explore more fully the issues sketched out above.

Notes

1. It was recognized that pragmatic considerations also argued in this direction. The majority of institutions in the HE sector had not previously been required to prepare an individualized staff record, and many did not have a computerized staff records system. There were serious concerns about whether these institutions would be able to introduce such a record on time: in fact, all institutions submitted data well.
2. For a more comprehensive analysis of staffing in higher education institutions, together with financial data including staff costs, refer to the annual Statistical Volume, *Resources in Higher Education*, June 1996 (and annually thereafter), available from HESA Services Ltd, 18 Royal Crescent, Cheltenham GL50 3DA, United Kingdom.

3

Managing the Employment Relationship in Higher Education: Quo Vadis?

Ewart Keep, John Storey and Keith Sisson

In 1992, two of the authors of this chapter (Keep and Sisson, 1992) produced a set of proposals for improving the management of the employment relationship in higher education in the UK, which was approvingly cited in the Committee of Vice Chancellors and Principals' own subsequent review (CVCP, 1993). Since that time there has been, at best, very patchy and halting progress towards implementing any kind of coherent strategy to safeguard, still less develop, the vital human resource which constitutes the heart of the HE system. At the level of the individual institution, there has often been plenty of activity, but much of it has been fragmented and ineffective. At national level, the pace of change has been snail-like; decision-makers seem attracted by a number of possible models, but incapable or unwilling to take the necessary action to put them into practice.

The chapter develops this argument in more detail. The first two sections outline the major changes which have characterized the system in recent years and identify the main associated personnel problems. The third sketches and evaluates a number of alternative solutions for managing the employment relationship and suggests what the most likely scenario will be. The fourth section offers some final thoughts on the way forward.

Changes in higher education and the associated problems

HE in the UK is profoundly different from what it was just a few years ago. There has not just been expansion on a significant scale, but also a transformation from a highly selective elite system into a mass education one. Between 1979 and 1993 the number of university students nearly doubled to 1.5 million, and the proportion of young people entering full-time HE rose over the same period from 12 per cent to over 30 per cent (DfE, 1994).

The removal of the binary divide has resulted in an increase in the number of UK universities from 38 to 72 (plus 50 colleges of HE).

With expansion have come concerns about quality assurance (of both teaching and research), teaching methods, the types of learning experiences required by students and the management of an increasingly diverse HE system. Perhaps most importantly, expansion has been accompanied by a reduction in the unit of resource. This has led to larger class sizes, fewer tutorial sessions and massively increased pressure on academic staff as well as reduced opportunity to probe the boundaries of knowledge.

Arguably, this adds up to serious erosion of the intellectual base upon which the viability of the system depends. Future plans cannot be predicated upon past levels of quality because much of this base has been spent and insufficient steps have been taken to replenish it. The basic problem is manifested in various ways: the increased proportion of part-time and short-term contract staff, a decline in relative pay and status, the loss of a whole generation of new scholars in some subject areas, the lack of attraction of an academic appointment compared with other commercial opportunities for many of the very brightest graduates. Last, but not least, there is what Halsey (1992) has described as the 'proletarianization' of the academic profession.

From the perspective of those managing the system, some of these features (most especially the last) may not appear matters of particular importance. Many quantitative indicators suggest that the system as a whole is more efficient. Moreover, the expectations of a greater proportion of the electorate for university places for their children have been satisfied without their having to pay higher taxes. Further, there are examples of the launch of 'quality management' initiatives, which suggests that the managements of at least some universities are beginning to take their responsibilities seriously (see below for further details).

Problem: what problem?

Evidently there is a danger of two sets of interest groups, with two different perspectives, simply talking past each other. A useful analytical exercise which can help to reduce, if not entirely avoid, divergent views is to compare HE management with 'best practice' in the private and public sectors. In knowledge-based industries, in particular, the critical centrality of human capital is seen as paramount in securing and sustaining competitiveness. The poverty of the 'Taylorist' and 'Fordist' formulae for modern conditions (i.e. hierarchy, bureaucracy and specialization) is well recognized. In place of conformity and simple duplication, sophisticated employers are looking for innovation, high commitment and high levels of skill.

How are these goals to be attained? The evidence (see, for example, Storey and Sisson, 1993) is that they require strategic insight and planning, investment in the stock of expertise, and the shaping of conditions so as to elicit commitment. Above all, it means someone in the system taking re-sponsibility for managing the totality of the employment relationship. At present, acceptance of such all-round responsibility is notable by its absence in HE. Rather, there is a series of isolated 'initiatives' (such as appraisal, total quality management, audits and hold-back) which do not on their own address the scale of the problem.

The challenges are massive. The problem of declining academic salaries is too well known to need rehearsing in detail here. Probably no other 'pro-fessional' group, however, in either the public or private sectors, has fallen faster or further in terms of pay and social status than have academics in the past 15 years. Perhaps as importantly, no end is in sight to this relative decline.

Also widely recognized is that stop-go recruitment 'policies' over the past 30 years have left a legacy of a skewed age profile. Currently, 85 per cent of teaching staff are over 35 years of age. The average age is 45 (for more details, see AUT, 1993; Keep and Mayhew, 1995). The bunching of staff in their fifties means that in a short time a large cohort will be retiring, but appropriate replacement policies have not been worked through.

Vacant posts can always be filled, as a recent report by the Higher Edu-cation Funding Council for England (HEFCE) calmly suggests (*Times Higher Educational Supplement,* 27 October 1995). The question its authors appear to neglect, however, is whether these posts can be filled by people of the same ability. As Keep and Mayhew (1995: 97–8) have pointed out, there is increasing difficulty in attracting sufficient well qualified candidates to train as secondary school teachers. The levels of qualification required to enter an academic career are more demanding, yet pay for academics trails that for school teachers. The normal operation of the labour market would suggest that the academic profession will find it hard to recruit well qualified entrants. Indeed, the current 'transfer market' in experienced researchers may, in part, reflect a realization that the supply of able young staff is dwindling (see Keep and Mayhew, 1995: 98–100).

A third problem is that of motivation and commitment. HE institu-tions have traditionally been able to rely on the personal dedication of academic staff to subjects and students. In addition to pursuing research and teaching, academics have traditionally taken on administrative duties to ensure the smooth running of their departments and institutions. In the process, they have assumed responsibility for their own careers and institu-tions, and have, in large measure, been truly ahead of their time in being 'self-managing'.

The irony is that just as cutting-edge practice in the private sector moves towards the 'self-managing' model, UK universities undermine their own ver-sion by imposing a fragmented set of practices which are sufficiently intrusive to erode mutual trust but not all-encompassing enough to provide a sus-tainable alternative. Many recent changes have threatened the balance of traditional arrangements. Thus, an increasing number of teaching and re-search staff are employed on short-term, temporary contracts. By the early

1990s, the overall proportion of academics employed in this way had reached 42 per cent. The universities have not been alone in facing turbulent and uncertain markets, yet few other employers of graduates have passed on that uncertainty so obviously as have HE institutions. Whereas other employers have tried to attract and motivate their graduate recruits with permanent employment contracts, high starting salaries and promises of rapid career advancement, 'many HE institutions by contrast take positive efforts to signal their minimal commitment' (Keep and Sisson, 1992: 71).

Staff on regular contracts may also be less willing in future to offer their former 'goodwill'. Increased workloads, fewer opportunities for meaningful interaction with students, the demands of audits on teaching and research, and the transactional mentality induced by performance-related pay are likely to undermine commitment and cooperation. Faced with resistance, if only in the form of 'working without enthusiasm', institutional managers may be tempted to respond with increased control mechanisms. The classic vicious circle of control and resistance could thus be triggered, as to some extent it has been in further education.

In the face of these developments, attempts to introduce 'total quality' programmes inevitably face an uphill struggle – a problem reflected in the fact that, in mid-1995, of the 72 universities and 50 colleges of HE, only seven institutions (or in some cases departments thereof) had achieved the Investors in People standard (HEQC, 1995). Notwithstanding the generally positive tone of those championing these programmes (see, for example, Clayton, 1993; Doherty, 1993; Geddes, 1993), there are good grounds for scepticism about their long-term impact. Commenting on a set of articles in a special edition of *Higher Education* on total quality management (TQM) in HE, Williams (1993: 373) notes that 'the papers do all seem to have one thing in common: they describe the introduction of TQM as a response to a crisis – financial, organisational, or social. Interest in it has also for the most part been born of corporate or individual frustration and fear.' TQM has much to commend it, but its success depends on trust, commitment and a supportive culture – features which may not be so readily available in the unfolding context described above. TQM certainly does not have an automatic effect.

As Fulton (1993: 163) notes, the move to mass education carries other consequences. One of these is the potential decline in attractiveness of the career to new recruits. He suggests that 'in larger systems membership of the profession as a whole is likely, *ceteris paribus*, to be less rewarding, mainly because the profession can make fewer claims for selectivenesss or exclusivity, and in addition, the salary bill, if borne by the state, is more conspicuously costly.' To make matters worse, in words he borrows from Halsey, the 'decline of donnish dominion' results not from the arrival of mass education *per se*, but from the failure of the profession to welcome it 'and embrace its implications' (Fulton, 1993: 163). This failure has led to a system which is too large to be sustained in traditional elite form, but too small to build the popular support characterizing higher education in the

United States and elsewhere. It is likely to bring about, suggests Fulton (1993: 163), further 'loss of status and worsening working conditions as well as relative loss of earnings, with obvious implications for the profession's potential to attract good new staff'.

Some solutions . . . and the most likely scenario?

It is possible to think of three main options for dealing with the challenges and the problems identified above: the 'strategic HRM' model, the 'professional' model and the 'networked employer' model. Each of these is considered in turn, together with what, on the evidence available, is the most likely scenario, i.e. more of the same.

Human resource management: a strategic approach

The starting point would be for the senior management team of each university to take responsibility for devising and implementing a human resource (HR) strategy. Someone must own the problem – or at least there needs to be a clearer view as to which parts of the problem belong to which stakeholder in the system. At the present time responsibility gets lost between the Department for Education and Employment, the employers' association (the Universities and Colleges Employers Association (UCEA), in practice often operating for universities through the CVCP), the funding councils and the individual institutions. All of the former have a role to play, but the main responsibility must rest with the employer.

The next priority would be to create a HR function capable of analysing the link between labour markets and institutional objectives. This function would embrace the senior university managers, who would have responsibility for integrating people management issues with all of the other key elements in corporate plans and would help to shape these plans with HR aspects in mind. They would engage in serious HR planning, with action at institutional level linked to that at national level, which would preferably be the responsibility of the CVCP. Analyses of supply and demand for academic labour would be undertaken. Steps would be taken to influence the shape and size of both aspects. Career plans might be put in place as one factor capable of influencing supply and demand. Within overall institutional policies and frameworks, central personnel expertise would be used to enable departments to develop and integrate communication, target setting, evaluation and reward strategies that fitted their particular needs. Further details can be found in Keep and Sisson (1992).

The assumption underpinning all of these measures is that a 'high commitment' model of HR is being pursued. If so, this would entail strenuous attempts to win back staff support and to enjoin staff in the shared vision. Piecemeal initiatives will not be sufficient. For example, research on the impact of staff appraisal in universities has suggested that overall the process has been 'largely ineffectual' (Haslam *et al.*, 1993). Much would be dependent upon overcoming a legacy of mistrust, suspicion and cynicism.

A further implication is that there would be a move from national to local bargaining. This opens up the prospect of diversity in subsequent arrangements. Local bargaining could result in gaps opening up in pay structures between institutions and even between subject areas in the same institution – this happens at the moment, of course, in the form of people of like qualifications being on different salary points, but seems to be 'acceptable' because it is not transparent. Some vice chancellors/chief executives may be tempted to move into individual contracts for academic staff.

For many, not least the AUT, such developments are anathema. The fundamental weakness of the present system of multi-employer bargaining, however, is that it enables the senior managers of universities to shirk their responsibilities. If, as in other sectors, national multi-employer bargaining were to end, it would be very difficult to carry on doing this.

A vision not broadly dissimilar to that outlined above informed the CVCP's Fender Report (CVCP, 1993) on staffing policies. Its recommendations included moves towards more local and single-table bargaining, a pay advisory commission to chart pay and labour market trends and the introduction of new mechanisms to reward teams of staff within institutions. In the three years since the publication of the report, however, relatively little concrete progress can yet be observed. Some recommendations, such as mechanisms for performance pay for teams, have vanished from sight. Others, such as a move away from national pay bargaining, the introduction of single-table negotiations at institutional level or the development of a unified national grading and job evaluation structure covering all university staff, have progressed very slowly. The idea of improved terms and conditions for fixed-term contract staff predated the Fender Report by several years, yet it was not until July 1995 that a draft agreement between the CVCP, the research councils and the Office of Science and Technology was finally issued for consultation. It is hard to imagine many other areas of the public sector, never mind the private, where progress on a major issue of strategic personnel management would take quite such a leisurely pace.

The professional model: back to the future

A second potential solution involves what might be termed the 'professional' model. It has many advocates among those who mourn the passing of what they perceive was the 'golden age' of British HE (the 1960s and 1970s). It has particularly strong support in the Association of University Teachers, where there is acceptance of the need for expansion, but rejection of what is seen to be the overly managerialist agenda of the HRM model associated with the Fender Report (see, for example, AUT, 1993, 1994; Triesman, 1994).

There are two main elements to this model. The first is a pay review body of the type enjoyed by the armed forces, school teachers, doctors, nurses, dentists and senior civil servants. The implicit argument for this is that academic salaries have fallen so far behind those of similar groups that any formal process of comparability cannot fail to halt the slide. The second is the need for academics to organize themselves on a professional basis. In this case the assumption seems to be that professional status equals high status and high pay – something which is not necessarily true, as the history of the professional engineering bodies attests all too clearly.

The second element is especially important because it chimes well with mounting external pressure upon HE to improve the quality of teaching provision. As Sir Ron Dearing, advisor to the government on the school curriculum and 16–19 education, and Chairman of the National Committee of Inquiry into Higher Education, has remarked,

> It has always struck me as odd, that the university teacher has not wished to establish him or herself in terms of professionalism, through some professional qualification in the art and science of teaching ... With the whole nation's future being so bound up with the quality of teaching ... it is of national importance that people of distinction should receive high advancement in the university community as a teacher, writer of textbooks and compiler of learning materials.
>
> (Dearing, 1995b)

Concerns about the absence of proper training for teaching duties within HE (and the imbalance between the weight given in promotion between teaching and research) have been echoed by Jeff Rooker (1993), the CBI (1995), the Association of Graduate Recruiters (1995), the Council for Industry and Higher Education (1995), Howard Davies (1995), Dominic Cadbury (*Times Higher Educational Supplement*, 26 May 1995) and, in rather more oblique terms, the Higher Education Quality Council (1994).

Major obstacles have to be overcome if either element is to be a feasible proposition. The government, for example, has refused to countenance the introduction of a pay review body, though both the main opposition parties are pledged to introduce one. Pay review bodies in other sectors, such as teaching and nursing, have also made life difficult for employers in recent years – it is too easy for the government to accept the awards but argue that it is up to the employers to finance them. This has led the CVCP (which until recently endorsed the idea of a pay review body for HE) to have second thoughts. In a letter to the *Times Higher Educational Supplement (THES*, 20 October 1995), the chief negotiator of the Universities and Colleges Employers Association (S. Rouse) casts doubt upon the CVCP's continued commitment to this goal. Rouse claims that an independent pay review body for HE is 'yesterday's solution to today's problem', but offers no clue as to what today's solution might be.

For the creation of a professional body for HE, the obstacles would appear to be even more significant. At present, the AUT is not a professional body in the sense that the accountancy institutes or the Law Society are. It is a relatively weak trade union that lays claim to represent a group that forms 'the UK's key profession' (Triesman, 1994: 1). Recently, the AUT has talked about the need for a system of training and accreditation for university teaching (Cottrell, 1995), and the AUT's executive has now gone as far as to call for universities to introduce formal and compulsory accredited qualifications for new entrants to university teaching (*THES*, 10 November 1995). This is a significant development, and the proposal, if adopted by universities, would take academics much closer to genuine professional status of the type enjoyed by lawyers and doctors. It will be extremely interesting to see how the AUT's membership and the vice chancellors react to this idea. In the past, there have been signs that many academics, while liking the concept of professional status, have not been enthusiastic to countenance anything so formal as compulsory entry qualifications.

Another problem is that the AUT's membership does not encompass only academics, but also librarians, computer staff and administrators. Trying to represent a broad group of occupations and skills under a professional banner is problematic – it would be hard, for instance, to envisage the BMA representing nurses, or hospital administrators. In its document *Promoting Professionalism* (AUT, 1994), the AUT itself argues that a university education is delivered by a core team of academics and support staff who make equal contributions to the delivery of courses.

A third difficulty is that, in marked contrast to law and accountancy, the most senior members of the academic profession, the vice chancellors, 'in general appear to accept little responsibility for the promotion of the profession to which they belong' (Keep and Mayhew, 1995: 103). Indeed, members of the CVCP have usually opted to assume the role of representatives of individual institutions (though without accepting many of the responsibilities towards their staff that other employers bear), rather than that of leaders of a profession. It is not clear either whether they would be keen to see a stronger professional voice seeking greater influence over the direction of the HE system.

Government hostility to the notion of professions, particularly within the public sector, represents a further hurdle. Professional groups, such as doctors and nurses, are seen as producer interests more concerned with maintaining restrictive practices and with the welfare of their members than with supporting innovative and cost-cutting reform of the public services. Thus, the government has so far set its face firmly against a General Teaching Council for school teachers. It is hard to see it being any more enthusiastic about a professional body for university staff, though it might be willing to accept the type of Teaching and Learning Board quango envisaged by MacFarlane (1993), which could act as a counterpart to the Teacher Training Agency.

A final observation is that the ideal time for academics to have made the transition to full professional status would have been in the years following the expansion brought about by the Robbins Report. Arguably, talk of moving to a formal professional model is taking place 30 years too late. The economic and political climate (with both large and small p's) is no longer so favourable towards professional groupings. Few groups, including journalists and many management functions, have been able to establish themselves in the way that the traditional professions have.

The virtual university, the networked employer

In the past five years more and more has been heard about the possibilities offered by technological advances in information technology, multimedia, telecommunications and the CD-ROM. This has led some to suggest that it will be possible to move from the traditional notion of the university as a physical entity, towards the idea of the virtual or distributed university (see, for example, Hague, 1991; Wright, 1994; Eisenstadt, 1995; Gell and Cochrane, 1995; Tiffin and Rajasingham, 1995; Yeomans, 1995). Examples of such an approach already in place or being developed in the UK include a virtual university for the motor industry (*THES*, 23 June 1995), plans for new universities in Swindon (*THES*, 4 August 1995) and Suffolk (*THES*, 14 July 1995), a virtual lab for robotics at the University of Reading (Greenhalgh, 1995), the further development of the Open University's open learning methods (Greenberg, 1995), the Learning Resource Centre at the Thames Valley University (Targett, 1995) and the Labour Party's University for Industry. In Spain, the Open University of Catalonia represents a working example of a virtual campus (Warden, 1995), and in the USA there are the National Technological University and the Mind Extension University (see Yeomans, 1995, for details).

The implications of such developments for staffing policies are not clear-cut. One school of thought suggests that, whatever the changes to the delivery of learning, 'the university's core resource will remain its academics and their expertise' (Wright, 1994: 101; see also Hague, 1991). Evidence from the USA, however, suggests that this may not prove to be the case. Core staff in the virtual universities are made up of a small group of administrators and technicians. The learning materials are devised by academics employed elsewhere within the existing university system. Tutors providing learning support are the peripheral workforce. At the National Technology University, all contributing faculty are subject to student evaluation, the lowest scoring fifth of staff being shed each year (Yeomans, 1995).

In the British context, the likelihood is that moves towards the virtual university would simply reinforce the already very strong drift towards the casualization of the academic workforce – at present, about 45 per cent of academic staff are on fixed-term contracts. Many vice chancellors give few signs of enjoying their role as employers. Developments allowing them to opt out of this tiresome responsibility altogether, by moving staff to self-employed status, or by simply hiring lecturers from staffing agencies of the sort that have already been established in the FE sector, might well hold a strong appeal. Indeed, the FE staffing agency, which was set up with the expressed objective of cutting FE teaching costs, by replacing part-time employees with hourly paid agency staff, has indicated a desire to expand its activities into HE. Developments in teaching delivery may aid this process, so that the ties between universities and those who deliver their teaching and research are yet further weakened.

While such an approach could, if applied with sufficient ruthlessness, undoubtedly reduce costs in the short term, it is highly questionable whether it would be a strategy that could be sustained in the long term if teaching and research quality were to be maintained at anything approaching their present levels. Moves towards new approaches to the delivery of learning none the less raise fundamental issues about new methods of working and new modes of employment. The implications of these need to be thought through, and properly managed, if the HE system is to avoid unpleasant and ultimately counter-productive side-effects.

More of the same: we'll muddle through

Perhaps none of the above models will be adopted in any coherent fashion. Many of those in charge of the system, whether in government, the funding councils or individual institutions, may simply delay confronting the staffing problems outlined earlier in the hope that something will turn up that will obviate them from the need for major change. On the available evidence, more of the same is the most likely scenario. It represents a 'default' option, whereby isolated fragments of some of the above strategies are adopted, with greater or lesser degrees of enthusiasm, by some institutions. Thus, one may expect further incremental improvements to the initial training of new entrants to the profession, further weakening of national bargaining, more performance-related pay and more casualization, but not a coherent HR strategy, let alone a full-blown professional body.

When confronted with the sorts of challenges raised in the opening sections of this chapter, senior figures within the HE system have a tendency to acknowledge that staffing is a problem area and that something must be done about it (by whom is rarely specified), and then to move on as swiftly as possible to the discussion of issues with which they feel more comfortable, such as the rearrangement of the funding formula or the criteria for research selectivity. The current rate of progress on implementing many of the recommendations of the Fender Report, the relaxed pace at which consideration of moves towards the formal professionalization of university teaching is taking place and the apparent absence of any coordinated strategy for promoting academic careers all attest to the reluctance of the key actors to face up to the scale of the problems.

Final thoughts

Outlined above are four directions which future developments in staffing in HE might take. We remain convinced that the first of these – moves towards a high-commitment version of developmental HRM – remains the option upon which it is most likely that sustainable development of an efficient mass system of HE can be built. However, we would emphasize three points.

First, moves towards this option do not simply mean implementing the agenda set by the Fender Report. The changes prescribed in that report represent some steps only along the path to the HRM model. Much more besides needs to be done, particularly at institutional level, to help teams, departments and different groups of staff to evolve detailed HR policies that suit their needs and goals. As best practice among large employers outside the HE system indicates (Storey and Sisson, 1993), the major role for any university HR function should be to act as consultant and enabler, rather than simply to design and impose monolithic procedures and solutions.

Second, moves towards the HRM model do not preclude exploration of a strengthening of professional identities and structures or of new approaches to assembling and maintaining a community of scholars. The training of university staff, particularly with regard to the performance of teaching duties and the discharge of managerial functions, remains a major weakness. It may well be that progress, particularly regarding teaching, can best be achieved by partnerships between staff and institutions, and between the CVCP and the AUT/NATFHE. Some form of professional training body might have a very useful role to play in helping to shape the overall structures and expectations within which such partnerships could operate.

Third, if proper HRM policies and systems were in place, it would make the exploration of new approaches to assembling and maintaining communities of scholars utilizing new technologies much easier to envisage. The growing internationalization and interdisciplinarity of research, the desire of students to learn at a pace and place of their own choosing and the potential for new methods of working and new lifestyles unleashed by technology all suggest that experimentation with new modes of teaching delivery, of research networking and of patterns of work are both feasible and desirable. However, as pointed out above, the great danger is that, in the absence of an enlightened approach to staffing issues, the virtual university will rapidly degenerate into a casualized and exploitative institution – not an end result from which staff, students or the community at large will benefit in the long run.

Our aim has been to underline the dangers of underestimating the importance of personnel issues in British HE. The problems have been repeatedly diagnosed (Keep and Sisson, 1992; CVCP, 1993; National Commission on Education, 1993, 1995; Kogan *et al.*, 1994), solutions suggested and policies and procedures to tackle them set out (Finegold *et al.*, 1992; CVCP, 1993; Warner and Crosthwaite, 1995). What has been missing has been concerted and coherent action on the part of those within the system whose responsibility it is to deal with these matters. As a result, universities as employers are becoming increasingly isolated, even within a shrinking public sector, in terms of their approach to staffing issues. Moreover, the costs of not managing the employment relationship, or of not managing it well, are becoming increasingly obvious, whether in terms of low morale or difficulties in recruiting and retaining staff of adequate quality. Teaching and research quality, and indeed the effective delivery of higher education, are at serious risk.

4

Does It Pay to Work in Universities?

Helen Murlis and Frank Hartle

Not for bread alone

Pay is not the main reason why people choose to work or pursue a career in higher education. But pay can be the oil in the works of any organization, or it can be the grit which prevents effective working. It may not be very high on the agenda for most people in universities most of the time. This is, however, a reality that can change very quickly and very uncomfortably with poor handling of any element of remuneration practice. The history of pay in universities is not without its moments of conflict, and for the future there are clearly strategic choices to be made in this area at both national and local levels.

In this chapter we look at the foundations for making choices over pay, starting with the nature of the reward contract and then looking at the remuneration trends currently influencing pay decisions, the changing nature of work and the likely impact of changing student motivations and perceptions. Finally, we look at the critical issues for reward policy development if higher education is successfully to ensure that it is staffed by highly motivated and committed people able to respond to the challenge of raising the knowledge base of the country as a whole. We do this against a background of significant recent change, notably a continuing rise in student numbers as well as changes to the mix of the student population and increasing pressure on running costs. These, and inevitably the pay issues, are part of the territory of the Inquiry into Higher Education undertaken by a National Committee chaired by Sir Ron Dearing during 1996–7 at the request of the Secretary of State for Education and Employment. We firmly believe that it is not possible to answer the question posed in our chapter title simply by looking at the engineering and technology of financial rewards and benefits. Pay is an art as well as a science and a subtle one at that. Managing it effectively involves looking at the broad employment environment for teaching, technical support and managerial roles as well as the financial architecture. The skills involved are more those of a good geographer than of simply an accountant or economist. There are many pieces to the puzzle of explaining why excellent people at all levels continue in considerable numbers to choose to spend a good part of their career in an area that is typically relatively lowly paid by professional standards.

Anyone summarizing motivation theory will say first that there is no single lever for maintaining or increasing motivation specifically in universities or elsewhere. The process is complex and depends on the following.

- Individual needs and aspirations, themselves infinitely variable.
- Both intrinsic and extrinsic motivating factors, about which it is unwise to generalize.
- Expectations about rewards, which vary in relation to individuals' previous experiences and perceptions of reward processes.
- Equity and fairness – the 'felt-fair' principle which applies in relation to comparison with others in accordance with what people believe to be the relative size and contribution of jobs and roles.
- Attributions – the subjective and sometimes distorted explanations people give of their successes and failures.
- Self-efficacy – the differences in the degree to which people believe in themselves and therefore, in pay terms, their worth to the organization.
- The social context – the influences that colleagues, management, organization culture and climate exert on commitment and the desire to perform well.

The second key message from motivation theory is the significance of expectations, goal setting, feedback and reinforcement as motivating factors. Both these messages militate against seeing reward purely as an economic contract. In the professions, and in higher education in particular, something that leading occupational psychologists such as Herriot (1992), Guest (1995) and others have come to call the psychological contract is also of critical importance.

This chapter is not the place for a rehearsal of motivation theory, but it is useful to consider just what the economic and psychological contracts may mean in the context of working in universities. We believe that this analysis provides a helpful framework for understanding how pay works in higher education and for planning sensibly for the future.

Key elements of the economic contract

In common with the rest of the UK public service, universities are relatively restricted in the elements of the economic contract available to them. Staff in higher education do not have access to the share options, large-scale bonuses and profit shares widely available in the private sector, and only very rarely to Inland Revenue approved profit-related pay schemes (such as that at the North East Wales Institute of Higher Education). The main elements are therefore:

- Base salary and pay progression – still largely negotiated either centrally or locally, and often set at levels that lag, for instance, behind jobs of equivalent size in the civil service.
- Performance rewards – introduced relatively recently and still very cautiously in an environment that is sceptical about organizational ability consistently and fairly to set, monitor and reward performance improvements, and where a range of research identifying the problems of implementation in the public service is taken very seriously.
- Team rewards – currently being explored and experimented with, and seen as better aligned to academic values but, realistically, not a panacea.
- Access to consultancy earnings – available lucratively to some and on a basis that varies quite widely from institution to institution.
- A teaching year of 38 weeks and a maximum of 550 hours of teaching responsibilities, as provided for in new universities, leaves some flexibility for many to supplement their earnings. But many staff in the older universities with less defined conditions and contracts have still greater freedom to pursue consultancy and the rewards this brings. In business schools and many scientific and engineering faculties, high-profile consultancy is a badge of success. In addition, partnerships with businesses are growing and go well beyond the traditional consultancy arrangements in nature, value and the opportunities they provide.
- Benefits – most importantly pensions and good early retirement provisions, generous annual leave, sick pay, childcare facilities, subsidized meals and social facilities.

Main components of the psychological contract

In universities the range of elements under this heading is typically at least as rich as it is in the private sector. Indeed, especially in knowledge-based industries such as information technology, the private sector may seek to replicate what it perceives as the appealing side of the academic working environment. For example, the Microsoft Campus in the USA is run very much on university lines as a collegiate culture fostering innovation and learning. The priority and importance of the elements listed below will vary from place to place and from one type of work to another but they show the essence of what we are looking at.

- Challenge – the opportunity to do or support leading edge fundamental research or take this into the teaching environment and enable students to achieve their full potential.
- Autonomy – working in an environment that fosters self-direction and motivation within what is affordable. University teaching staff value academic freedom highly – much as this may be in conflict with some of the messages in the developing economic contract (see above).
- Quality of working conditions – by no means universal, given a maintenance

backlog of £2.5 billion recently identified by vice chancellors, but clearly part of the picture where good recent investment has been made. Quality of working conditions also, of course, means the possibility of spending long periods of time reflecting on research and the issues emerging from it, as well as networking across the world in the quest for new knowledge.

- Quality of management – again patchy, but there is a growing managerial focus on enabling high performance among the best of our institutions.
- Quality of colleagues – at best the exhilaration of working with some of the best minds in the country in a particular area, as well as developing them or supporting leading edge research.
- Status – working in universities is still highly regarded in the UK. 'Professor' is still a high-status title, satisfying a strong need for status based on intellect.
- Power – over internal management as well as across a broader academic spectrum.
- Recognition – for quality research, teaching, publications and contributions to the life and management of the institution. Some universities have successfully developed specific recognition programmes for lifetime academic achievement. Others use endowments and fellowships for the same purpose.
- Training and development opportunities – at all levels, the chance to improve career prospects and personal employability in the context of a 'learning organization' where continued upskilling and broadening of experience are highly valued.
- Career opportunities – clearly linked to the above, both within a single institution and in the broader community. Staff may also join a university in a technician role to fund a higher degree taken part-time, with an eye to short-term financial support and longer-term academic gain, in the process diminishing the 'class structure' of universities.
- Effective performance management – clear and well communicated processes for planning, managing and coaching as well as reviewing and recognizing performance improvements. Peer group reviews of academic contributions are an important cornerstone of this, a point neglected when 'top down' appraisal is considered.
- Conferences, extra support for projects in resources or kind – all highly valued, as are the travel and international reputation-building that go with them.
- A balanced life – recognition of the value of and support for balancing work and family commitments as well as contributions to the community.
- Convenience of location – accessibility both to work and to local amenities is important. At more junior levels, for example, the difference between a 5 and a 15 minute bus ride from home can affect choice of employer. At more senior levels, relative remoteness and housing costs are key elements of the decision process.
- Honesty about needs and requirements on both sides. In transactional analysis terms (Berne, 1967), this is an adult–adult employment relationship,

where the type and durability of the relationship is explicit in relation to what the organization offers and seeks and what the individual can contribute and is looking for. This means being honest about whether the contract on offer really is a core/career focused contract, whether it is project based/short term or whether it is part-time, enabling perhaps a limited high-level contribution (from, say, a visiting professor) as part of a mutually beneficial arrangement.

When one is making career choices or moving jobs these elements will loom at least as large as the financial deal on offer. All too often, in our experience, the psychological contract and its importance are neither fully recognized nor articulated. We believe that the psychological contract is worth researching and communicating as a critical element in managing good employee relationships at all levels. This should mirror the work already done in many places to attract the best students available in the market place.

Trends in reward systems

The past 15 years have seen unprecedented change in reward practice in both the private and public sectors. Not all the thinking is new, and some key trends, like performance-related pay, have been around since employment replaced slavery. Below we summarize the key trends that are influencing pay system design in the UK and outline the kind of impact they are likely to have on the UK academic environment. They can be divided into external environmental influences and the internal factors that are changing the nature of work and reward practice.

External influences

- Internationalization of activity leading to greatly increased competitive pressure. Universities are busy creating strategic alliances with other institutions around the world, and this must influence perceptions of performance and reward, not just among teaching staff but in the way contracts are managed and support staff are deployed.
- Progressive decentralization and devolution of control for pay down as far as is compatible with homogeneity of activity, unit size, cost effectiveness and management capability to take ownership of operational decisions. This is happening across the UK public service at different speeds and with differing degrees of success. Universities are the latecomers in the process – with the opportunity to learn from the lessons of others.
- Technological advance creating a growing demand for a highly skilled and qualified workforce – resulting in skill shortages even where unemployment among the unskilled workforce is growing.

- Affordability. Strong financial pressures on pay systems have created an environment in which the message is 'do more with less'.
- Increased employee mobility between organizations, notably where market pressures are strong.
- A growing emphasis on the 'portfolio career', where, especially for professionals and managers, it is now considered preferable to have gained experience with a number of different employers before achieving senior levels.
- Loyalty to profession or specialism tending to dominate over loyalty to employer.
- The emergence of flatter, more fluid, delayered organizations, more able to respond quickly to competitive pressures but offering significantly different career prospects from the promotion-based systems of the past. The impetus to respond to this in higher education has been nicely summarized by Mike Fitzgerald, Vice Chancellor of Thames Valley University: 'We need to move from control through rules and systems which tend to create rigidity, to management through values, where we develop shared values which create frameworks within which people can find direction without being told and controlled. To achieve this we need to establish an organization which is looser, and based on networks, rather than one which is rigidly hierarchical and based on functions. Management will need to be much more about the shaping of the context in which others work and operate, and within which they have more power, authority and responsibility. Managers will no longer be supervisors. They will be a resource for others' (Fitzgerald, 1995: 12).
- The emergence of a new employee mix. The previously dominant pattern of the male breadwinner is quickly giving way to growing numbers of single parents (the product of continuously rising divorce rates and changing social standards), women who choose to continue their career and raise a family and healthy, flexible-minded older people who either wish to continue working beyond normal retirement age or are embarking on second careers in their late forties or early fifties. There is a firm economic base for policies covering equal opportunities and the management of diversity in the workforce.
- Increasing employee financial literacy. The financial revolution of the past decade, the growth of house ownership, individual shareholding (generated to some extent by the privatization of public utilities as well as the expansion of all-employee share schemes) and the growth of personal pensions options have all contributed to the development of a workforce that is now more financially aware and questioning.
- As a result of the above, growing demand for more focused and tailored reward packages that reflect the differing needs of employees at the varying stages of their life and match varying personal circumstances. Contrary to common belief, this has not, even in the private sector, led to widespread adoption of so-called 'cafeteria compensation'. Instead it has led to greater flexibility in individual benefit provisions in areas such

as company cars and pensions – in ways not generally available in the public sector.

Internal influences

Within organizations, including universities, many changes are influencing the way in which pay is managed, as follows.

- The breakdown of old established work boundaries and demarcations, as the result of either technological change or new organizational structures born of the push towards more flexible and cost-effective operations. This is having the effect of breaking down the 'class structures' of many employment environments.
- In organizations where project working and flexibility are dominant requirements, the disappearance of fixed and defined jobs in favour of more loosely structured and flexible roles which change in relation to current needs, whether they are managed by contracts or through flexible longer-term roles.
- Much greater emphasis on the value of both formal and 'on the job' skills acquisition, reflected in the rapidly spreading use of competencies to define the proficiencies needed in a given role and the indicators for successful performance, and in the focus on planned career moves that encompass both lateral and vertical progression. Pay and performance management systems are adjusting to this as they seek specifically to reward personal development. This is slow to develop in universities and, notably among technical and support staff, there is much work to do.
- Greater individualization of the employment relationship as the emphasis on personal contribution has grown and direct union involvement and a broad collective focus have declined.
- As something of a counter-balance to the above, growing interest in team working, team effectiveness and ways of rewarding team contribution and collaborative behaviour in environments where this is of strategic importance.
- The development of new working patterns, such as annual hours, use of short-term contracts and outsourcing, designed to improve flexibility and control employment costs as well as to optimize use of the available labour pool. This has to be balanced against the differing levels of commitment and focus that short-term arrangements can generate.
- Broadening of pay structures and the introduction of unified approaches to grading, within frameworks that provide for effective cost management as well as greater flexibility and the breakdown of traditional hierarchies.
- A much increased emphasis on the quality of pay management and associated processes as this area has moved from the purely administrative to the actively strategic element of organizational activity. The burden of this is shifting from personnel to line management, and the development of

pay literacy and pay management capability among line managers is clearly critical to success. With this has come increasing stress on alignment with organizational strategy and values, simplicity and communicability of design and the defensibility of pay decisions across the whole organization.

The changing nature of jobs and roles

In the public service, as in the private sector, the culture has, at least in part, been held together by the existence of long established and traditional hierarchies. These have been underpinned by job and grade structures to which grade labels have been attached, which give the whole institution a 'shorthand' (e.g. senior lecturer, clerical officer) for defining people and staffing needs and for mapping promotion and career paths. Such structures are now changing rapidly and in places disappearing. In the UK civil service, for instance, all the old grade labels may begin to disappear after 1 April 1996, as both senior management reviews and local pay delegation allow new structures, labels and career patterns to emerge. Often these patterns are built using a more flexible concept of role (e.g. team manager, as embraced by HM Treasury), rather than reinforcing hierarchy or even specialism. The same is happening in the NHS and in local government. It is also beginning in universities, although the current central pay bargaining arrangements and the job levels and grades enshrined within them tend to act as a brake on change.

This development calls into question the use of conventional job evaluation and grading approaches based on the evaluation of every job and, typically, heavy administration procedures to support the process. But the need to manage internal and external relativities on a defensible basis remains. New approaches are emerging which combine the investment in competencies with role definition and the development of agreed performance measures and criteria. Such approaches may be based on generic roles (e.g. lecturer, laboratory technician) or they may be job family based (e.g. clerical, secretarial, technical support, teaching, research). In this case definitions, often called role profiles, are produced participatively for each job family as the foundation for development planning, performance management and the mapping of career progression. Role profiles for each level in a family can be measured using any suitable analytical job measurement methodology. This provides a framework for understanding the nature of the gap between role levels and between levels in different families to enable sensible lateral moves to be made. It is of critical importance to avoid turning job families into rigid occupational groups which tend to prevent rather than explain and foster flexible moves. It is also important to keep job family definitions up to date and to ensure that they evolve to match organizational change.

Initiatives on competency-based role definition from the centre and local projects within universities are moving work structures into this territory. If experience in the private sector or in the civil service is anything to go by, growing flexibility will result. More importantly, new approaches will produce a much more holistic view of work and the capabilities needed for effective performance.

This should enable better quality recruitment and career management, more focused development and training and the development of a performance focus that goes well beyond the quantitative and captures the essence of effective performance in the academic environment (more on this below).

More effective performance criteria and management

Despite the concerns commonly voiced within higher education about performance-related pay, the performance agenda remains. It is perhaps unfortunate that pay has under the current government agenda been seen as the main catalyst for performance improvement. A wide range of attitude survey and other research focused on evaluating the effectiveness of performance-related pay schemes suggests otherwise. Not that it is wrong to pay for performance, but the most significant organizational 'wins' come from improved performance management. In the public service in 1996 there is very little money available to fund sharper performance rewards. This hard economic reality provides little respite and leaves little time for universities to focus on improved performance management, assess and test out approaches which fit the culture and deliver real performance improvements. Some encouraging starts have been made in a range of institutions, e.g. a scheme for the top management staff at Nottingham Trent University and a quite well established scheme looking at a number of performance dimensions, including peer group and student feedback, at London Business School.

Better performance management means more effective recognition for success. Effective performance management in the mid-1990s is much more than a well run 'top-down' appraisal scheme. In our experience, the majority of annual appraisal schemes either do not work or under-perform.

All too often, success is defined in terms of whether all the forms are returned completed on time rather than whether the processes involved have delivered identifiable performance improvements in terms of agreed results and personal development.

Under-performance is too frequently tolerated. It is often easier to give individuals a middle performance rating in the hope that they can be moved to another area where they may perform better (but usually do not) than to tackle the underlying problems. The manager reviewing performance can get away, sometimes for years, with failing to confront real performance issues, sometimes forcing colleagues to work round a difficult individual and under-perform themselves in the process. Solving this depends on clarity about the nature of good performance, effective training in giving performance feedback and support for managers tackling problems that may have persisted for many years. It also means taking 'stakeholder' views on performance as a direct support for personal development.

We believe that improving performance management improves the quality of the psychological contract. Our experience to date suggests that, at its best, performance management can be used to:

- integrate current management and developmental initiatives;
- communicate and translate blueprints for change within organizations;
- translate corporate strategy and values into measurable or observable actions and results;
- reinforce and reward actions and behaviours which support key organizational goals;
- help to develop the managerial and staff capabilities that will bring about and sustain desired change;
- embed a performance focus into 'the way we do things around here';
- create a more positive, forward looking, and dynamic culture.

This cannot be achieved in the short term; nor can it be delivered without investment. Perhaps the most important investment is time, and to begin with, time spent at top management level on strategy clarification and learning the skills of more effective performance management and team working. This means building awareness of successful management style, understanding what is required to produce a motivational organizational climate, how to coach other senior colleagues as well as staff in the levels below and how to focus and agree targets to produce continuous performance improvement.

Working on this area is much more about processes than systems, and process skills have to be learnt. They may not naturally reside in professors of mathematics or readers in geology, or even in the psychology faculty.

Universities do not normally have these skills in much greater abundance than a major multinational or a government department. But like the latter, some are obtaining significant pay-backs in terms of improved motivation and higher performance where they have invested in skills development among already successful and senior people.

Taking account of changing student needs and motivations

Just as in the private sector, where customer focus and customer feedback become ever more important, so in universities levels of student satisfaction are now taken seriously. In an increasingly diverse student population, a wider range of needs has to be met. Measuring student satisfaction levels is an increasingly important feedback mechanism, both to help to adjust the scope and teaching methods for courses and to help individual teaching staff to improve their performance.

It is our view that it is important to develop and validate measures of student satisfaction and use them for the performance debate. We do not, however, advocate their use as a component in assessing individual performance rewards in the first instance. Experience with management training colleges in the private sector, for instance, suggests that it is easier to get good feedback for courses that are fun rather than for those that are hard and challenging. Many private sector organizations are beginning to use the concepts of the 'balanced scorecard' and 'performance pyramids' in order to define a set of broad-ranging measures of performance.

Typically these measures would embrace performance indicators directly related to the following:

- the 'bottom line' (for example, increase profit by X per cent, increase margin by Y);
- shareholders (for example, increase return on investment by X per cent);
- employees (for example, improve organizational climate results in specified ways);
- customers (for example, improve customer satisfaction survey results in specified ways).

Clearly it is time-consuming to develop these sets of comprehensive measures and costly to have systems which provide the relevant information, but evidence gathered from organizations which have gone down this path suggests that such systems are becoming a valuable and valued tool for offering the performance management improvements that really do make a difference.

Critical issues for future pay policy development

Unless the Dearing Inquiry makes strong representations to the contrary, there is little hope of changing the balance of pay in higher education or the reality that universities have fared less well in terms of pay increases than school teachers. This does not, however, remove the need for more effective reward management within the range of pay and other rewards that are available. The answer to the question 'does it pay to work in universities?' is therefore not just about reward levels, it is about the effectiveness of reward strategies and management and the processes that go with them.

Effective and successful reward strategies in the public service appear to depend on:

- a well articulated link between organizational strategy, the way people are managed and what they are paid to achieve;

- a sensible fit with the culture that the organization has and/or wants to develop;
- an agreed pay philosophy, which underpins all actions taken to further reward strategy achievement;
- both long- and short-term plans about what will happen when and for what reason, linked to how ability to manage new approaches will be developed and maintained;
- a managed pace of change within either an internally agreed or, as often happens in the public service, an externally set agenda for new ways of working;
- effective and continuing consultation with and communication to all parties involved (this needs to be aligned to the new values being developed as well as to be open, honest and credible);
- processes in place from the start to monitor how changes are working out in practice, evaluate results and implement changes in direction swiftly, while admitting honestly where initiatives have not delivered to expectations (being able to say you were wrong is generally a sign of strength).

All of this points to greater levels of decentralization and flexibility over pay in higher education. But cohesion also matters. The most recent public sector lesson here lies in the senior civil service, where proposals made in a consultative document covering pay arrangements for top civil servants were overturned to a significant degree by the Senior Salaries Review Body in February 1996, when it was realized that this might lead to greater diversity of practice than is prudent for a service where career mobility between departments and agencies needs to be fostered and protected. This points to the need for very clear frameworks for decentralization and a mapping and sharing of practice as it develops.

5

Which of Us Has a Brilliant Career? Notes from a Higher Education Survivor

Gaby Weiner

Two events especially have drawn attention to the changing notion of career in higher education: the abolition of tenure in 1983 in the old universities and the introduction of new lecturer contracts in 1991 in polytechnics and colleges of higher education, which transferred into the new university sector in 1992. Both signalled a fracturing and reconstitution of what it means to work in higher education and a shift in emphasis from the individual to the corporate, and both have profoundly affected how higher education staff have come to think of their professional careers.

My experiences of working in higher education (included later in the chapter) – as a late entrant, a woman, on the wrong side of the binary divide and in an applied academic area – may be seen, perhaps, as illustrative of changing contexts of career choice and progression. Do we still see career as 'structured into ordered sequences ... frequently arranged as a hierarchy of increasing income and prestige' (Abercrombie *et al.*, 1984: 27)? Or has it become something else? This chapter explores these issues by identifying shifts, in the term 'career' itself, in those who might consider themselves to be on a university career track of some kind and in the current nature of academic work.

The chapter is divided into five parts. The first considers the concept of career generally: how it has been understood in the past and how it may be viewed as a configuration of personal choice and structural imperatives. The second part examines who in higher education may be said to have a career and the proliferation of roles for university workers, particularly in view of the fact that the system itself is increasingly dominated by short-term planning, financial crises and necessarily swift responses to government policy turns. The third part focuses on changes in the nature of academic work and its apparent intensification, while the fourth provides a brief autobiographical overview of one apparently non-conventional career which has ended up in higher education by virtue of a 'winding track' rather than the usual 'straight road' (Elgqvist-Saltzman, 1992). The question to be addressed here is whether the notion of academic career can adapt to both 'straight' and 'winding pathways' and, if so, how. The final section attempts to pull the debates on career together to suggest possibilities and pitfalls for the future.

Concept of career

Conventionally, careers have been understood 'as the sequences of jobs performed by individuals in the course of their working lives' (Abercrombie *et al.*, 1984: 27), with the attendant characteristic of financial reward for increased professional knowledge and experience. Careers may be seen as *structured*, i.e. a series of ordered sequences, or *unstructured*, i.e. character-ized by movement between jobs 'of an apparently haphazard nature' (Abercrombie *et al.*, 1984: 27). In both cases, peak earnings tend to occur in the thirties, with little hope of advancement thereafter. Occupationally based careers, such as those of many staff in higher education, tend to be more stable and predictable, with progressive and structured career routes, rising pay and upward social mobility.

More recently, however, it has been suggested that the notion of career should be applied more inclusively to involve all adults of working age, whether or not in employment (School Curriculum and Assessment Author-ity, 1995); thus, voluntary work can be said to be part of a career plan. Here, then, career is perceived as arising principally from individual needs and interests, and as a consequence of autonomous decisions and aspirations.

It would seem that such changing and broadening of what it means to have a career reflects two dimensions of the debate. First, the balance between individual choice and the needs of the labour market has altered as a consequence of the shrinking public sector, seen, for example, in demands for 'efficiency savings' and 'downsizing' in organizations such as universities and the civil service. Second, there has been a major restructur-ing of white-collar occupations, such as banking and financial services more generally – sectors hitherto having well delineated and progressive career structures. Thus, for many professional and white-collar workers, steady career progress or a 'job for life' has become a thing of the past.

Nevertheless, despite attempts at redefinition and labour-market in-stability, 'career' continues to be viewed by most as a series of upwards or sideways moves between and within occupations, usually of a professional nature. It has within it implications of long-term and/or lifelong plans aimed at reaching a target job destination shaped by individual choice and experience. As mentioned above, it is clearly also structured by wider polit-ical and economic contexts which shape labour market changes and re-quirements: as Ball and Goodson (1985: 11) put it, 'by definition individual careers are socially constructed and individually experienced over time'.

Where careers are viewed principally as individual experiences, efforts are made to chart work histories, investigate aims, abilities and personal career trajectories and elicit perspectives on what happened and why (e.g. Furniss, 1981; Powney and Weiner, 1992). The main purpose is to establish, from the perspective of the actor (or careerist[1]), how and why certain apparently personal choices are made.

Where careers are viewed principally as a result of structural patterns, occupations are presented as offering a typical sequence of positions, together with rules and conventions for their allocation – which then facilitate or inhibit career progression (Acker, 1989). Thus, Furniss (1981) understands the traditional North American academic (or faculty) career as progression from the high school diploma to bachelor degree, master's or professional qualification and doctorate, through to eligibility for the tenure track to assistant and then full professor. Another view, following Lawn and Ozga's work (1981) on school teachers, is that university lecturers (and other staff) are workers with a career structure for a few based on a lack of one for most of the others. Alternatively, the impact of chosen discipline on career in higher education may be a principal focus, with the emphasis on how the novice is inducted. In his study of senior and junior academics in a selection of university departments covering a dozen disciplines, Becher (1989: 106) suggests that this induction is primarily a 'continuing process of selection and socialisation to the pivotal norms of the field governing criteria for truth, and how it is to be achieved, communicated and used and secondarily to peripheral norms governing personal life-styles, attitudes and social relations.'

In Becher's view, this form of initiation has tended to produce career inertia, owing to, on the one hand, the need to create and affirm unique areas of expertise and, on the other, the fact that career advancement is generally geared towards teaching (for the first permanent post) and then administration (for later promoted posts), rather than towards research. Becher's research concentrated on elite institutions, emphasizing the differing expectations and initiation processes of individual departments and subject specialisms.

What might be termed the conventional (or inert?) academic career trajectory frequently leads, according to Becher, to a mid-life or mid-career crisis when academics are in their late thirties or early forties. Whether remaining intellectually engaged or experiencing 'burn out', boredom or exhaustion, at this stage of their work life they are confronted by a number of alternatives.

> The main question which is posed at this point concerns whether or not to continue working within the same specialism, whether to switch to another one, or whether to begin the process of moving away altogether from active research ... The most important consideration must be what relative career gains and losses are likely to result from deciding to make a move.
>
> (Becher, 1989: 114)

Academic inertia has also been challenged to some extent by the departure of the modern university from its earlier characterization as a community of scholars with shared patterns of education and training, apprenticeship and socialization, to a rather more heterogeneous and diverse place of work. However, the existence of a community of scholars, according to Harman (1990), remains a 'potent myth', despite the changes to modern universities. Middlehurst (1993: 49) characterizes these changes as having 'disciplinary and structural heterogeneity [within] ... the present managerialist and market pressures of the external environment and the conflicts of territory and interest present within institutions.'

With the creation of new higher education structures, the need to generate new markets, new areas of expertise and new academic 'stars', a higher education career may come to be seen as the way in which academics develop and alter their perspectives, interpretation and strategies in response to changing circumstances. Indeed, recent research assessment exercises illustrate one of the main shifts of academic work in recent times, whereby productivity is measured according to research and publication, rather than teaching and scholarship as in the past. Another shift is the increasing impact on the everyday lives of academics, administrators and students of centrally directed imperatives (whether as a consequence of government policy, HEFCE requirements, research council bidding strategy or university procedural changes).

Examination of the concept of career in higher education has generally, as we have seen, focused on academic and related posts. There have been fewer discussions about the careers of administrators and other university workers who are principally concerned with 'the well-being, coordination and regulation of the whole institution: its diverse staff; its range of activities and resources, particularly finance; its extensive plant and equipment' (Middlehurst, 1993: 109). These may be senior 'career' administrators, faculty, departmental and course administrators, secretaries, technical support staff, canteen staff, cleaners etc. The main factors governing the work of such staff, particularly at the lower levels, is that they are more likely to be women (and/or from minority ethnic groups), on short-term or part-time contracts, low paid and lacking a progressive structure for career advancement (Farish *et al.*, 1995). Thus, it is they rather than academics who are more likely to think in terms of 'job' rather than career.

Whose career?

Higher education in the UK has been affected by structural, cultural and demographic changes in recent years, which have profoundly affected the staff who work within the sector. For example, the accelerated expansion of student numbers in the early 1990s and the abolition of the division between the universities and polytechnics in 1992 created for more individuals the possibility of having an academic or administrative career track.

This involved increased career opportunities for particular groups of individuals, specifically women, though other groups, such as minority ethnic staff, appear to have benefited less from the changes. As in other countries, there is in the UK a higher proportion of female academics in the 1990s than in previous decades, though they are still in a substantial minority, are less likely to be tenured and are more likely to be on temporary or short-term contracts, to be promoted slowly and to have low salaries than their male counterparts (Becher, 1989; Stiver-Lie *et al.*, 1994).

Female administrative and other support staff, being more office-bound, tend to have a higher visibility than their academic sisters. As office workers, they are typically thought of as keeping the organization running on a day-to-day basis, yet they remain in subordinate, lower-status and lower-paid positions. For example, in the 'new' university studied by Farish *et al.* (1995), a 1993 internal report showed that

> women represented 47% of the total staff at the university, with over half (51 per cent) of female workers employed in such 'traditional' female occupations as cleaners, catering staff, library staff, clerks, typists and administrative assistants. Indeed, categories of staff such as clerical assistant, clerk, typist, receptionist, administrative assistant and personal assistant were *exclusively* female . . . 92 percent of female manual workers were employed at the lowest grades . . . while three quarters of the men . . . were employed in the three top graded manual posts.
>
> (Farish *et al.*, 1995: 53)

Significantly, in the same university, the department with the highest concentration of minority ethnic staff, most of whom were cleaners, was campus services.

Those who are aware of such patterns of employment, and suffer from them, are more likely to advocate stronger institutional back-up to guard against discrimination. Thus, Farish *et al.* found that,

> at Metropolitan University, women staff often found themselves in a minority (especially in the academic sector). It is therefore not surprising that many of the women academics we spoke to, or made contact with through the questionnaire, conveyed strong views on the importance of promoting equal opportunities, combined with a powerful sense that on a number of occasions discriminatory practices were preventing women from reaching their full potential. In contrast, their male peers . . . appeared fundamentally uninterested.
>
> (Farish *et al.*, 1995: 136)

Moreover, there is now a wider spread of occupational categories available in higher education: for example, newly created posts related to the expansion of enterprise and marketing services have attracted employees from the private sector with public relations backgrounds; and the development of information technology (IT) has created new requirements for

IT technical support to both students and staff, and for librarians with advanced information retrieval skills.

Another example of widening career opportunities in higher education is the expanding number of research staff in the new university sector which, according to a recent survey (Hart, 1995), currently constitute approximately a third of all full-time academic staff, though they are still fewer than in the old universities. The same survey of research staff by the National Association for Teachers in Further and Higher Education (NATFHE) suggests that the enhanced academic status that the new universities have gained from research has come at a price. For example, the survey found that:

- average pay is lower than the starting salaries of researchers at the old universities;
- the majority are on fixed-term contracts, affecting the quality of research as well as personal lives;
- the research assessment exercise was perceived to favour the old universities, and short-term traditional research;
- researchers liked their work, but not the way they were treated by the institutions;
- almost half of those surveyed who wished to stay in research did not intend to remain in the new university sector (Hart, 1995: 16–17).

Nature of university work

As career opportunities have opened up for some in the university sector post-1992, this has been accompanied by an intensification of work for others who have worked in the sector for some time. This intensification has been caused, among other things, by higher student : staff ratios (SSRs), new forms of course delivery and qualification and more bureaucratic forms of corporate planning. For example, in 1970–1 the university SSR in Great Britain was 8.5 to 1; in 1980–1 it had risen to 9.5 to 1; in 1988–9 it was 11.5 to 1 and by 1990–1 it was 12.3 to 1. SSRs in the polytechnic and college sectors had always been higher than the 'old' universities, increasing from 13.5 to 1 in 1986 to 15 to 1 in 1990 (Miller, 1995). At the time of writing, SSRs are likely to be even higher unless current trends towards expansion are reversed. According to Miller (1995: 51), the increase in staff : student ratios in the 1980s was unprecedented: 'the rise in university staff/student ratio has been exponential, at nearly 11 per cent in the first half of the 1980s and 19 per cent in the second.'

Intensification of work is also the consequence of increased pressure on academic staff across the sector to do more research and to publish. However, given cash limits, and increased pressure elsewhere in the system, as mentioned above, whether more means better is a moot point. As Miller (1995: 51) reflects, 'more research is being done with the same or scarcely increased resources, but it is difficult to assess if quality is being maintained.'

So while, on the one hand, more academics are currently in a position to pursue a career, on the other, the restructuring of universities has resulted (at least for some) in a reduction in career satisfaction and progression. In Carroll and Cross's (1989) survey of stress in universities, increased stress was reported by over three-quarters of the academics, with 62 per cent expecting their jobs to be yet more stressful in the future. Nearly half expressed the view that job satisfaction had been lower in recent years, with fewer than a quarter indicating higher levels of job satisfaction than previously. Sources of job dissatisfaction included conflicting and increased work demands, inadequate resources, the absence of promotion prospects, a lack of public recognition, job insecurity, a lack of autonomy and isolation from colleagues (Carroll and Cross, 1989).

The specific nature of the restructuring of higher education and its impact on working conditions provide a clue to the other sources of increased stress and anxiety. There is an increased density and heightened bureaucracy within modern universities, which profoundly affects the day-to-day lives of staff. Participation, communication and policy-making have all become more complex and difficult as the university administration moves typically to a three-tier framework: the departmental, school or faculty committee structure; the collegial system of academic committees, assemblies and councils; and the centralized management system, with the increasingly powerful vice chancellor and senior management team (Miller, 1995). This has resulted among other things in greater demands on all staff in terms of paperwork and administration, course analysis, evaluation and review, action planning and development, expanded quality procedures, the need to generate outside income and so on.

Those who seem to survive and indeed flourish in the new social and work relations of universities are the youthful, the energetic, the entrepreneurial and those with few domestic commitments who are able to work long hours. It is clear, therefore, given what we know about differences in lifestyles between men and women and between different social groups, who will be likely to benefit from this changed work ethos.

One career: winding track rather than straight road

If, indeed, the cards are stacked against the career progress of some groups working in universities, the development of a broader and more inclusive conception of career might well be helpful in making different work and career patterns more visible. A recent 'life-line' study of women graduating from secondary schools in Sweden in the 1950s and 1960s (Elgqvist-Saltzman, 1992) provides a clue to alternative conceptualizations. It was found in this study that women's educational and career development was generally uneven and fragmented: more of a 'winding track' than a 'straight road'.

It was found that women's vocational careers were surprisingly similar – in spite of different educational, social, and regional backgrounds and settings. Most women had chosen 'female professions', most worked part-time and only a few had leading positions. Many women expressed educational plans for the future and many planned for professional careers in their late forties and fifties. A lifelong education model, where education was attributed different functions at different phases, was revealed.

(Elgqvist-Saltzman, 1992: 47)

Perhaps, then, individual career trajectories such as my own may reflect not only changes in university conditions but also the different life chances of female and male workers. For example, I had four years out of the labour market when my children were young. I also initially chose a 'female' career (school-teaching), which left me free to look after children in the school holidays. In fact, I moved into the university sector relatively late in my career, after having had a number of mini-career starts as a local authority clerical officer (before marriage), time at home, late entry into teacher training as a young 'mature' student, a short period as a primary teacher, a year out to do a master's degree, employment as a researcher in an independent educational research organization and several other periods of short-term employment.

My first regular job in higher education was at the Open University, as a temporary and then permanent course administrator. I had previously established a minor academic profile on gender issues in education as leader of the first national project on the subject, and was allowed to build on this, providing it did not detract from my main administrative responsibilities – in reality, I had to work a double shift to pursue my academic career. In 1982, most course administrators and secretaries in the university were female and most lecturers were male, though when I pointed this out, I was viewed as somewhat of a malcontent and trouble-maker. Because of my interest in social justice and gender issues, my awareness of inequalities in the system was perhaps sharper than others'. For example, I noted the existing career structure, which seemed designed mainly for men, and also the small, often covert, incidents of discrimination and unequal power relations which affected the everyday lives of all staff. These appeared to fuse together to bolster men's career advancement and simultaneously to block the personal career development and work choices of women. However, for me as an individual, working at the Open University brought substantial benefits: I was fortunate to work with some exceptionally gifted individuals and, perhaps as important, was encouraged by the nature of the university's main work (the production of distance learning materials) to develop and extend my writing and communication skills.

After a few years, I was allowed to switch from administrative to largely academic duties because of gaps in the academic workforce and support from other female academics: first to work on a master's course and then to become a staff tutor in London. During this time I also enrolled for a part-time PhD, though it took me eight years to complete because of the demands of my 'day job'. Unlike mainstream academics, I was expected to be primarily office-based and therefore could use only leisure time and annual leave to pursue academic study.

I realized that I would be unlikely to gain promotion at the Open University principally because of my relatively lowly entry point, so for this as well as other reasons, in 1989 I crossed the binary divide by moving to the Education Department at South Bank Polytechnic (now South Bank University). Significantly, among the reasons I was appointed to South Bank (with a substantial salary increase) was that as an ex-mature student I would have a greater understanding of the problems experienced by, and the opportunities available to, the largely mature student intake. At South Bank, I taught mature student teachers who had similar social backgrounds to my own, contributed to the establishment of a master's in education course and sought involvement with a variety of projects relating to equality issues in education. I joined a mainly teaching department, and though the workload seemed high, I was able to complete my doctoral studies and continue to publish.

The late 1980s and early 1990s was a period when interest, never strong, began to turn away from equal opportunities and social justice issues (particularly in schools), so I was compelled to shift my research interests elsewhere; for example, by changing focus to post-compulsory and higher education. I was successful in gaining several research grants, which allowed me to develop a higher research profile and, after one rejected application to become a reader in 1990, I was appointed Professor of Education in 1992.

I have since become head of department (for a three-year period) with a heavy administrative burden, but still have a wish to develop new research areas; for example, the politics of academic publishing, for which I recently gained a research council grant. I have come, rather later than other colleagues, I suspect, to the mid-career crisis point identified by Becher, as new researchers and academics begin to challenge the ideas and work of the previous generation.

So currently my career might be viewed as a winding track which has, unexpectedly, provided me with a fairly senior post within a new university. As a latecomer to higher education, I none the less have experienced during my years at the Open University and South Bank an increased workload and all the attendant problems arising from the doubling of student numbers during a relatively short period and the increased bureaucracy of the sector. Nevertheless, compared with most women and many men, I am relatively privileged. My work has brought me into contact with a wide range of undergraduate and postgraduate students and university staff (at South Bank and elsewhere); I have been fortunate to be a part of an enormously stimulating intellectual network which traverses countries and continents (electronic mail being a recent valuable asset in helping to maintain contact with distant colleagues); and I have also been able to visit other countries and compare other education systems and cultural frameworks.

How my status and quality of scholarship (and salary) compare with those of colleagues in other universities (new or old) or with other comparable professions is difficult to estimate, though, for example, my conditions of service do not include study leave to pursue research (as is the case in some other universities). Moreover, as a woman, I still feel a certain 'otherness' in the presence of male colleagues. In the institutions (schools, research organizations, higher education) in which I have worked, my immediate bosses have generally been men, and senior hierarchies have been virtually exclusively male and white. This has not appeared to change over the years either in my own experience or more generally (see, for example, Powney and Weiner, 1992; Heward and Taylor, 1993; Farish *et al.*, 1995; Arnot *et al.*, 1996), despite the proliferation of institutional equal opportunities policies.

Perhaps my experience of being on the less privileged side of the binary line illustrates the disadvantages and also the advantages of being in such a position. For me, like others who have been provided with hitherto un-anticipated career avenues, the recent transformation of higher education has been largely beneficial; though what I recognize as academic work or an academic career is clearly different from and, to some extent, less privileged than that of earlier times.

Considerations for the future

This chapter has attempted to point towards the need for new thinking about what is meant by career. Earlier definitions of academic career have implied early entry, specialization, sequence and progression, continuity, linearity, security and privilege. In contrast, the work of university administrative and support staff has conventionally implied orderliness, security and, perhaps, the relatively high status attached to white-collar workers in elite institutions.

For both groups, times have clearly changed. New types of university have recognized different forms of expertise and greater diversity among staff, although, particularly in the old universities, the straight road or structured pathway to a specific occupational destination may still be available for some. For others, particularly women (whether academic or administrative), a winding or unstructured path might be a more accurate definition of career progress, involving multiple or late entry, lack of continuity, more diversity, opportunity and insecurity, and a weak sense of eventual occupational destination.

An added factor is that, as universities have expanded, often becoming a major employer in the locality, several members of the family might find work there. Thus the university might simultaneously create wider access for some to employment in a broader range of jobs; and, for others, potentially diminished career opportunity owing to restrictions placed on geographical mobility. A possible outcome of this might be, however, the reconceptualization of career as that of a winding track within one institution.

Another possibility is that movement within the sector towards modularization, semesterization, accreditation of prior learning, independent learning and so on will create new academic and administrative career structures, reflecting a hierarchical binary divide *within* higher education institutions. New forms of academic provision will be produced at undergraduate and vocational levels, pushing conventional academics towards research and postgraduate teaching.

For all these reasons, the only safe prediction is that to have a university career will continue to mean different things to different people, and to shift and mutate to meet the ever-changing concerns and interests of the modern university. Old elites will, no doubt, continue to survive and flourish at the time that new institutional power bases will seek higher status within the new order. These in turn will continue to offer, for potential university workers, a heady yet confusing mix of career opportunities, the eventual destination of which is likely to be increasingly impossible to determine.

Note

1. A term generally used critically to imply the sacrificing of principle to ambition rather than its dictionary definition: 'one intent mainly on personal advancement and success in life' (Fowler and Fowler, 1964: 180).

Part 2

The Work

6

New Liberty, New Discipline: Academic Work in the New Higher Education

Richard Winter

Introduction

In organizing these thoughts on the current experience of university work, I am reminded, at first, of an observation which impressed me twenty years ago: a good theory always explains how any given social role is necessarily associated with a characteristic, structurally determined form of pain. But I will also keep in view another principle, that institutions are to be understood as offering 'a specific relation . . . and distribution of *enablements* [as well as] constraints' (Wagner, 1994: xiv; following Giddens, 1984), in order to explore some opportunities for creative development which may be detected lurking ambiguously, as it were, behind (or even within) the pain.

Admittedly, this approach could be immediately accused of wilful optimism. It might be argued, instead, that in general the typical current experience of work can be fully understood simply as one of subjection. Thus, one might point to the subjection of staff to untrammelled managerial power, in which key features would be the crippling of trade unions, the dismantling of staff rights and the establishment of chief executives in the role of feudal barons, attempting to extort the maximum level of 'productivity' that staff can be forced to endure.[1] A second 'subjection theory' would focus on the encroachment into higher education of market relationships, converting what were formerly the 'crafts' of curriculum construction, research and teaching (expressing the direct cultural authority of the 'professional' educator) into a series of exchange relationships determined by principles of competition and profitability.

Nevertheless, it must be admitted that, however appealing such lines of argument may seem, they remain somewhat simplified and schematic. As I have argued elsewhere (Winter, 1995), the management task is inherently ambiguous, ultimately relying on the very forms of initiative which its attempts at 'coordination' seem destined to stifle; and although market relationships do threaten to debase communication with the promotional rhetoric of 'selling', they also have the potential for decentralizing decision-making and thus for 'empowering' the citizen/consumer. In this chapter, then, I treat such general interpretations as a tacit background awareness, and my explicit focus is instead on the details and ambiguities in current higher education phenomena, starting from issues in current theories of the culture and structure of organizations, and concentrating on the pains and opportunities surrounding the recent introduction into university work of three features with which I have recently been particularly involved: (a) modularization; (b) competence-based curricula; and (c) the accreditation of students' work experience.

The notion of 'modern' organizations

Universities are (and always have been) organizations: they hire staff, establish management structures, allocate resources and attract customers by marketing goods and services. (The same could be said of the medieval church.) We may feel that in many respects this needs to be understood as a metaphorical description ('customers'?), but similar reservations might be expressed on behalf of hospitals, charities, government departments, orchestras etc. The argument I wish to make, therefore, is simply that universities as organizations reflect (to some degree) the form and culture of other contemporary organizations, and that the basic forms of organizational life current in a society embody (in some sense) societal conceptions of authority, rationality and communication. Thus, by considering some aspects of current theories of organizations in general, I hope to gain a broad theoretical perspective on our experience of employment within specifically 'academic' organizations.

A recurring theme of writers on organizations is that of ubiquitous and rapid change, a sense of needing to respond to an 'unpredictable' environment and of living in a permanent state of uncertainty: 'Successful management is dependent on . . . dealing with change and realising that in today's interdependent and complex world, there are no certainties on which to cling' (Aspden, 1994). Aspden is conducting a general review of the current state of management theory, and his analysis contains an underlying note of anxiety and nostalgia, which is echoed in the title of Charles Handy's detailed account of current organizational structures, *The Age of Unreason* (Handy, 1991), as well as Tom Peters's 'international best seller', *Thriving on Chaos* (Peters, 1989). In more measured tones, Heckscher suggests that we are in the midst of a long-term historical shift from the 'bureaucratic' (hierarchically ordered) organization described by Weber (see, for example, Weber, 1964; originally 1922) to a 'post-bureaucratic organization', which he characterizes as 'interactive', in that its decisions are based on dialogue and the persuasive use of 'influence' rather than on positional authority (Heckscher, 1994: 24–5).

The basis for much of this sense that the experience of organizational life has suddenly become fundamentally unpredictable is the sudden powerful influence of information technology, which dramatically increases both the manipulability of knowledge and social access to knowledge, and thus undermines the extent to which static authority structures can control information:

> Since electronic information appears to evade the laws of what might be termed Weber's Newtonian universe – it can be everywhere at once, manipulated instantly and effortlessly – it can be said to be fundamentally opposed to any outward manifestation of structure . . . [Hence] managers and executives brag about the elimination of hierarchy and the turn to *non-structured* arrangements of people and information.
>
> (Nohria and Berkley, 1994: 119, 121)

The possibilities of this newly liberated, barely structured organization of work roles and knowledge, celebrated by, for example, Zuboff (1988), lead to urgent advice that organizations must, if they are to survive, abandon 'traditional authoritarian' forms and become 'learning organizations' (Senge, 1993: 3–5) or 'learning companies' (Pedler *et al.*, 1991). However, the urgency of this advice is ironic. 'Learning organizations' may be theoretically conceivable, because of human creativity and adaptability (Senge, 1993: 4) and because our conceptions of knowledge now embrace systematic uncertainty and contingency (Rorty, 1979, 1989; Prigogine and Stengers, 1985); but Heckscher (1994: 17) is adamant that the post-bureaucratic organization as such does not exist: 'To my knowledge there is no concrete example that truly exemplifies the type – certainly not in business, certainly not on a large scale or for more than a short period.' Moves towards 'decentralization', total quality management and 'participation', he argues, are better understood simply as attempts to make hierarchical bureaucracies more effective (Heckscher, 1994: 28–9).

Behind the insistent rhetoric of the new 'interactive organization', therefore, and in spite of its apparent technological basis, there are inherent contradictions which make its realization in practice highly problematic. For example, an interactive organization may emphasize that decisions are to be made through 'dialogue', but they nevertheless need to solve the problem of power and authority (Heckscher, 1994: 37) since organizations always (as the term itself implies) have the task of *coordinating* decision-making. Heckscher's answer here is that the outcome of organizational dialogue must be the *legitimation of consensus* (Heckscher, 1994: 39ff) and that this requires an exceptionally high degree of mutual trust (Heckscher, 1994: 25). But this is, of course, not an answer but a restatement of the question: what are the procedures which will enable the new interactive freedom of individuals to be coordinated in such a way that the practical outcomes of dialogue will be perceived and 'trusted' as indeed 'consensual' rather than, yet again, imposed? Handy, for example, recognizes that within the new organizational order, 'flexible' workers on part-time contracts will have no basis for either loyalty or commitment, and that the 'fairness' of these contracts relies on managers to 'resist the temptation to exploit the monopoly power of the organization' (Handy, 1991: 79–81). No wonder, then, that the 'learning organization' is more of a pious ideal than an operationalized reality.

This enables us to see the necessity of understanding the nature of modern organizations within a more complex conceptual framework than merely a Pandora's box of new freedoms. In a recent analysis, Peter Wagner interprets Western history since the industrial revolution in terms of a continual dialectic between two key processes: on the one hand, the development of new forms of 'liberty' and, on the other hand, corresponding shifts in 'disciplinization' (Wagner, 1994: 6); a barbarous coinage, to be sure, but one which expresses the suggestion that the development of new dimensions of freedom generates attempts to 'contain' and restrict those freedoms, i.e. to *order* them, through shifts in conceptions of rationality and morality, shifts in *norms* for organizational relationships and shifts in conceptions of valid knowledge. Wagner's basic argument is that what provides the dynamic for historical change is precisely this ambiguous and intimate relationship between a 'drive' for the development of liberties and the elaboration of corresponding 'disciplines'.

It is in these terms, therefore, that I shall try to analyse some typical current developments in higher education, but first I would like to add one further dimension to the general argument. Heckscher presents his discussion of post-bureaucratic organizations in terms of a conflict between the liberty of dialogic interaction and the discipline of consensus, and he takes this to be easily intelligible as the basic problem of 'democracy' (Heckscher, 1994: 39). But this, I would argue, is both outdated and simplistic. The current issue for democracy is no longer the negotiation of 'consensus', since it is precisely consensus which seems elusive, part of an endlessly lamented 'lost' sense of order and discipline. Instead, the problem is how to develop 'decentralizing' procedures for the coordination of 'pluralistic' societies (see Hirst, 1994), so that *differences* may be fully accepted. Now, differences imply strongly defined identities, and identities (particularly collective identities) are constructed in terms of an 'Other', as the focus of outwardly projected feelings of hostility (Mouffe, 1993: 2). Hence, the recognition of differences, within a pluralist structure, involves recognizing conflicting interests, and this, as Mouffe argues, is the current political problem of democracy: 'The liberal claim that a universal rational consensus could be produced by an undistorted dialogue . . . is only possible at the cost of denying the irreducible antagonistic element present in social relations, and this can have disastrous consequences for the defence of democratic institutions' (Mouffe, 1993: 40).

Hence, in order to grasp the nature of organizational structures, we must accept that the order which coordinates the new interactive liberties must be understood in terms of procedures for handling conflict, as the necessary precondition for constructing consensus. Indeed, the rhetoric for the new interactive organization is itself usually put forward as part of a necessary strategy for survival against competitors (Senge, 1993: 4), so that even in its own terms the new liberty of the flexible, continuously learning organization is part of the new 'discipline' of the global market – the ultimate mechanism for managing conflicts of interest. Thus, in the next three sections I discuss aspects of current university work in terms of: (a) increasing liberties; (b) corresponding elaborations of 'discipline'; and (c) inherent conflicts of interest.

Behind the analysis lies an awareness of the sort of general challenge presented by Ronald Barnett in *The Idea of Higher Education*:

> Higher education is not an ivory tower; even if it wished, it could not be one . . . Higher education has been sucked into society, at least into the fringes of the state apparatus, and with this incorporation, knowledge has been institutionalized and colonized . . . The question then, which an educational theory of higher education has to answer is: What ought we to do to see that a higher education fulfils its emancipatory promise . . . ?
>
> (Barnett, 1990: 77–8)

But is there not here also a tone of lament, for a 'lost' ivory tower? The phrasing ('sucked into', 'colonized', 'emancipation') suggests a general sense of a new and regrettable conflict between higher education and 'society'; in the following analysis, by way of contrast, I shall try to explore (following the general argument outlined above) examples of what may be considered both 'incorporations' and 'emancipations' and thus to emphasize that some important conflicts, forming an integral part of our experience of organizational relationships, also lie within the university.

Modularization

Modularization threatens to break up the hierarchical and sequential structure of academic disciplines in order to permit increased liberty in the construction of individualized programmes of study, corresponding to the variety of students' interests and expertise. Modularization may thus be seen as part of a recognition that an overall grasp of an academic discipline may be approached in different ways, depending on the learner (Swann, 1992), and that there are alternative ways of conceiving of the structure of any given discipline (Lenoir, 1993). However, this increased structural liberty leads potentially to fragmentation, and thus to the curtailment of the relationship between a given lecturer and a given student in relation to any particular set of ideas. For students this may have advantages, in that it might reduce the specifically educational danger of 'dependency' (often so close to a form of oppressiveness), but it could also lead to the loss of a sense of guidance embodied in a strong role model. For tutors this curtailment is more likely to be felt as an unambiguous loss, since it reduces our sense of being able to exert a significant influence in the formation of our students' cultural identities, and thus to a loss of the opportunity to exercise cultural authority. Worse, if the modules we teach are to recruit enough students to remain 'economically viable' within an ever-diminishing resource base,[2] we may feel under pressure to 'popularize' our material and thus to demean our expertise. In terms of both of these arguments, therefore, modularization seems to 'empower' students at the expense of staff.

However, following the general argument of the previous section, we can expect to find, within modularity, new expressions of order which counter-act ('discipline') the students' new-found liberties. Most obvious, perhaps, is the notion of 'coherence', with which programme coordinators circum-scribe the potential liberty of students to permutate any combination of modules. Hence, one can envisage conflicts between students arguing the coherence of their proposed choices, and staff rejecting certain requests as lacking a proper foundation in a 'disciplined' structure. Furthermore, given a growing awareness of historical contingency and change in the constitution of disciplines (Messer-Davidov *et al.*, 1993), we might also anticipate conflicts surrounding decisions as to whether a certain module is to be compulsory within a pathway: some staff may resent the classification of their particular specialism as 'optional' by influential members of an 'oligarchical' coordinat-ing committee, whom they may suspect of promoting their own or their political friends' expertise as more 'central' (see Michels, 1959: 389, on 'the iron law of oligarchy' within ostensibly 'representative' organizational pro-cedures).

A modular curriculum, then, like any other organizational structure, needs to manage a balance between liberty and order, and is thus likely to become a site for conflicts between 'managers' and 'managed' in relation to its various decisions, even where particular individuals shift between these two roles on different occasions. At a more general level, the administration of modular curricula requires a massive centralization of information, in order that (in theory) it may be easily and equitably made available to *all* concerned, whenever and wherever it is required. In this way, it empowers not only students but the administrators of the centralized system; this in turn is likely to sharpen conflict with tutorial staff, who thereby experience a strong sense that their specialized and creative activity has been newly subjected to further external control, and (moreover) control by those from whose specialist professional perspective the operational requirements of a computerized 'system' will seem more urgent than the educational require-ments of the teaching/learning process.

This centralizing tendency extends beyond mere information-gathering, however, to include such basic procedures as the assessment and timing of modules, and this can lead to quite sharp issues of educational principle. For example, in order that *all* students may be able to select *any* module into their individualized pathways, system managers may urge that all mod-ules need to be 'delivered' within a similar time frame and be graded according to a given numerical scheme, so that any combination of module results can be arithmetically manipulated to create an overall award outcome.

But a single format may not be equally appropriate for a wide range of academic disciplines and learning contexts. For example, staff responsible for musical performance, professional practice development or work-based learning may find numerical marking of students' work highly inappropriate, and part-time students may need a longer and more flexible time frame for completion than full-time students. In many ways, then, modular systems will generate conflicts (among staff) between different versions of order and freedom: between the need for modules to be administratively 'the same' (so that a wide variety of choices can be accommodated) and the need for modules to be 'different' (so that a wide variety of work can be accredited).

Perhaps the most educationally significant problem of 'order' created by the new liberties of modularity concerns the nature of educational 'levels' or stages. Modularity liberates the structure of a given student's pathway to a qualification from the constraints of a single large-scale 'course' following a prescribed sequence of topics and activities; but since qualifications, by definition, are supposed to represent a publicly agreed level of achievement, this seems to mean that within a modular system every module within the set of options must in itself express a particular educational level. This not only requires a tightening of the rules for the presentation of small-scale units of learning; it is also rather embarrassing, since an examination of the guidelines and marking criteria used in assessing different academic levels conspicuously fails to show detailed specifications of those levels: on the contrary, it suggests that academic assessments are made in terms of a broadly similar set of categories at A level (the pre-university school examination), throughout the three years of undergraduate study and through to the master's degree (Winter, 1993, 1994a). In other words, the increased freedom of modular structures has revealed the need for the new (and hitherto largely ignored) discipline of providing a clear differentiation of educational levels.

However, by presenting us with this issue in starkly unmistakable terms, modularity may have done us all a favour, simply by ensuring that we begin to address it. For example, we may be forced to recognize that the specification of the educational level of every module across the whole disciplinary spectrum may be impractical. (Stages of mastery are conceived differently in different subject areas, highly complex material can be superficially 'mugged up' and even the most basic matters can be tackled 'critically'.) We might then, however, conclude that it is not actually necessary to specify the level of all modules (new liberty!) as long as we also introduce the rule (new discipline!) that all awards must include in their latter stages an 'integrative module' (requiring students to write reflexively about what, in personal terms, they have gained from the various modules they have undertaken) and a 'project module' in which students formulate and undertake a personal programme of investigation (see Winter, 1994a). The learning outcomes for such modules, I suggest, could be articulated at a number of different levels which would identify specific educational achievements across disciplines.

Both types of module have the advantage of clearly offering students scope to demonstrate their abilities (and their limitations) as learners in ways which embody directly a set of general educational values. For example, in the study referred to, the criteria that did differentiate higher education work were a wide range of reading and the linkage of individual experience and theory in the development of a responsible personal stance (Winter, 1994a: 98), which begins to encapsulate some of the key values of higher education. Modular programmes might thus enable us to divide our assessment work into those occasions when we are emphatically focusing on these values (or a more refined version of them which might emerge from further research) and other occasions when we are not. In this way we might achieve greater confidence in our ability to achieve them and greater credibility for our claims to have done so. As a set of values, even in this rudimentary formulation, one might argue that they implicitly combine educational principles with those of the citizen in a democracy. They thus have a particular relevance for the 'political' dimension referred to earlier, and thus for our conception of the relationship between higher education and society (see the quotation from Ronald Barnett above).

Competence-based curricula

In principle, a competence-based curriculum specifies in detail the required outcomes of learning, and leaves students complete liberty as to the learning process by which they acquire the capacity to demonstrate those outcomes (Jessup, 1991). Again, we see that it represents both a new form of liberty and a new form of discipline. In general these are distributed 'asymmetrically': it is students who acquire the liberty not to attend any particular educational 'event', but it is staff who are now called upon to specify in exhaustive detail the assessment criteria which previously were happily allowed to rest on the intuitive application of individual expertise:

> Examiners have tended to hold *in their minds a personal sense* both of the course objectives (which have served as a surrogate set of criteria) and of the overall performance of the relevant set of candidates. In neither sense, though, are the standards (the criteria or the peer group performance) normally set down analytically on paper.
>
> (Barnett, 1989: 33; emphasis added)

Not unexpectedly, the new discipline of specifying educational outcomes has met with resistance. Newman (1994) claims that 'Marking schemes are for dullards' and that they represent 'a failure to engage [*sic*] the purposes and standards of higher education'. There is also the fear that if the basis of academic assessments is made public, as competence-based curricula require, it will become difficult for universities to disallow students' appeals against academic judgements, leading to the danger of embarrassing litigation, especially if students manage to join the growing list of 'service users' whose rights are embodied in a 'charter', expressing 'the principles of public service', namely 'setting, monitoring and publication of explicit standards for . . . services' (see *Times Higher Education Supplement*, 4 September 1992: 1).

It can be argued that the absence of formally specified assessment criteria gives academic staff too much power in the making of sensitive and crucial decisions, and also renders universities incapable of responding effectively to criticisms such as 'falling standards' or lack of comparability across subjects and across institutions (see Yorke *et al.*, 1996). From this point of view, the new discipline of competence-based curricula could be an opportunity to 'put our house in order', i.e. to subject our assessment processes to a long overdue rigorous analytical scrutiny, and thus to contribute to our own professional development and enlightenment (see Winter, 1994b).

For this, of course, 'competencies' need to be rescued from their tendency to fragment the educative process (Ashworth and Saxton, 1990; Norris, 1991), but our recent experience at Anglia with the ASSET Programme (Winter and Maisch, 1996) suggests that it is feasible to combine the assessment of specific practices ('competencies') with a second, general dimension of assessment criteria expressing 'holistic' educational values, such as ethical and affective awareness, the mastery of bodies of knowledge and a reflexive commitment to the learning process itself. This 'two-dimensional' analytical specification of assessment outcomes may offer a way out of a current dilemma: a focus on fragmented detail (often rejected as 'missing out' the core of the educational process and achievement) or a reliance on global impressions of 'quality' which leave educational outcomes in a state of mysterious unpredictability.

In the past, higher education has rationalized its position within this dilemma in terms of an opposition between 'education' and 'training'. But the recently presented rationale for competence-based curricula can help us to go beyond the well worn terms of this formulation. In particular, its educational argument concerning student choice and access (see Jessup, 1991: Chapter 1) implicitly draws our attention to the power dimension of our work as academics, especially in the area of assessment, where (I fear) our own desire to preserve the current extent of our autonomy and discretion leads us into conflict with the desire of our students to increase their control over an experience which may have dramatic consequences for their future well being. From this point of view, the still widely heard arguments concerning the unpredictability of educational outcomes and the 'intuitive' nature of the educational judgements may be read as placing the 'liberty' of academic staff at odds with the political discipline of democratic accountability.

Accrediting work-based learning

Competence-based curricula are frequently combined with the accreditation of work-based learning, as in the work of the UK National Council for

Vocational Qualifications (NCVQ). This threatens a double 'disciplinization' of the liberties of academic staff: the pre-specification of learning outcomes (see above) together with a learning agenda set by employers. However, the relationship between universities and the NCVQ approach is extensively discussed elsewhere (see, for example, CVCP, 1995), so in this section I focus on the implications of accrediting work-based learning as a separate general curriculum principle.

Work-based learning is relevant not only in courses leading to an explicitly vocational/professional qualification. Periods of work placement are increasingly being introduced into higher education generally: science students may work in laboratories, literature students in libraries or theatres, historians in museums etc. This is a recognition that for all students higher education is intended as a preparation, rather than a retreat or a postponement. Indeed, one important point to bear in mind in debates where 'academic' values are contrasted with 'employment' values is that in defining and promoting specifically academic values universities are (quite understandably) engaged in elaborating an appropriate mode of selecting and training their own future staff, i.e. as part of a 'professional training', for employment as university teachers or researchers.

But where we, as academic staff, are concerned with organizing, facilitating and evaluating students' work in employment contexts other than the university, our students' activities suddenly lie beyond our own experience, leading to a loss of confidence in the relevance of our expertise, and hence in our ability to guide, instruct and assess. The inclusion of students' work-based learning within the system of academic accreditation therefore seems at first like yet another instance of academics' loss of professional authority, of our subjection to external controls. However, there is a broader view, which suggests that the more direct connection of the worlds of the university and the workplace potentially expands the scope of academic work, in ways which combine recent thinking about the structures of knowledge and about the 'emancipatory' function of higher education.

In order to make this argument, let us start from Gramsci's notion of 'the intellectual'. Gramsci distinguishes between the 'traditional intellectual' (e.g. the priest) and the 'organic intellectual' (the professional 'knowledge worker' with a specific role 'organically' related to the social system of administration and production; Gramsci, 1971: 5–7). Gramsci's formulation appears to preserve a simple dichotomy between, on the one hand, claims to universal truth and, on the other hand, elaborations of a merely practical, situationally specific expertise. Debates concerning the nature of higher education have long been cast in terms of this distinction (e.g. Kant, 1979; originally 1798; Newman, 1982; originally 1852), but the distinction itself is problematic (see Derrida's, 1992, critique of Kant) and, as Gramsci himself notes, ideological and political (Gramsci, 1971: 7). Let us, therefore, instead, take seriously the increasing body of work which suggests that forms and conceptions of knowledge are historically contingent (Kuhn, 1962), that they emerge from the challenges of innovatory practical tasks (Hoskin and

Macve, 1993), as a result of which academic disciplines arise, combine, split and decline – as social structures (Klein, 1993) – and that definitions of validity and methodological adequacy are shifted and elaborated as the process whereby communities of innovatory practitioners respond to the practical task of deciding whose accounts of novel events are 'trustworthy' and on what basis (Shapin, 1994). From this point of view, the academic accreditation of work-based learning is not simply the 'colonization' of university knowledge by 'the state' or 'society', as the quotation from Barnett, above, seems to imply, but also the expression of an epistemological libera-tion, the liberation of our conceptions of knowledge from the realm of the sacred (where it is divinely ordained and theologically controlled) to the secular realm of human history (where we ourselves develop it through our interactions with others).

This line of argument has two interesting implications for the nature of our work as university teachers. To begin with, a social, practice-based epis-temology reinforces the significance of the student's experience as the site where 'knowledge' is constructed, so that the teacher becomes a facilitator/ mentor rather than an expert instructor. This in turn means that the emo-tional dimension of learning needs to be more fully recognized as constitu-tive of the educational experience – not only the defensive anxieties of learners faced with the challenge posed by novel experience to their exist-ing conceptualizations, but also the processes of 'transference' and 'counter-transference' in which learners and teachers project on to each other, within the tutorial transaction, the emotional residue of other relationships. In other words, the new epistemology dismantles the hierarchical, subject expertise-based authority structure of 'teaching' only to introduce the new discipline of 'counselling'.

Second, if knowledge is seen as arising from social practices, it becomes possible to reinterpret the traditional 'problem'of the relationship between the university and 'society'. Ronald Barnett has recently suggested four key terms which sum up the central features of higher education: understanding, interdisciplinarity, wisdom and critique (Barnett, 1994). His basic argument is that these terms represent a 'lost vocabulary' within a version of higher education excessively dominated by the 'skills' and 'competencies' of voca-tional employment. I wish to argue, in contrast, that the absence of these virtues is attributable with equal plausibility to the lack of a direct connec-tion between knowledge and social practice, and that a practice context for learning is more likely to contribute to their presence, as follows. (a) Practice situations always require us to *work with* a body of knowledge and remind us that knowledge is embodied in 'understanding' as part of an 'active . . . engagement' (Barnett, 1994: 110); only in an examination room is credit sometimes given (to students with particular mnemonic facility) for 'mere knowledge'. (b) Practical situations always have such complex-ity that effective action demands the application of more than one 'type' of knowledge, each of which may be elaborated separately as 'an academic discipline' within the institutional structure of a university. Practical action, in other words, always presents the opportunity, and often the necessity, for 'interdisciplinarity'. (c) The practical application of knowledge is always problematic, a matter of judgement, and thus requires Barnett's third category, 'wisdom'. (d) However, the realm of social practice is not a site for the 'consensual' negotiation of a single unified rationality; rather it is an arena for conflict between competing persuasive rhetorics structured by power relations, and this brings us once more to the specifically political dimension of the argument and to Barnett's final term, 'critique'.

Although we may recognize a plurality of provisional and socially situated rationalities, when it comes to action we necessarily find that we must make choices and justify them, even though we are prepared to modify them in response to further events, further evidence and further arguments. (This in itself merely echoes the well known work of Donald Schon (1983) cited by Barnett himself: '*Every* student is or should be a reflective practitioner' (Barnett, 1990: 160).) But we need to go further than Schon, because in making these choices we will also need to analyse 'critically' the apparently plausible versions of reality promoted and manipulated by political authorities, by scientific and industrial establishments, and by the competitive marketing of products and services by rival institutions, including universities. Again, the 'liberation' of regimes of knowledge (as represented by the academic accreditation of activity within organizations of production) also challenges us as university staff to formulate ('disciplining') criteria as a basis for making important ethical and cognitive judgements. In other words, the addition of 'critique' to the accreditation of work-based learning requires us to bring together a definition of higher education and a definition of responsible and autonomous citizenship, both for our students and for ourselves. And in both cases we will find ourselves supported (albeit with typical ambiguity) by the managerial rhetoric of the 'learning organization' (see above), in which it is recognized that an effective organization needs an independently critical stance on the part of each member of its staff.

Conclusion

All this risks seeming somewhat grandiloquent; nevertheless, it does reflect quite precisely the sorts of themes and issues which have arisen in my own (and colleagues') recent grapplings with the practicalities of establishing a modular, competence-based honours degree course based on the accreditation of work-based learning (see Winter and Maisch, 1996: Chapters 4 and 8). What I am intending to suggest, overall, is simply that the new influences upon higher education do not necessarily need to be simply resisted as losses of essential liberty and painful impositions of external control, although I do not mean to deny the reality of our current experience of both pain and loss. Rather, I have tried to argue that these new developments may also be seen as pointing the way towards the creation of new formats for higher education, which take advantage of new conceptions of knowledge and inevitably require new organizational arrangements. As such they may be seen as not as intrusions into the ivory tower, like so many Trojan horses, but as opportunities for a series of exciting sorties into the societal fray. As academic staff we may not have (and never have had) the power base to act as 'emancipators', but we retain the fundamental duty to act as 'critics'. The 'new' higher education both summons us and enables us to reinterpret, to reinvigorate and, indeed, to extend that role.

Notes

1. One of the factors which suggests the analogy between the feudal baron and the modern chief executive is simply the level and structure of their economic reward, with its routine 'golden handshake' guaranteeing their own economic security, come what may. This must reduce any sense that the security of the chief executive's position is dependent on the general level of staff morale, a state of affairs which would seem to contravene many other current theories of effective management structures.
2. This is a reminder of a further aspect of the current general experience of higher education: the apparently never-ending diminution of resources. The introduction of unrestricted market relationships of the 'global economy' leads to what Gregory Albo calls the 'vicious circle of competitive austerity' (Albo, 1994: 147), as Western economies attempt to drive down expenditure in competition with each other and with the low wage economies of the 'Third World' (Portillo, 1995). Hence, in the pursuit of ever-receding goals of 'productivity', governments continually drive down university funding and reduce the 'unit of resource' available for individual students, while, at another level, there is the threat of a competitive 'credit war' between universities (on the analogy of a 'price war' between commercial companies) to inflate the credit rating of programmes and thus, again, to reduce the resourcing of any given programme.

7

Professors and Professionals: on Changing Boundaries

Sheila Corrall and Ray Lester

Introduction

Academic support services are essential to the business of higher education – not quite a legal requirement, but very unlikely to be dropped entirely. However, the scale and scope of their operation has always been open to question, and never more so than at present, when trends elsewhere are towards downsizing, delayering and decentralizing specialist corporate functions, that are often viewed as value-adding services by those involved but as burdensome overheads by their supposed beneficiaries. Professional 'support staff' – a description that seems self-contradictory to the uninitiated – have an uneasy relationship with their academic colleagues, which veers from critical dependence to indifference or resentment, according to their perspective. At best, academics acknowledge their importance and accept their existence but are reluctant to pay for their upkeep. More often, they see them as underachieving, overpaid supernumeraries, whose jobs are part of an unnecessary bureaucracy and prime candidates for replacement by smart machines.

The professors are right to ask questions, but such debates are seldom conducted in constructive terms, or at the strategic level. There are all sorts of anomalies, a common example being the apparent disparities in grading and status of different professional groups. (It is not uncommon, for instance, for library staff holding both first and higher degrees in addition to professional qualifications to be appointed on clerical grades, while their administrative and computing counterparts with less practical experience and fewer formal credentials are on academic-related scales.) This is an important issue for those directly concerned, but there are more fundamental questions requiring consideration, which will in turn illuminate other areas. Key issues include: what these support services actually or potentially contribute to academic activities; how information technology will affect future development and competitive positioning; and whether there can be

Figure 7.1   The working environment

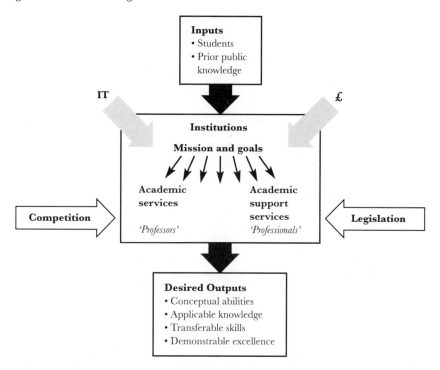

a generic model for service provision, resource allocation and institutional planning.

We pursue these issues with specific reference to information services, from the perspective of library and computing service directors. We shall not explore directly the activities of other professional groups, but we think our argument will have some relevance and resonance for other specialists/ administrators. Our particular area of focus will be the blurring of bound-aries and convergence of interests and activities between 'professionals' and 'professors'.

Environmental imperatives

Our starting point is the institutional environment in which academic support services are currently provided. Our model (Figure 7.1) shows the primary inputs as students and prior public knowledge, and suggests that the desired outputs can be broadly categorized as applicable knowledge, conceptual abilities, transferable skills and demonstrable excellence. The inputs include a complex mix of student types (undergraduate, postgradu-ate taught and research, post-experience, full-time and part-time, sandwich, distance learners etc). The outputs relate to both teaching/learning and scholarship/research processes, and will be manifested to differing degrees in the people who leave or stay in the institution and also as publications or other artefacts. These desiderata have been influenced significantly by shifts in thinking about the nature and purpose of higher education and the importance of teaching and research assessments as indicators of excellence.

We see the activities of higher education institutions grouped under two general headings of academic services (provided by 'professors') and academic support services (provided by 'professionals') with their particular shape determined by the distinctive mission, goals and priorities of each institution. The former is a convenient label for not only those formally titled 'professor', but also readers, lecturers and other academic members of the institution; the latter covers here almost everything else that supports academic activities, from administration to estate management, although we shall take libraries and computing services as our primary examples. The blurring of boundaries among the different services and the nature of the para-academic role at the centre of this model are the key areas for exploration. Such issues have been the subject of discussion over a lengthy period – several decades, in the case of the academic nature of support services – but the situation currently facing us is in many ways so different that a fresh perspective is needed to tease out the fundamental questions.

The environmental influences on higher education at present are well known and need not be documented here in detail. Institutions are under continuing pressures from government to prove their worth, in a climate of public expenditure cuts, a weak national economy, a legislative environment increasingly affected by European developments, competition on a global scale, the empowerment of the consumer or customer through the quality movement (and Citizen's Charter) and assumptions about massive improvements in efficiency and effectiveness through the application of information technology (IT) – and business process re-engineering. The change from an elitist tradition to a mass market for higher education but with much more selective funding for research, and the prospect of similarly divisive outcomes from teaching assessment exercises, have thrown the whole system into turmoil, but we can anticipate a gradual shake-out over the next few years which will return us to a stratified system – perhaps not so very different from what preceded the removal of the binary line.

The economic and electronic imperatives are the significant driving forces. Economic pressures have been with us for a long time, and IT has also been heralded as a potential transformer of organizations for decades, but developments within the past few years (especially advances in networking) have brought us to the point where the forecast revolutionary changes in working practices are actually happening. Libraries and computer centres are among the most visible examples of services transformed by technology, but they have not been immune to other environmental factors. Indeed, the primary impetus for the Joint Funding Councils Libraries Review Group (1993) chaired by Professor Sir Brian Follett was concern about capacity – particularly physical capacity – to cope with growth in undergraduate student numbers. A detailed account of these environmental forces and their implications is beyond the scope of this chapter; the issues have been fully discussed and documented elsewhere, both in the context of the Follett review and more generally (e.g. Corrall, 1995).

Service assumptions

Before we consider the roles and relationships of 'professors' and 'professionals' in this context, it is pertinent briefly to remind readers what library and computer services have traditionally contributed to academic work. The traditional university library service has, in recent years at least, taken the form of a centrally managed facility (though often delivered through more than one service point, e.g. site/branch libraries). Standard offerings include: study facilities; general reference collections and subject-oriented collections of books, journals and reference works; lending services, including short loan arrangements for material in high demand and inter-library loans for 'non-core' items; photocopying services or facilities; and enquiry points. These basic services are generally supported and supplemented by various activities and additional offerings, such as online catalogues, printed guides to services and resources, instruction to users in various forms, information services (including current awareness) and access to personal computing facilities.

User perceptions and preferences have inevitably varied, but they have tended to place a higher value on the collections and related facilities and been less likely to demand or defend investment in the value-added services in which professional staff take particular pride, although the latter have often been appreciated by recipients, especially students. A significant trend in library provision has been the shift from a 'holdings' to an 'access' strategy, generally linked with developments in IT and electronic publishing, and often associated with stronger management to cope with economic constraints (Corrall, 1993). Copyright, which has long been a difficult issue with printed publications, has proved even more troublesome in the electronic environment, involving library staff and users in complex licensing and leasing arrangements, often requiring negotiation on a title-by-title basis.

On the computing side, there has been a similar scepticism about professional services beyond the basic job of getting the equipment installed and operational, although academics have been more ready to acknowledge the technical complexity of the work involved and accept the need for professional specialists. The historical model of central mainframe services, with specialist operators carrying out jobs for departmental users, long ago gave way to the now familiar decentralized pattern, but where a need for specialist help with applications was identified, this tended to be met by employing programmers in departments (which suggests a significantly different user view of library and computing support).

As the decentralization of processing power to the desktop has continued, this has reinforced the academic view that all they want from a central service is an infrastructure that works, with a minimal number of (expensive) professional intermediaries. Computing services have thus often had a hard time convincing colleagues of the benefits of providing central support services such as help-desks, and even more difficulty arguing the need for higher-level staff in planning and developing – as opposed to running and maintaining – the network infrastructure, which is assumed to require little thought or expertise. As with libraries, students have shown more interest in the central services available; indeed, as the PC revolution has progressed, student demand for help has grown in parallel with academic disdain, creating tensions and strains within the system.

Just as 'quality' has become the buzzword in higher education generally, 'convergence' has emerged as the big organizational and political question for library and computing services in particular. The Follett and Fielden reports (Joint Funding Councils Libraries Review Group, 1993; John Fielden Consultancy, 1993) have given further impetus to such discussions, with Fielden especially assuming that the trend of library and 'information/ computing' services coming closer together will continue and become 'universal in some functions' (John Fielden Consultancy, 1993: 22). Fielden's contribution to the debate is notable for drawing a distinction between 'organizational or formal convergence' and 'operational or informal convergence'. The report also predicts and defines 'a new form of convergence . . . "academic convergence" through learner support' (John Fielden Consultancy, 1993: 24), and raises some pertinent questions about the staffing and skills implications of such developments. However, the picture offered is both short-sighted and incomplete; it is constrained by the time boundaries set by Follett (the review's limited planning horizon and the timetable for the report's completion) and it concentrates on support for students with rather superficial treatment of support for research.

Boundary disputes

Our model here is more complex than Fielden's, as it explores the shifting boundaries between academics and library/computing professionals along several dimensions, in relation to both teaching and research, and in the context of short-term as well as longer term changes.

Our first point of departure is to argue the need for a tripartite view, where we identify three types of player, broadly categorized as the 'professor' (a person appointed on the basis of his or her academic specialism) and two species of professionals: the 'content' professional (whose particular expertise is in the organization of information, the data) and the 'conduit' professional (an expert in the technology itself) (see Figure 7.2). The professionals can be approximately equated with the traditional library and computing specialisms respectively, but to label them thus is to ignore

Figure 7.2 The three players

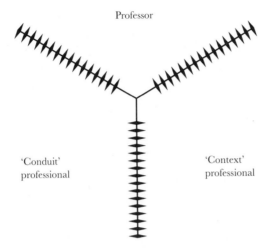

shifts that are already taking place, and it is more appropriate to think in terms of 'information specialist' and 'IT specialist' without presupposing them as defined by possession of particular sets of professional/technical qualifications, or knowledge and skills. Despite growing support for the notion that there are so many common job elements among library and computing personnel that the distinctions are almost trivial (e.g. Woodsworth *et al.*, 1992), we believe that this is a valid and useful classification, while acknowledging that some professionals may combine competencies from both areas.

The complexities of the model emerge as we consider the blurring of boundaries between these three types of players, represented by eight examples of 'hybrid' professionals. For convenience, we have given these examples labels reflecting some roles undertaken or titles used in universities in the past and present (see Figure 7.3).

On the boundary between the academic and information specialist, we have identified not only the traditional subject librarian (Fielden's candidate for an enhanced para-academic role) but also the research assistant, who approaches the border from the other direction and works from a departmental base.

The *subject (site) librarian* will probably have a formal qualification in librarianship and possibly a degree in a relevant academic discipline; he or she will certainly acknowledge a responsibility to have an understanding of the structure of the literature in the chosen field, and some grasp of its terminology and concepts. This job typically involves advising on the selection of books and other information resources to support teaching and research, providing user education or information skills seminars (especially for undergraduates) and answering subject-related enquiries, including helping users to search CD-ROM or online databases. The postholder may

Figure 7.3   Some specialist roles

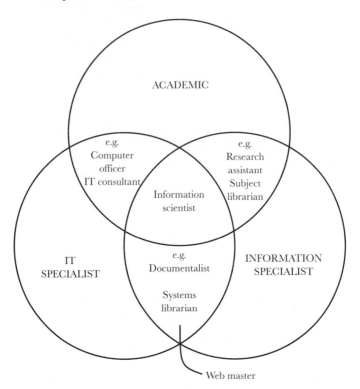

be based at a reference desk in the part of the library where materials on the specialism are concentrated, or at a separate departmental or faculty library; in either case, liaison with the relevant academic staff will be an important aspect of the job.

The extent to which an academic dimension to the post is explicitly defined will vary: in the former polytechnics, the title tutor librarian was often used to signal the teaching role associated with instructing students in the use of the library and its stock; in the older university research libraries, it was not uncommon for subject librarians to pursue their own research interests (for example, compilation of scholarly bibliographies) alongside their work in supporting library users. It has never been entirely clear on what basis such posts claim to be 'academic-related', not least because in practice the numbers of genuine subject specialists (as opposed to information specialists) have tended to be relatively low if we use an academic qualification in the subject as one of the criteria. On the other hand, there are examples of information specialists who have managed to integrate their information skills work with academic programmes by organizing their inputs to coincide with specific student assignments and delivering them in tandem with academic colleagues; in some cases, library staff have helped to shape changes in teaching methods and course contents, by, for example, alerting academics to opportunities for project work presented by new electronic information sources.

Current opinion on the subject/information librarian role is confused. Fielden argues against academic-related conditions of service (because he favours a single integrated grading system for professionally qualified and other library staff), but he sees the para-academic role of learner support as critical to future success, and recommends formal agreement of the boundaries of responsibility with relevant academic staff. Heseltine (1995) has strongly criticized 'the whole concept of subject librarianship', but he supports the development among library staff of 'a much wider range of teaching and communication skills' (in addition to network skills, technical competencies and awareness of information resources) to turn them into 'professional educators'. His model assumes wholesale convergence of all academic support services, with functional specialists (rather than subject- or faculty-based teams) and training as a prime example. He has previously argued (Heseltine, 1994) that librarians' success in imparting lasting generic information skills is as yet unproven.

This debate has been with us for some time, and our views have not changed in essence over 15 years (Lester, 1979, 1984). In principle, user education in a university library must be driven by the needs of the academic discipline, and ought to be led by academic staff – ideally carried out by the lecturers themselves, with librarians at hand to advise on more technical aspects of information organization and management if required. The whole focus should be on integrating information handling with academic course work and not teaching library or information use for its own sake or in isolation. Library and information systems should not be so difficult to use that this becomes a substantial subject for study in itself by people for whom it is not a primary concern. In practice, librarians have more often than not had to take the larger share of this work, as many academics have proved either unwilling or unable to do so. Ironically, although we are now working in an environment where information systems have been designed much more with the 'end-user' in mind, it will be some time before so-called 'user-friendly' systems are easy to search both efficiently and effectively. Users commonly still need help with the technology to gain access to networked services, and also professional advice on search techniques, especially for more complex searches.

The *research assistant* is a player often overlooked in the debate on the level of library support required by academic staff. This is the researcher appointed on the basis of his or her academic qualifications, probably with a fairly narrow remit within an academic department or research group, and almost certainly no explicit responsibility for information work. However, in practice, these people often fulfil such a role by conducting literature searches and seeking out relevant material for professors. While we can point to examples of academics calling on library staff to act as research assistants when they lack support within departments, experience suggests that they are more likely to seek academically qualified people (rather than information specialists) when making such departmental appointments.

Academics often question the costs and benefits (to them personally) of the library having subject/information specialists, claiming that the research support supposedly offered is an unnecessary or irrelevant luxury and arguing that the money would be better spent on periodical subscriptions. Professional opinion is quite divided on this: although many libraries aspire to provide tailored support for both teaching and research, success in the latter area is much harder to measure, and therefore to justify (especially financially). Some libraries (notably in the United States) have introduced multilevel subject-oriented support, which ranges from basic reference queries through more in-depth enquiries to appointment-based advisory and consultancy services, which are open to both students and staff, but with the latter aimed particularly at researchers (Hammond, 1992; Massey-Burzio, 1992; Rinderknecht, 1992). Others have contented themselves with meeting and greeting new academic appointments, making them aware of facilities and resources available, and perhaps offering some current awareness or alerting based on profiles of research interests. In practice, few libraries are staffed at a level which enables them to do this systematically; provision has therefore been patchy, with the predictable effect on user experiences and reactions.

In the past, the subject/information librarian was often able to make a distinctive contribution by carrying out online searches for academics, but the upsurge in 'end-user' searching (in the library or at the desk) has dramatically reduced this role to a point where it has almost disappeared completely. It seems unlikely that the library will fulfil a substantial mediated research support role in the future, as the combination of networked self-service access and availability of research assistance within departments will obviate the need.

On the boundary between the academic and IT specialist, we have chosen the two illustrative roles of computer officer and IT consultant. Despite a longer history of separate faculty and departmental libraries, the decentralization of academic computing support in recent years (largely precipitated by the PC revolution and the networking of processing power to the desktop) has generally resulted in much reduced central computing or information systems functions during a period when libraries have tended to become consolidated as centrally managed services, albeit with distributed access. The focus of campus computing services has shifted away from computing *per se* – hence the frequent change of name to IT or information systems – to planning and management of the network infrastructure, support for shared facilities (including student PC laboratories) and a range of advisory services, which like their library counterparts emphasize training, facilitation and self-help, rather than operating equipment on users' behalf.

The type of *IT consultant* we are concerned with here on the boundary between the central service and academic departments is likely to have a significant customer-service dimension to his or her work, and the job may well be defined in terms of support for a particular department or faculty. Some university IT services have reorganized to create separate divisions for network/facilities management and user support, with the latter organized along similar lines to library liaison and subject-based activities. (In so-called converged or merged services, this is generally the area where operational convergence has come closest to fruition, with information and IT specialists working together as a team.)

The IT consultant role typically involves: advising on the choice, purchase and installation of hardware and software; providing training in IT skills (especially for undergraduates); and solving application and equipment-related problems, including helping users to access networked software and other facilities (for example, library services). The academic dimension of this sort of work is perhaps less obvious than for library counterparts, but the recent trend towards making computer literacy/IT skills modules compulsory components of degree courses has clearly strengthened that aspect. The potential overlap with library staff in both the information skills and networked resources areas can cause understandable confusion for users, who are often unsure where to go for help with day-to-day problems (for example, obtaining access and instruction in the use of services like the nationally networked Bath Information and Data Services).

The role of *departmental computer officer* is particularly associated with academic departments which have a discipline-based interest in IT (for example, computer science, electronic engineering) and a long tradition of employing their own computer people because of their specialist needs and heavy dependence on such equipment. The growing use of IT in many other subject areas, combined with the shift to distributed processing, has led to similar appointments in departments ranging from pharmaceutical sciences to business and management studies. These people often perform similar roles to the centrally based IT specialists, including advice on equipment purchases, user support and training, as well as day-to-day maintenance and trouble-shooting. The decision to invest in specialist staff at the departmental level will depend on factors such as size and physical location, degree of dependence on IT and the level of service available from the centre. However, the nature of the job tends to vary with the subject discipline, in terms of both technical complexity and academic role. Computer officers in laboratory-based departments are often expected to do a significant amount of teaching and also to carry out their own research in the subject discipline, whereas in other areas the academic-related work is more likely to be limited to IT skills training (like the computer centre staff).

Approaching the border between libraries and IT/computer services, we find the professional traditionally known as the *systems librarian*. These people will usually be professionally qualified librarians, often with a technical services background (for example, cataloguing), who have gained knowledge and skills from experience of working with library 'housekeeping' systems. However, with the new generation of library systems running on industry-standard platforms and the growth of networking and PC-based applications, this role is changing significantly and the more technically advanced libraries have seen the need to have someone capable of taking a strategic management responsibility for all IT-based systems in the library, rather than relating it too closely to technical services. The extensive and intensive use of IT by libraries, and particularly the introduction of local CD-ROM networks, has resulted in many libraries establishing a systems team, which will often include their own IT specialists (akin to academic departments' computer officers) as well as library/information specialists with an aptitude for IT.

The latest addition to this group is the new breed of network support officers, often based in the library, but recruited on the basis of either information or IT expertise. Specific examples include the *web master*, who concentrates on Internet (and Intranet) support. It is worth noting that, in some institutions, posts of this type may be completely outside the library/computing services and linked with university/public relations functions.

Coming from the other direction – but probably less common now in the days of slimmed down central units and online help facilities – there is the *documentalist*, defined here as someone in a central computing service who looks after documentation (for example, maintaining collections of software manuals and training aids). Although there are known examples of qualified information specialists fulfilling such roles, it is more common to find a non-specialist doing this job.

At the centre of our model sits the professional who combines information (library), IT (computing) and academic (subject) specialisms: the real *information scientist*, which is actually rather a rare breed in higher education institutions, although quite common in industrial research units. These people tend to be found in industries where specialist knowledge of the subject content is essential and IT systems are so integral to the organization of information that it is best to combine the expertise, and they are most commonly found in the pharmaceutical and chemical sectors. They clearly have a potential role to play in academic research centres, and it is interesting to speculate why such appointments have not generally been made; perhaps this is because academics have not been convinced of the benefits of such investment in the information infrastructure, for these people can generally command rather higher salaries than the typical post-doctoral research appointment.

Stakeholder priorities

What will the university library of the future look like, in terms of contents, location, services and (therefore) staffing? Our model predicts a spectrum of provision, with the information resource mix varying from discipline to discipline, ranging from on-site holdings of published print materials (probably quite extensive in many humanities subjects) to local access to remote electronic data sets (likely to predominate in the hard sciences). The term

Figure 7.4   Desired future states

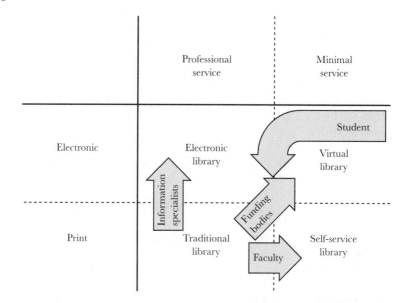

electronic information sources will cover a multiplicity of different publishing media and delivery modes, as well as informal and semi-published communication. Although the ownership and copyright aspects seem intractable problems at present, these will eventually be resolved; likewise, current technical difficulties with access will be sorted out, so that the future user will not need sophisticated searching skills.

The electronic and economic imperatives will ensure a definite move away from the traditional print-based professionally staffed library. We suggest three possible scenarios, representing the preferred future of different stakeholder groups (see Figure 7.4).

The electronic library is the model favoured by information specialists. It involves a progressive shift from print to electronic provision, which will bring complex challenges along the way, but assumes a continuing role for large numbers of information professionals – perhaps even an enhanced 'para-academic' one – as expert navigators, organizers and instructors. (For example, Fielden envisages subject librarians or their future equivalents becoming more involved in assisting academic departments with both course design and the development of teaching materials.) There may be several variants on the basic professional service model: some foresee a 'relayering' of staff structures, with library assistants moving into an 'upskilled' para-professional role as quasi-information specialists, taking on the bulk of cataloguing and enquiry work; others forecast substantial delayering, with information and IT specialists contributing genuine value-added services, but the only other significant categories of staff being front-of-house receptionists and low-level support personnel (to restock paper copiers, printers etc). The former is in effect an evolved version of the learning resource centre model, which tends to be associated with newer universities or those with a particular focus on undergraduate education; the latter represents a more revolutionary view of the academic library as an information centre of the type more commonly found in the industrial and commercial world.

The self-service library is the model that appeals to faculty. This is the true self-service library, with minimal staffing – not the style of self-service advocated by professionals, which requires their presence as educators, facilitators and helpers. The shift envisaged here is in effect from payroll to periodicals, with substantial staff cuts seen as the answer to the twin problems of continuing increases in both the numbers and prices of titles published. The extreme version retains a large number of serials in print format, both current issues and extensive backruns of bound volumes, including both primary and secondary literature, as well as generous purchasing of monographs and expensive reference works in hard copy. In this scenario IT supports the print library by enabling more economical and efficient housekeeping (using bought-in cataloguing records, self-service requesting, issue and return of books) and more effective information provision (through better search facilities, access to other libraries' catalogues, networked services etc.). It assumes that systems are relatively user-friendly and trouble-free, and the main staffing requirement will be attendants and a handful of administrators. This model is particularly favoured by research-oriented staff, but also by teaching staff who wish to redistribute the budget to allow more extensive purchasing of student textbooks and longer opening hours, but without the expense of professionally staffed service points.

The virtual library is the model favoured by our paymasters, at both national and local levels, but especially the former. The funding councils have invested heavily in the national IT infrastructure, both in the network itself (and its subsequent enhancement to SuperJANET) and in a series of initiatives and programmes intended to promote the take-up and exploitation of new technologies in the context of teaching, research and administration/support services (notable examples being the Management and Administrative Computing initiative, the Computers in Teaching Initiative, the Teaching and Learning Technology Programme and the Electronic Libraries Programme). While investment in the network infrastructure has been acknowledged as a huge success in terms of its impact and benefits, many of the initiatives have delivered considerably less than anticipated by their authors. The Electronic Libraries Programme, initiated as a result of the Follett Report, has a budget of about £15 million over three years and at the time of writing has led to around 60 projects (involving more than 90 institutions) intended to improve information delivery and to explore new methods of scholarly communication. Irrespective of the technical outcomes of the programme, the Follett initiative has already had a significant impact in highlighting problems and suggesting possible solutions offered by technology, and bringing these to the attention of key opinion formers – administrators and academics – at all levels within institutions.

Although the Follett Report acknowledges that, 'In practice, most libraries will continue to combine traditional media with electronic media for the foreseeable future, and the purely electronic or "virtual library" will be rare', and its outcomes also included substantial funding for projects supporting more traditional library activities, there is no doubt that the report is associated in most people's minds with a move towards the virtual – or at least the electronic – library. The initiative has roused hopes and fears among various constituencies, and it has put libraries under much sharper scrutiny than before. It is difficult to assess whether on balance it has won more support for future investment locally, or reinforced polarization of views on the campus; either way, it seems clear that the 'traditional view' is now widely accepted as inadequate for the challenges of today and tomorrow.

How and where does the *student* fit into these scenarios? Although increasingly likely to be paying customers, students – individually and collectively – are least likely among the stakeholder groups identified to exert a direct influence on future developments. The preferred model for students is probably a mix of all four scenarios: they want the latest technology at their disposal, but also abundant supplies of recommended textbooks in the hardcopy format with which they are most familiar; they like the idea of self-service facilities (preferably around the clock) with minimal staff intervention so that they do not have to queue at issue or enquiry desks, but at the same time if they have difficulties they want to be able to get personal help from someone who really knows what he or she is doing. Inasmuch as most institutions will probably opt for a 'mixed economy', students will get what they want in general terms; however, with budget pressures continuing, and competition on and off the campus growing, how they fare in particular institutions will depend on who holds the balance of power. Traditionally, library staff have tried to protect and support student interests, and the attention now paid to learning support services in Teaching Quality Assessments should assist these efforts; however, the Research Assessment Exercise may begin to exert even stronger influence in the opposite direction. If institutions move significantly in the direction of devolved budgeting, we can envisage a situation where the level of service available might vary considerably from department to department, depending on how they choose to allocate funds between books and periodicals – and between salaries and other library expenditure.

A generic model?

The Follett Report confirmed the view that there is no accepted appropriate level or percentage of institutional expenditure on library services (and the same principle applies to support services generally). Although not a surprising conclusion in the current political and economic climate, this contradicts a suggestion of the last major British report on university library provision that, in order to provide facilities comparable to those in other developed countries, annual spend would need to represent 'approximately six per cent of the total university expenditure' (University Grants Committee, 1967). Inter-institutional comparisons tend to be fairly meaningless in this context as there is so much individual variation (for example, in the mix of academic disciplines, physical distribution of facilities, financial practice in treatment of overheads etc.).

The relative priority given to teaching/learning and research, and the nature and number of disciplines covered, must affect both the level and type of provision considered as essential or desirable, and the way that services are organized, which in consequence will reflect other management arrangements within the institution. Follett and Fielden, while not making explicit recommendations on the subject, convey a fairly strong message on the inevitability of much closer working arrangements between library and computing services. It is also interesting in this context to note the comments of Professor Follett, recorded in an interview published about two years after his report went to press, confirming a personal preference for 'flat structures, with the librarian and head of IT both reporting to the vice-chancellor, because at the end of the day, you have to have a librarian to run the library and an IT person to run IT' (Worley and Follett, 1995: 22).

The current pressures for convergence – in addition to the implicit steer from the funding councils – include anticipation of cost savings in a climate of continuing budget constraints, partly founded on assumptions about duplication of effort and overlap of service roles arising from the increased use of IT by libraries and the development of networked services. Experience has shown that many factors influence the decisions made by institutions, including: institutional size; geographical dispersion; the history, culture and range of services involved (for example, academic and administrative computing, audio-visual and educational technology services, telephony, reprographics); commitment to an 'access' strategy; penetration of networking and PCs; and the skills base of staff. More specifically, personality factors and opportunities created by departures of existing service heads (rather than a planned strategic review) are often the triggers which prompt a rethink.

Arguments in favour of convergence include: the greater flexibility offered by a combined budget; the potential for improved responsiveness through joint planning and management of services; and more effective staff deployment, with common help desks/enquiry points, joint induction and training sessions and shared academic liaison roles. Against this, critics have expressed concerns about dilution of expertise and loss of professional identity. Co-operation and teamwork among library and computing staff will clearly become even more important in the future as the technological dependence of libraries increases; in addition, as the size of central computing units decreases, their viability as separate operations must be questioned.

Ultimately, it is for each university to decide what sort of support services it requires, and how best to achieve this; professionals and professors must work together to determine needs and priorities in relation to institutional and departmental missions and objectives. As yet there is a lack of hard data on whether the quality or standard of library/information/IT services is a critical success factor in attracting either students or academic staff to higher education institutions. Academics often cite periodical subscriptions as crucial in securing the appointment of good research staff, but we think this probably applies only in extreme cases of holdings that are widely known to be very extensive (or depleted). For students, we feel that impressive IT (rather than library) facilities are more likely to represent a competitive advantage.

Conclusions

We already have virtual computer centres, and the virtual library is almost with us now – and certainly a distinct possibility within our professional lifetime. Irrespective of whether a university has substantial holdings of printed materials, the electronic imperative raises important questions about distributed facilities and decentralized management. In particular, it has subjected to renewed scrutiny the roles and responsibilities of professionals engaged in academic support activities: the 'priesthood' of central computing staff disappeared with the demise of mainframe computing, and professional librarians are now similarly threatened. Academics have long been suspicious of the so-called academic-related nature of this work, considering that these jobs are primarily about maintaining the infrastructure. The situation has become further confused with the blurring and shifting of boundaries not only between 'professors' and 'professionals', but also among the professionals themselves.

We believe that there are sound reasons for retaining the concept of the centrally managed library and information service, which includes commitment to a corporate approach to planning and developing the IT infrastructure. For the foreseeable future (ten to fifteen years) users will still need considerable help in obtaining access to the information they need on both technical and legal/economic grounds: the British Library Working Party on Electronic Publishing listed ten different types of user support and training inputs potentially required by individuals and groups for 'self-service' access to electronic information systems, and also drew attention to the evolving but difficult regulatory environment facing library staff (Vickers and Martyn, 1994).

Eventually we expect many of these problems to be resolved, and even in the short to medium term some student user needs may be met via computer-mediated learner support (Levy *et al.*, 1996). In the longer term, although there will still be a need for some user support and training, this could conceivably be provided online from a remote off-site source (for example, through video-conferencing), although we still envisage this role being fulfilled by professional information specialists. However, while the totally decentralized information service may be technically feasible, economies of scale will be lost in the process unless there is some central coordination and control of site licences for both software and datasets. Moreover, there will still be crucial policy issues relating to information use, intellectual property rights and data protection that will require institutional decisions within a strategic framework.

More specifically, in the long term we predict some downsizing and delayering of the professional cadre of information specialists involved in supporting particular client groups. Where this type of support is currently related to specific academic departments, in future this is more likely to be justifiable only at the level of faculties or schools, but the role will be critical. A key responsibility will be to anticipate and manage shared interests in information access which cut across traditional subject boundaries to ensure optimum value for money from institutional investments in information resources, however this is charged and funded. While interdisciplinary research and scholarship as reflected in cross-department and cross-faculty interests in electronic journals or datasets are perhaps the most obvious example here, the same principle applies to developing strategies for managing access to software and data generated internally within the institution.

Finally, on the question of changing boundaries, we expect the situation to remain fairly fluid among the professionals. We have already seen significant shifts within libraries, between library and computing people, and more gradual blurring of boundaries with other support staff (including those in registry, public relations and planning functions). As the electronic and economic imperatives continue to drive us towards more novel ways of working and further restructuring, the professionals will regroup and require even wider skill sets, with some becoming more specialized and others developing new combinations of skills.

But we do not subscribe to the para-academic model advocated by Fielden and others; the value of the professionals' contribution must be defined in terms of their own specialist knowledge and skills. For information and IT specialists, the core competency is in information management – in the content and conduit respectively – but we must also acknowledge that while this competency is necessary to deliver effective information services, it is not sufficient, and information workers will also need personal qualities and abilities in several other areas to offer a truly professional contribution to their institutions. The professors in turn will need competence and confidence in managing information in the electronic era, without becoming information specialists. The way forward must be on the basis of mutual respect and partnership, rather than each trying to usurp the other's role.

8

Managing How Academics Manage

R. J. Johnston

Prolegomenon[1]

Stand in the corridor of the average university department for a day – starting at 07.30 hours. Soon some of the academic staff will arrive and go to their rooms, perhaps pausing to make a cup of coffee and have a brief conversation with a colleague. Others will arrive during the morning; there will be a peak at around 09.00 but with some turning up later – even not putting in an appearance until the afternoon. Soon after midday, some will depart; the peak for leaving will be around 17.00, but some will stay much later and lights will continue to burn in some rooms long into the night.

Some doors will remain open most of the day, and their offices will have a steady stream of visitors. Others will remain closed, but during specified 'office hours' a small queue of students wanting to consult the staff member will form. During the hours they are on the premises, some staff will frequently leave their rooms – to visit the library or an IT centre, perhaps, or to give a lecture, conduct a class, attend a seminar, participate in a meeting, consult with a colleague or go to a common room for coffee or a snack. Go into their rooms while they are there, however, and you will find some reading, some writing or typing, some computing ... or even just thinking.

At the end of the day, when synthesizing your observations, you will find it hard to identify a general pattern, except that many work very intensively over long hours (although some don't appear in their offices at all, if you check you will undoubtedly find that they have been working elsewhere), that at some times life in the department seems very frantic and that the purpose of it all is not easy to discern. And if you asked them to show you what they had done during the day, some could produce nothing, some little more than one sheet of prose, others a large pile of assessed scripts and so forth. Furthermore, if you had asked them to keep detailed diaries, you would have found that most undertook a wide range of different tasks during the day, rarely spending even as much as an hour on one, and that their concentration was frequently punctuated not only by visitors but also by telephone calls and (for a number at least) the arrival of faxes and e-mail messages, some of which called for an immediate response.

Introduction

> The presidency is an illusion. Important aspects of the role seem to disappear on close examination. In particular, decision making seems to result extensively from a process that decouples problems and choices and makes the president's role more commonly sporadic and symbolic than significant. Compared to the heroic expectations he and others may have, the president has modest control over the events of college life. The contributions he makes can easily be swamped by outside events or the diffuse qualities of university decision making.
>
> (Cohen and March, 1974: 2)

The task of institutional managers in universities (vice chancellors and their equivalents, plus those who work alongside them) differs from that of their contemporaries in most service industries, let alone those working in production industries. Not only may there be no tangible outcome, but the quality of the service offered is very largely evaluated by those who deliver it; academic staff success as teachers, for example, is assessed by the exams and other assignments which they mark, albeit with the oversight of external examiners. Furthermore, the institutional manager cannot set explicit targets: one cannot direct a department to produce so many first-class degree graduates, or an individual to undertake research which will win a Nobel Prize or election to the British Academy. A university (defined throughout this chapter as an institution whose staff are employed to undertake *both* teaching and research) comprises a large number of professional staff whose independence is not only prized (and not infrequently stoutly defended) but also necessary; without it, their ability to explore the frontiers of knowledge would be substantially constrained. Furthermore, the outcomes of their explorations are in many cases genuinely unpredictable, both in the short term (one cannot be sure that a scientist's experiments will succeed, for example, however strong the underpinning theory) and over longer periods (the utility of work may not be realized for many years after it has been completed). There can be general evaluations of the quality of what is undertaken and delivered, and in addition there may be widely held images of the standing of individuals, departments and institutions. All that the manager can aim for, therefore, is attractive images and success in the external evaluations, plus 'satisfied customers': those who consume the research outputs and participate in the teaching programmes.

The university manager's function, therefore, is to ensure that the institution's academic staff carry out high quality teaching and research, and are recognized externally and rewarded for that. This cannot be achieved by setting explicit goals, whose achievement can be tracked, except that certain outcomes of the regular evaluation exercises in British universities (the Research Assessment Exercises and the Teaching Quality Assessments) can be aimed for. The manager has to work *with* staff to establish an ethos in which excellence is pursued and to manage the university's resources so that success is attainable.

A further difference between universities and many other service industries is that the university's two basic tasks – research and teaching – are undertaken by the same individuals. (Although a greater variety of contracts is now in place, the core of the British university as defined here is provided by the large cadre of teacher-researchers.) Research and teaching are complementary in a university's *raison d'être*, but they are also in conflict, to the extent that time spent on one is not directly time spent on the other; constructively managing that conflict, and thereby ensuring high quality productivity in both, is thus a particular role for managers in those universities whose mission statements claim that original research underpins their student teaching and learning strategies. A further peculiarity of the university is that although much of the infrastructural management is undertaken by a separate cadre, and support services are provided by 'non-academic staff', a substantial volume of the administrative work associated with the teaching and research functions is (has to be?) undertaken by the academic staff themselves. This introduces a further call on time, which exacerbates the conflicts.

The three basic tasks of academic staff – teaching (the preparation and delivery of lectures and other classes, the setting and marking of assignments, the supervision of student work and the range of informal consultations with students), research and administration – are all labour-intensive, and although each can be partially facilitated by investment in non-human resources (such as IT), the scope for time saving is limited. Time management is a major consideration for those working at all levels within universities, though for many it is implicitly rather than explicitly exercised. My concern here is with the role of institutional managers as managers of others' time, in which they give few, if any, explicit directions on how much time should be spent on each task, for some of which at least (notably research) identification of valid time constraints and deadlines is very difficult. (You can realistically and properly require staff to turn up on time for their classes, to return assessed assignments to agreed deadlines, and to return marks to an exams office by a given date, but not to have so many papers published in recognized high quality journals within a specified period, for example.[2]) To achieve the goals of recognized high-quality teaching and research, therefore, all that institutional managers can do is:

- establish, sustain and enhance an ethos in which those goals are pursued by all, which includes an accepted reward system;
- appoint and retain staff who are committed to those goals and able to pursue them;
- ensure an adequate infrastructure;

- provide the resources which allow the individual academic staff members to pursue the goals effectively and efficiently.

I concentrate here on the last of those four.

University vice chancellors are required to be both resource managers and academic leaders, two very distinct skills which do not necessarily reside in the same individual and which are not always easily developed by a person who has one but not the other. A vice chancellor who cannot or does not provide leadership through interpersonal and communicative skills, and has no close associate who can provide them, is less likely to motivate academic staff to the achievement of high quality than one who does. Similarly, one who does not sensitively allocate the resources which departments apply to their tasks of teaching, research and administration is unlikely to get the best from those departments.

Because the academic staff member's three basic tasks of teaching, research and administration are labour-intensive, the basic resource to be allocated and managed is time. A major task for university managers is to provide academic staff with sufficient time to manage for themselves, so that they can be successful researchers and teachers.

A second feature of those three basic academic roles is that the quality of the work done is difficult to evaluate, despite continuing efforts to develop credible and acceptable methods. Like the United States' Supreme Court Justice who claimed that he could not define pornography, but knew it when he saw it, we know when we encounter good research, good teaching and good administration, but often find it difficult to defend our judgements, especially to critics from outside the universities, in particular politicians and others concerned with benefit–cost analyses of investment in higher education. The role of institutional managers in time management necessarily involves making such subjective judgements when selectively allocating resources.

Time and 'quality time'

Most academics on 'general contracts' in those British universities established before the 1990s (on which this chapter focuses) have relatively loosely worded terms and conditions of employment, which define neither the number of hours per week that they are expected to work nor, in some cases, the number of weeks per year. In most cases, too, there is no contractually defined allocation of time among the three basic tasks: a typical contract in a pre-1992 university (i.e. an institution with that title prior to the Act which allowed polytechnics and colleges of higher education to apply for the title, which all of the former successfully did), for example, may only indicate that the employee is required to conduct research and to undertake those teaching and administrative duties allocated by his or her head of department – with a grievance clause indicating what to do if dissatisfied with that allocation. Thus, how much time each academic allocates to each task, and the total number of hours he or she works in an average week, depend on a combination of personal dispositions, institutional and departmental ethos and external pressures. Similarly, there is no formal indication of what might be considered unsatisfactory performance in any of the tasks.

The great majority of staff appointed to the pre-1992 universities will have had recent experience as postgraduate and, in some disciplines more than others, postdoctoral researchers, and a continued research career is central to their personal aspirations, as well as the expectations of those who appointed them.[3] Many will have some teaching experience, usually in the delivery of material and assessment of assignments but not more generally in the management of student learning; until relatively recently, they will have been provided with very little 'training' to prepare them for that role. They have been expected to develop as competent teachers, allocating scarce time to learning new skills at the same time as employing them, while also establishing themselves as independent researchers (which in many disciplines involves learning the skills of grant winning and grant management as well as successful report and paper writing); administrative skills are expected to develop spontaneously, through experience and observation.

Quality time

The pursuit of careers as university researchers and teachers involves a variety of intellectually (and thus physically) taxing activities. For most individuals involved, such pursuit requires intense concentration, which is readily broken by interruptions that hinder the creative process. (A few can break off an activity to deal with another matter and then return to it with no difficulty. Most cannot, and it is not a skill that can be 'induced' through training, though experience helps somewhat.) To be creative, therefore, they need 'quality time': unbroken periods which can be committed to a task.

The concept of quality time is readily understood with regard to research work, but is equally applicable to teaching (and also to some, though not all, administrative and managerial tasks). Certain of the activities involved in research – such as data collection in the field or laboratory – necessitate the allocation of unbroken periods of time. Many others benefit from it: in teaching, for example, reading and synthesizing material in preparation for classes, the preparation of handouts, the design of laboratory and field experiments and the preparation of assignments, let alone their evaluation, all benefit from 'quality time' allocations. Thus individual academics will want to structure their daily, weekly and annual working arrangements to allow as much quality time as possible, thereby best enabling them to produce high-quality work. How they do that will vary substantially, but for most it will involve one or more of the following.

- Organizing substantial blocks of time each week – whole days or at least major parts of days – which can be devoted to a particular task without interruption (save *in extremis*). For many, this may involve being away from their workplace office: in the field, at a library, in a laboratory or in a privately furnished (and paid for) study at home.
- Arranging for substantial blocks of time, a term or a semester perhaps, which can be devoted to a single task. This is more often associated with research than with either teaching or administration.
- Negotiating that large blocks of time spent on one task – usually, though not invariably, a major administrative role – will be compensated later with a period when attention can be focused virtually exclusively on one or more of the others.

None of these can be done unilaterally; each requires compromise (sometimes after conflict) because one person's time allocation almost certainly substantially influences what others do, and when.

Each academic staff member's personal time management affects the overall work of his or her department, and can have both negative and positive consequences for what others are asked to do. Departmental heads are thus crucial, both in negotiating arrangements that satisfy all of their colleagues – as far as is possible – and in winning resources for the department which allow good time allocation policies to be implemented. They can only do that within the overall context of institutional ethos, policies and resources.

Institutional managers can have only a marginal impact on how individual academic staff members manage their time, and little more on the allocation of tasks and roles within departments which impinge upon that. Their main function is to ensure that resources are obtained and allocated so that sufficient time is available to the departments and their members to pursue their assigned tasks and roles: thus, *a principal task for institutional managers is the allocation of resources to departments so that sufficient time is available for the pursuit of excellence in teaching and research, which will be recognized externally as of the highest quality.*

Time, money and resource allocation

Time is money, which is centrally allocated in most institutions; successful department heads (in their colleagues' eyes, at least) are those who win favourable financial allocations from their institutional managers. This may involve opportunistic bargaining in the light of events and opportunities, but it is in the institution's best interests that resource allocation procedures are both transparent and fair, and have been designed to promote the institutional mission. No institutional leader should wish to create administrative tasks simply for the sake of doing so, and the leader will want to minimize spending under that head while providing a good administrative infrastructure. And if excellence is at the core of an institution's teaching and research objectives, its resource allocations must reflect that goal.

Time is money, which is needed to buy human resources, so the best resourced departments (all other things being equal) are those which have the most money allocated for the employment of academic staff, relative to the work expected of them. The more time available for preparation, delivery and evaluation of teaching and for involvement in the student learning process, the better its quality, so that, *ceteris paribus* yet again, the lower the student : staff ratio the more time available per student, and the easier it is for departmental managers to release blocks of quality time within which academic staff can pursue their research while not skimping on their responsibilities to students.

Central to this allocation process are the economies of scale, whose very existence, let alone extent, is contested by many within universities. There are some limited economies of scale in teaching activities, which mean that maintaining its quality calls for a slightly declining amount of extra time for each additional student above a certain threshold. To some extent, the size of a lecture class has little influence on either the time needed for its preparation or the quality of its delivery; but the same cannot be said for tutorial classes and seminars, whose quality as learning experiences decline with size, and there are similar intellectual diseconomies with laboratory and field classes too. Other activities central to the teaching operation (setting and marking of assignments, supervision of individual student work and informal consultation with students) benefit little, if at all, from such economies.

There are undoubtedly diseconomies of large scale, however: large numbers of students mean heavy assignment, supervision and other loads which cannot necessarily be shared among several staff, especially when there are tight deadlines to be met, as is increasingly the case with assignment evaluations. Much more important, however, are the diseconomies of scope associated with small scale. Small departments face particular problems, including the following.

- Problems with the provision of degree curricula. Most departments have to cover a certain amount of basic subject matter if they are to provide a viable degree scheme in a named discipline. The smaller the number of staff members available to do that (even if the student : staff ratio is relatively favourable), the greater the span of material each individual will have to cover, which calls for a great deal of quality time if high-quality teaching is to be delivered.
- Problems with individual time management. The teaching and administrative demands in small departments make it more difficult for individuals to be granted quality time to promote high-quality teaching and research (such as a day a week without formal teaching or administrative duties, let alone a term/semester every seven or so released from any formal responsibilities for those two roles) than is the case in larger operations.
- Problems of intellectual isolation. When making their staff appointments, small departments will have particular concerns to ensure subject

matter coverage for their degree programmes, which may well mean that each individual has no colleague working in a very similar research area (an increasing problem given the ever-greater fragmentation and specialization of research activity). In many disciplines, this will hamper the research process, since individuals will have nobody knowledgeable who is readily available to listen, comment and contribute significantly (on which, see Clark, 1993).

- Problems of administrative overload. There are economies of scale in most administrative tasks, and also basic activities whose size is invariant with a department's size. A faculty board meeting lasts the same length of time for the representative of a department with eight staff and 50 students as for the person from one with 25 and 300 respectively, but the former has many fewer colleagues with whom the burden of attendance can be shared over the years.

The introduction of IT has not significantly improved individual efficiency (i.e. saved time substantially) in any of these, and I doubt that it can. Whereas increasing a department's size in terms of student and staff numbers may not produce substantial benefits above a given threshold, therefore, attaining that threshold is crucial; thus, *institutional managers should ensure that departments are sufficiently large to benefit from the available economies of scale and to avoid the diseconomies of scope associated with small units.*

This is the first important step towards ensuring that a department can deliver high-quality teaching and research; its staff must have the resources available to allow the allocation of substantial blocks of quality time to each activity. (I should stress that I am only referring here to the size of departments and not to the size of their institutions; my preference with the latter is for small institutions with carefully designed academic structures comprising linked departments which are large enough to achieve the economies of scale and scope outlined here.)

Within this overall policy objective, issues of institutional mission and policy provide a context within which departmental and individual goals can be pursued. These include explicit, and implemented, policies which reward excellence in both teaching and research, but also – and to many academics perhaps more importantly – policies which protect and enhance the provision of the quality time within which they can pursue their individual career interests; given an overall collegiality, individual career success should also be best for the advancement of the institution's interests. These can include:

- minimizing administrative demands and ensuring adequate staffing, so that academic staff are not called upon to undertake tasks which make poor use of their time and expertise;
- sensible and sensitive timetabling of the use of teaching facilities, so that departments and individuals can plan their time management within a known and accepted institutional framework;
- encouragement of curriculum design which optimizes the use of resources,

without unnecessary duplication of offerings in the name of 'student choice';

- provision of 'quality time slots' for teaching and research which allow uninterrupted concentration for substantial periods on particular tasks, such as study leave, available to all with certain caveats, and special leave both to promote particular goals and to allow staff to 'catch up' after undertaking onerous administrative responsibilities;
- ensuring an infrastructure within which academic staff can pursue their individual and departmental goals.

All of these institutional policies require money, in addition to the creation and maintenance of an ethos which aims at sustaining and enhancing quality in teaching and research. The role of institutional managers is the winning and allocating of the money needed to implement such policies.

University funding, efficiency gains and quality

The allocation of block grant income for teaching and research to British universities is tied to activity levels, which thus encourages growth; the situation varies somewhat among the four countries, and I concentrate here on England. The methods by which that income is distributed are full of anomalies, however, which make the pursuit and delivery of high quality teaching and research difficult.

Teaching

Income for teaching is distributed on a per capita basis, with the amount varying by subject: the largest sums per student are for the clinical disciplines and the lowest for the humanities and social sciences. (The money is obtained through two routes – part is in the block recurrent grant from the funding council and part, via local governments, from fees – which exacerbates administrative difficulties.) There are incongruities, however, among which the most important are the following.

- The income per undergraduate student (normally registered and provided with tuition for only 30 weeks a year) is the same as for postgraduates on taught courses, who are enrolled for 50 weeks. This makes the encouragement of postgraduate education difficult, especially taught courses which are increasingly in demand for a wide range of careers. High-quality postgraduate teaching makes expensive claims on staff time, because at least part of it in most cases involves one-to-one supervision of research work for a dissertation during the summer vacation (substantial parts of which are the only long-term quality time available for staff to conduct their own research). This is especially so if only a proportion of the department's staff are qualified to deliver any one course (which therefore creates a particular

difficulty in small departments, where only one person may be qualified and able to deliver a specialized course or supervise a particular
piece of research); this encourages both short-cuts and the cross-
subsidization of postgraduate teaching from income 'earned' for undergraduate education.
• Furthermore, the income per student is not the same for all institutions.
There was equalization of the per capita sum among the then-existing
universities in the early 1990s, but at the same time institutions were
encouraged to recruit additional numbers on a 'fees-only' basis (at about
two-thirds of the full sum in the best year). Those which recruited heavily
in this way – in order to increase income, which in many cases was necessary to maintain spending commitments let alone allow investment in new
infrastructural and staff resources – thus reduced their average income
per student, which became the basis for future allocations. As a broad
generalization, therefore, the more students recruited in the early 1990s,
the lower the 'unit of resource' received per student later in the decade.
Meeting both popular demand and the government's wish for expanded
HE provision has thus made it more difficult for those institutions which
did so to sustain high-quality provision.

The first of these anomalies is not currently being addressed, whereas
the second is being tackled so slowly that it is unlikely ever to be removed
under the current funding regime. At the same time, the amount allocated
per student by the government to the funding councils, and hence to the
institutions, is subject to annual efficiency gains of some 3 per cent per
annum, and the reduction in available money is being exacerbated by other
policies. The government's argument is that any service industry should be
able to achieve such gains through increased productivity, and especially so
in labour-intensive activities such as university teaching and research (though,
interestingly, it has blocked proposed salary increases to reflect the large
productivity increases which staff have delivered through the substantial –
at least 25 per cent over five years – increase in the student : staff ratio).
Given other rising costs plus the government's withdrawal of separate capital funding, the real per annum efficiency gains are very much greater than
3 per cent, so that universities are forced to make very significant annual
economies in a labour-intensive 'industry' which, as indicated above, does
not enjoy substantial economies of scale in many of its activities, while it
suffers diseconomies of small scale.
The need to cope with these income reductions persuaded many university managers that the only way to sustain the quality of their teaching
through the 1990s was to expand student numbers, and because of the
freeze on additional recruitment of full-time undergraduate students since
the mid-1990s, most could only do that through either or both of expansion
of postgraduate provision and recruitment of overseas students. The result
is usually more work and, at best, a constant real income; staff numbers
rarely grow substantially and student : staff ratios inexorably deteriorate:

the pressures on staff increase and the amounts of quality time reduce. But not to grow necessarily means surviving on less income, and with the same number of students the work demands increase. An institution will probably lose if it grows; it certainly will if it doesn't; and whatever the outcome, its staff will have more demands put on them, which makes sustaining quality teaching increasingly difficult.

Facing up to these issues is a focus of much debate within universities. New teaching and learning strategies for coping with larger student numbers and deteriorating student : staff ratios are being promoted and experimented with. Departments are both restructuring course offerings (reducing 'contact hours' for staff and limiting options for students) and changing their employment strategies (such as employing graduate students and other part-timers on low incomes to undertake an increasing number of teaching responsibilities) in order both to protect quality time for teaching by their full-time academic staff and to sustain the amount of quality time that can be devoted to research.

Research

Income for research is allocated to universities as a component of the block grant and is constituted as a series of department-by-department calculations, for which the main terms in the formula are:

- the 'unit of resource' for research allocated to each discipline;
- the number of research-active staff in the department;
- the perceived quality of the research undertaken in the department, as evaluated in the regular research assessment exercise (RAE) peer reviews, which grade departments on a scale from 1 (the lowest quality) to 5.

The intent is that the 'bigger and better' the department the larger its allocation, but there is one major anomaly in the system to date: the size of the 'unit of resource' (basically the amount of money allocated per staff member in a department with the lowest grade that receives funding) bears little relationship to the cost of undertaking research in the discipline (on which, see Johnston, 1993). As a consequence, for example, departments of physics get much less money than departments of chemistry with the same grade and number of staff.

The formulae are transparent, and the emphasis on 'bigger and better' is widely appreciated (bigger departments certainly performed better; Johnston *et al.*, 1995). To increase their income, therefore, institutional and departmental managers pursue strategies that allow them both to grow and to achieve higher grades; the two interact in many cases, with many believing that a major step to getting a higher grade is to import one or more 'stars', researchers whose presence will substantially assist in, if not ensure the success of, that search for grade promotion.

This is a zero-sum game, however. Those who win must be balanced by those who lose, because there is no additional money available; even if the average perceived quality of research in a discipline improves (i.e. the average grade awarded increases), the outcome will be a smaller unit of resource. An institution is in the situation with regard to any discipline/department whereby:

1. If its size and grade are maintained, it will only retain the same income if all others do too; any increase, however slight, in either or both of the average grade for that discipline ('grade drift') or the average size of department being assessed ('size drift') will produce a reduced unit of resource and so a decline in that department's contribution to the university's income.
2. If it increases its size, but not its grade, income will only increase if there is very little or no grade and size drift. The most likely to benefit in such circumstances are departments with high grades which grow, while those with low grades do not. Given some grade and size drift, however, the best that a department which grows but keeps the same grade can hope for is maintenance of its income level, and that outcome is unlikely.
3. If it increases both size and grade, income will probably be maintained, and may even increase if the growth and enhanced grade are substantially above the average for the discipline.

The conclusion that managers will draw, therefore, is that to suffer a reduction in grade will be disastrous, to maintain one's grade will probably lead to a reduction in income, whereas to increase one's grade could mean more.[4] They will also conclude that growth in the number of researchers is highly desirable (not only in academic staff but also, because of the formula's terms, in research assistants and students), especially if staff can be recruited who will substantially assist in the search for a higher grade. Thus the two years preceding the 1996 RAE saw the development of a very active academic transfer market, whereby institutional managers invested heavily in the recruitment of 'stars' to enhance their RAE prospects, sometimes at inflated salaries.

Financial evaluation of these strategies indicates that the investments in growth and recruitment are unlikely to be rewarded by commensurate returns. Grade and size drift are likely in most disciplines, which will mean that those which increase their size and grade may sustain their income, but no more; much more likely is that they will lose less income than those which lose grade and/or don't grow (or even decline). The managers are in cleft sticks, however, because they know that if their departments neither grow nor gain a grade (heaven forbid that they lose a grade point), they are bound to lose income. The university will lose if it wins; it will lose even more if it doesn't (even if it stands still).

All this feeds back into time management, because the likely outcome for many institutions is that their share of the research component of the block recurrent grant will decline, whereas those for whom it grows slightly may well find that the expenditure commitments made to achieve the RAE successes increase more than the returns. As a consequence, the demands on academic staff time will increase – more research students to supervise, more research assistants to oversee, more undergraduate teaching, more administration – and the ability to provide quality time for both research and teaching will be reduced accordingly (as will the institution's ability to invest in the necessary infrastructure for both). For the system as a whole, the likely outcome is that the greatest losers are the highest rated departments, with obvious implications for the national research effort. Individual universities will experience problems of declining incomes in their perceived 'best' departments and problems of sustaining activity there as the degrees of freedom in time management are reduced (not to mention those of sustaining morale where academic success leads to financial failure).

These problems are exacerbated because the concept of efficiency gains ('newspeak' for public expenditure cuts) is now being applied to the funding of research as well as teaching. Whereas its relevance to teaching can be appreciated (some small economies might be achieved at the margin, and productivity increased without necessary losses of standards), even if the demanded level and its continued application is not, its application to research is much less obvious. It boils down, in the end, to a demand that one thinks more efficiently and effectively – or, in starker terms, more quickly. (The only alternative is fewer people doing research.) Given the absurdity of the former proposition, then the conflict between teaching and research for the allocation of quality time will be exacerbated – and teaching will probably be the sufferer, for a variety of reasons associated with both individual and institutional prestige and enhancement as well as the many anomalies and contradictions of the current funding system in British universities (on which, see Jenkins, 1995; but also Johnston, 1996).

Evaluation

> The American college or university is a prototypic organized anarchy. It does not know what it is doing. Its goals are either vague or in dispute. Its technology is familiar but not understood. Its major participants wander in and out of the organization. These factors do not make a university a bad organization or a disorganized one; but they do make it a problem to describe, understand and lead.
>
> (Cohen and March, 1974: 3)

Many implications can be drawn for university managers; I focus here only on how they can evaluate how (or even whether) successful they have been. Three measurable indicators of success are immediately apparent:

1. The institution's average (weighted?) grade in the latest RAE, or some aspects of the raw data which can be reduced to that score (such as the percentage of departments getting grades 5 and 5*).

2. The institution's average score in the Teaching Quality Assessments, or some other manipulation of the raw data.
3. The institution's block recurrent income, divided into its research and teaching components and expressed as a ratio. (If the denominator is the number of academic staff, then a high ratio – pounds per staff member – for the research component will indicate a 'good performance', and thus high quality research; a high ratio for the teaching income will indicate a high student : staff ratio, however, which is more likely to indicate low- than high-teaching quality, especially as there is a strong correlation between research grade and outcome of the Teaching Quality Assessments.)

The problem for the institutional manager is twofold; how to identify the desirable outcome, and then how to achieve it.

In some ways, that problem is similar to the one Hayek (1988; see also Sayer, 1995) identifies with both socialism and state planning in a mixed economy. He contrasts an economy with what he calls a catallaxy. In an economy, as he defines the term (such as a factory), the institutional manager has a clear goal: to produce a good or service which is saleable at a given price and will yield a profit on the investment. In technical terms, there is an objective function to be maximized, and resources (human and other) are allocated accordingly. In a catallaxy, on the other hand (such as the public sector in a country such as the UK), a vast number of 'economies' (or 'enterprises') are competing for resources and no objective function can be specified; there is no 'best' allocation of funds among the many competitors, so the selected distribution is the result of a subjective process only. As a consequence, the resource allocation decisions are based on judgements (often political and ideological), no optimum can readily be identified and the outcome cannot be evaluated against predetermined criteria. The price signals in a market system influence patterns of supply and demand and thereby determine what is produced and bought. You can plan the division of labour within an economy on economic criteria, therefore, but not within a catallaxy; you can determine the most efficient way to make cars which are competitively priced, but only market operations can determine – through expressed preferences (which are always changing) – the relative volumes of, say, foreign holidays, video recorders and CD players that will be traded.

The three university performance indicators set out above cannot readily be presented as explicit goals and reworked into an objective function. Even if the latter can be specified, a resource allocation programme which will ensure its optimal achievement cannot be identified. Subjective judgements have to be made regarding whether, for example, investing in a further staff member in department X is more likely to result in a higher RAE grade than a similar investment in department Y, and because controlled experiments cannot be conducted, the correctness of the decision can never be tested. The difficulties are compounded with teaching, because whereas the external judgements on research quality are made (albeit subjectively) on 'products' (papers in refereed journals etc.), with teaching quality the decisions are made subjectively on the basis of impressions, notably of performance in a small sample of 'classroom' situations, which by their nature are unrepeatable and 'unnatural' (Johnston, 1996). A university is a catallaxy, therefore, not an economy; it cannot be 'managed' in the way that a factory can.

Finally, even if the institutional manager could identify a tractable objective function, it may not be possible to achieve it, because high-quality research and teaching cannot be subjected to 'scientific management' (like the time-and-motion studies widely used in Fordist economies). Training programmes, recruitment and selection policies, infrastructural support, institutional ethos and continuing education can all be provided for the academic staff, but although these might be necessary conditions for success, they are not sufficient. People cannot be programmed into thinking great thoughts, and certainly not thinking great thoughts to a timetable;[5] people cannot be programmed into conducting stimulating teaching on every occasion. In effect, all that the institution manager can do is back hunches – whether in allocating resources or making appointments – because what is being managed is, in effect, unmanageable. It may not even be a catallaxy, but rather an 'organized anarchy', as described by Cohen and March (1974) in their seminal study of the American college/university president.

In their description of the university as organized anarchy, Cohen and March contend that

> Efforts to generate normative statements of the goals of a university tend to produce goals that are either meaningless or dubious. They fail one or more of the following reasonable tests. First, is the goal clear? Can one define some specific procedure for measuring the degree of goal attainment? Second, is it problematic? Is there some possibility that the organization will accomplish the goal? Is there some chance that it will fail? Third, is it accepted? Do most significant groups in the university agree on the goal statement? For the most part, the level of generality that facilitates acceptance destroys the problematic nature or clarity of the goal. The level of specificity that permits measurement destroys acceptance.[6]
>
> (Cohen and March, 1974: 195–6)

And even if some acceptable, measurable goals could be agreed, they too would have to submit to critical tests, such as: 'First, is the goal consistent with behaviour? Does the imputed goal produce the observed behaviour and is it the only goal that does? Second, is it stable? Does the goal imputed from past behaviour reliably predict future behaviour?' (Cohen and March, 1974: 196). They will probably fail, leading Cohen and March to conclude that:

> College presidents live within a normative context that presumes purpose and within an organizational context that denies it . . . They accept the presumption that intelligent leadership presupposes the rational pursuit

of goals. Simultaneously, they are aware that the process of choice in the college depends little on statements of shared direction.

(Cohen and March, 1974: 197)

Thus their power is exercised through resource-allocation processes which are based more on hunches than rigorous analyses and which are subject to general evaluations only. Hunches are crucial, of course, and have to be based on careful evaluation of the financial realities involved in making resource allocations, set in the context of experience. That is why being an institutional manager is not enough, and why being a leader as well is crucial – a point undoubtedly taken very seriously by those who appoint vice chancellors.

Summary

It is probably a mistake for a college president to imagine that what he does in office affects significantly either the long-run position of the institution or his reputation as a president. So long as he does not violate some rather obvious restrictions on his behaviour, his reputation and his term of office are more likely to be affected by broad social events or by the unpredictable vicissitudes of official responsibility than by his actions. Although the college library or administration building will doubtless record his presidency by appropriate portraiture or plaque, few presidents achieve even a modest claim to attention 20 years after their departure from the presidency; and those who are remembered best are probably most distinguished by their good fortune in coming to office during a period of collegiate good times or growth, or their bad fortune in being there when the floods came.

(Cohen and March, 1974: 203–4)

Management is an imperfect science – but some management is a more imperfect science than others. University management falls close to the more imperfect pole, because the institutional goals – high-quality research and teaching, sustained by efficient and effective administration – are not conducive to the critical path analysis which characterizes the operational environment of a Hayekian economy. Management is crucially involved in the resource allocation process which has been the focus of this chapter, but it is insufficient of itself: it must be associated with stimulating leadership, a supportive, collegial ethos and a great deal of serendipity. In a nutshell, it is paramount to appoint excellent people, give them good working conditions, make clear what your (realistic) expectations are, sustain them through the bad times, celebrate with them during the good and hope for the best.

When we move from the abstract to the particular, we identify the contextual problems involved in achieving these general goals. I have focused here on the resource allocation processes that managers have to operate in the context of government funding mechanisms for British universities, including those of the funding councils. These, to be kind, are full of anomalies and are not conducive to the achievement of high-quality outcomes. The core resource for producing high-quality outcomes is time, and particularly quality time; unless university managers have sufficient of that to distribute, then any other policies they implement are unlikely to produce the sort of quality outcomes we all want from academic staff and their students.

Notes

1. My stimulus for this section comes from Massey and Allen (1995), to whom apologies for pinching the idea.
2. A recent trend in British universities, stimulated by the regular Research Assessment Exercises (RAEs), is for targets to be set, since each of the last two exercises has asked all staff to nominate their 'best' four pieces of work over the previous four to six years. Since the RAE panels comprise small numbers of experienced academics assessing the work of large numbers (perhaps eight panel members assessing the work of 1000 staff, i.e. 4000 pieces), they are unlikely to have read the great majority of them and will not have time to during the assessment period. Thus they have to rely on secondary indicators, such as the perceived quality of the journals in which they are published – hence the pressure to publish in your discipline's 'top' journals.
3. Some of the staff in the post-1992 universities (the former polytechnics and colleges of higher education), notably in the arts and social sciences departments, had similar backgrounds and aspirations to their counterparts in the pre–1992 universities, whereas others, especially in the applied sciences and professional subjects, had work experience outside higher education and were more committed to teaching and learning and to applied research. Conditions of employment were different in the latter institutions, and the conduct of 'pure' research was rarely a requirement: there was usually less stimulus to undertake research and infrastructural support was weak. Many did develop research careers, however, as exemplified by their departments' successes in the 1992 RAE.
4. There is a major problem here. If a department already has the highest grade, no upward step is available. This has been recognized by the funding councils with the introduction of a new 5* grade for the 1996 RAE. But departments in England which attain that new grade will apparently get the same amount of money per capita as those which are awarded grade 5. The almost certain consequence of that decision will be that departments which achieve the new highest grade, and are marked out as the best in the country, will lose money while gaining in charisma – they will only gain financially if they have grown very significantly in size and all of their competitors have decreased equally substantially (if not more).
5. This supports the argument that the RAEs promote 'normal science' (as defined by Kuhn, 1962) rather than innovatory or revolutionary science, in which the risks of failure are greater. They promote 'run of the mill' enquiries, whose outcomes are relatively certain from the outset and from which 'respectable'

publications are virtually ensured, rather than more speculative, original pieces – a situation that might also be associated with the expansion in the number of universities and academic staff employed to conduct research.

6. Perhaps if their book had been widely read in British universities, less time would have been spent in recent years devising mission statements, most of which are so general that they are devoid of any real meaning for the staff to whom they apply.

9

Work's Committees

Ian McNay

Editor's introduction

For the unsuspecting reader this chapter might come as a surprise – but that alone would not justify the unusual device of an editor's introduction. The introduction is included simply to protect the author, who might otherwise lay himself open to the charge of academic deviation or what might be seen as the same thing, flippancy. If you are surprised at the tone of this chapter then you have forgotten, or skipped, the introductory chapter to the book, where all was explained. Please do not trouble to turn back at this stage. Instead, think of this chapter as a committee meeting at which you have just arrived, in time-honoured fashion, without having read the agenda and papers in advance.

Think of the editor as a committee secretary who, knowing your habits in these matters, has thoughtfully laid an executive introduction on the table in front of you, obviating your need to refer back to the chapters circulated in advance, and enabling you to bluff your way through the meeting regardless.

All you need to know, as the chapter begins, is that the author has done exactly as his editor requested: to try to combine wisdom with wit. We hope there is some of both. The book's first chapter noted that, alongside academic analyses of higher education work, there was an equally longstanding tradition of academic caricature, stretching at least from F. M. Cornford to Laurie Taylor. 'What everyone knows' about higher education is that it is beset by committees, in which most people spend hours while someone takes minutes. We need to access this everyday knowledge about working in higher education if we are to achieve a sufficiently rich picture of work to make it credible. At the same time, you deserve to be spared the kind of struggle involved in trying to write an interesting straightforward account of the work of committees.

Ian McNay accepted the challenge to produce an alternative view of 'work's committees', so much an alternative that, as you enter the chapter, it seems that the meeting is almost over.

Introduction

> The time approaches
> That will with due decision make us know
> What we shall say
>
> (Macbeth, Act V, Scene 4)

It had been a long meeting.

The internal evidence is strong: those there rushed off afterwards, late for other meetings; the group was barely quorate. Pratchett (1987) suggests that this is a normal situation, though his record of university meetings suggests that those with a different gender balance were bigger, much bigger. The final piece of evidence is the agenda item they had reached: date and place of the next meeting. 'When,' said the chair, 'shall we three meet again?'

Several Shakespeare plays are parables of universities. The opening of *King Lear* is based on the aftermath of the meeting to review the portfolios of pro vice chancellors; *Othello* shows what can happen without an equal opportunities policy and a good appeals procedure for internal disciplinary matters. Marlowe's Duchess of Malfi, in yearning 'to spend two days with the dead', obviously had fond memories of the joint senate/council residential retreat. Others, more ancient, were prophetic: Caesar's division of Gaul into three parts was a result of a committee compromise between the supporters of a national binary system and one based on four integrated regional sub-systems.

Modern literature also has its classic committee moments from higher education: the Council for National Academic Awards (CNAA) validating committee visit in *Wilt* (Sharpe, 1978); the assessment board in *The Lyre of Orpheus* (Davies, 1988); the academic promotions committee in *Moo* (Smiley, 1995). And, of course, C. P. Snow (*passim*).

Constitutional clarity

> Bloody business.
>
> (Macbeth, Act II, Scene 1)

In a recent exercise with senior staff in a modern Scottish university, the statement 'too much staff time is spent in committees' scored a mean of 7.4 on a scale where 9 meant 'strongly agree'. Only one person disagreed, and then only marginally. The same group scored 7.2 for the statement 'good teams are more effective than good individuals' and, conversely, only 4.2 for 'good individuals are more efficient than good teams' – 13 out of 21 disagreed. Yet committees are only a specialized subset of teams, so why the dissatisfaction with them? I suggest that it is because their remit is unclear, their meetings are often automatic, not strategic, and their control is poor. In some cases they should not be meeting at all.

All is but toys.

(*Macbeth*, Act II, Scene 3)

The witches' next meeting, with Macbeth, would not be necessary nowadays. Apart from the social bonding (one role for a committee) before the real business started, it could have been done by fax or e-mail, since its purpose was simple information transmission. As we retain lectures to do that inefficiently in a teaching context as a protective device, perhaps we keep committees to do it out of that same fear: of creating time to do the things we've been alleging we can't do when, in truth, we can't do them anyway with all the time in the world. The witches' only excuse was that they were 'performing', which in Tuckman's typology comes after 'forming', 'storming' (as in 'thunder, lightning or in rain'?) and 'norming' (Tuckman, 1965). You must have been to one of these 'have I got news for you' committees. Look at the minutes: 'noted . . .', 'noted . . .', 'noted . . .', 'noted . . .' That is, at least, one better than 'received . . .', which, in turn, is better than 'reported . . .', which implies that some spoke and none listened.

Bring me no more reports.

(*Macbeth*, Act V, Scene 3)

The witches were at least listened to. One had obviously trained as a registrar because outcomes were known in advance. The policy scenario was clear; the plans were developed; executing them was, as ever, a bit messier. Committees are full of policy makers; often empty of those who have to implement, when the two phases have to integrate with and inform each other.

Be bloody, bold and resolute.

(*Macbeth*, Act IV, Scene 1)

Resolution is another function of committees: remember the branch committee of vultures in Disney's *Jungle Book*, with their recurrent refrain, 'What're we gonna do?' There is some research (Stoner, 1961; Wallach and Kogan, 1965) that suggests that committees take bolder decisions because responsibility is dissipated around members; not these days when the corporate management have taken over committees and their decisions resemble those of the Soviet politburo or the Tory Party conference. Decision and resolution imply choice; often TINA rules (as she did under Margaret Thatcher), and there is too much work and, perhaps, fear involved in opposing and developing proposals to prove that there *is* an alternative.

These deeds must not be thought
After these ways; so it will make us mad.

(*Macbeth*, Act II, Scene 2)

Developing alternatives takes time but it is surely better to be slower and right than to be quick but wrong. Deadlines for outside bodies are often used by chairs in three ways: to speed debate down the wrong path; to stifle extended discussion; and to blame an external force for the deficiencies. This is called positive leadership by some. I call it 'parasitical power' – legitimacy is leeched off some other body, creating a dependency culture rather than one of self-sufficiency.

There are, conversely, committees set up to delay decisions or divert an issue into a siding. Cornford's (1908) 'principle of unripe time' is still prevalent. Procrastination is then the order of the day and, by comparison, timeless test matches, drawn, and ended only when the touring party's boat was leaving, seem like time trials in the Tour de France.

> We should have . . . desir'd . . . good advice
> In this day's council; but we'll take tomorrow.
>
> (*Macbeth*, Act II, Scene 4)

In the early 1970s, one polytechnic of my experience set up a DipHE committee and another a year later to review its report. Two years after that an implementation [*sic*] committee was set up. The polytechnic provided two officers to the Association of Colleges Implementing DipHE (ACID). It never did offer a DipHE: the role of the senior committee was suppression of its recommendations. The succession of delaying committees served another purpose: to occupy the curriculum subversives and preserve conservative approaches in the departments whence they came.

Then there's 'what do you think of this?' – the consultative committee. In the old days, departmental consultative committees were supposed to be a channel for external members to feed in ideas as 'users' of a department's wider services. They were community representatives. Not for long: the committee agenda was seized by the head of department and the external members' role turned through 180 degrees to be ambassadors *to* the community, not *for* it: back to 'have I got news for you'. The same is true of internal consultative committees: they drift to senior managers telling/selling, not listening.

> oftentimes, to win us to our harm
> The instruments of darkness tell us truths,
> Win us with honest trifles, to betray's
> In deepest consequence.
>
> (*Macbeth*, Act I, Scene 3)

So the list continues. *Negotiating committees*: audience participation in blood sports as David and Goliath meet in arm wrestling or worse across a table. *Safety committees*: required by law, but when did yours last meet or report? *Examination committees*: rubber stamps at £40 per person per hour (at least).

Scene: first year exam committee, engineering.

Dean: [*in the chair*]	Next, McIntosh. He is just one mark down in maths: not a problem, Dr Sugar?
Dr Sugar:	In maths, an exact science, a fail is a fail is a fail.
Dean:	He's two marks short of the total for a compensating pass. Jim, he has 62 in engineering drawing; could that be 64 or is judgement on drawing precisely inflexible?
Jim: [*previously primed*]	I suppose it could be 64.
Dean:	Fine. Pass by compensation. Now, McPherson . . .
Dr Sugar:	But . . . but . . . but . . . but.

Departmental and faculty committees often combine several of these functions but are not clear which at any one point. A problem with general purpose committees is that they tend to drift into just one – the 'get it off my chest' committee – where the *obsessive* push their idea (or grievance) yet again, the *possessive* bewail intrusions into autonomy or the perversion of good ideas they started, or the need for private personal space (a sort of protest and survive tactic), met by the *dismissive*, for whom there hasn't been a good idea, or at least one that hasn't failed, since the Planning Committee for Deluvian Survival, and even then their refrain was 'Ark at him – rain!'

The *obstructive* may or may not be there. At one university where I studied policy development I was told that the deans' behaviour at senate was predictive: if they kept quiet, or weren't there, policy initiatives from the senior management team would never progress to commitment and implementation despite apparent consensus. Faculty level committees would condone defaulters or conspire with them. Harmony was illusory: it wasn't even 'satisficing' (Simon, 1976). That is where the decision taken was the first one not to have the committee say 'no', never mind progressing to a positive 'yes'. So the committee process was ineffective, with each side blaming the other. The VC's comment was that 'all new ideas start with my staff. There have been great policy initiatives, but they have got bogged down.' Meanwhile, most members are *passive*, with the active staff likely not to be there. The latter are self-empowered and do things; the former feel disempowered. They think representative democracy should give them a say, but they never seem to work out how to say their say. They then blame some malevolent external force for their impotence or incompetence.

A final committee role, in some systems, is *scapegoat*. Senior managers have a hot potato and set up a committee to whom they delegate (i.e. abdicate) the decision. If it works, their genius is demonstrated; if it doesn't, they were nowhere near the scene of the crime. Nominated members have an acute decision to make: what is the cost–benefit analysis of refusing to serve (this person is disloyal, uncommitted) or of serving without success (incompetent)?

Chairs I have sat under

So clear in his great office.

(Macbeth, Act I, Scene 7)

Chairing committees is a crucial role. The bureaucracy of committees has an inbuilt tendency to indecision or to standardization or equal misery depending on the issue; chairs have to push them to strategic selectivity.

We still have judgment here; that we but teach
Bloody instructions, which, being taught, return
To plague the inventor.

(Macbeth, Act I, Scene 7)

We all have our styles:

- The *actor manager*, flamboyant, oratorical, charismatic even. Better suited for big occasions where he (it's usually a he) can stand rather than sit and can orchestrate other role players as they pop up to do their bit.
- The *philosopher king*, who believes it is better to travel enquiringly than to arrive. He or she will indulge in Socratic dialogue in a peripatetic fashion, walking all round an issue to view its many facets.
- The *flight lieutenant*, a reluctant chair who adapts flight strategies so that someone else can be in command: referral and deferral are the prime tactics.
- The *anal retentive*, tightly controlled, formal, obsessed by procedure not process, task not mission, and restricting the imagination of the group by an inability to tolerate even slight disorder. He or she may indulge in rites of personal hygiene as an obsessive action.
- The *paranoid*, for whom any comment is a criticism, any suggestion a challenge, any question a revolutionary challenge.
- The *hippy happy anarchist*, also known as *laissez-faire*, for whom time is passed, not spent, and timetables are a control device of a capitalist corporate bureaucracy. So is 'firm' – think of its alternative meanings – so that formless is good even though the people perform less. This may not be as purposeless as it seems. I advised one general meeting where the chair allowed constant interruptions to speakers who refused to give way, so that, at times, four people were talking at once. No decision was reached, as the meeting broke up in disorder, which was the chair's desired outcome.
- The *benevolent dictator*, who may smile and smile and be a villain. The sort in my acquaintance who, after 20 minutes' debate of an issue, would pull a paper from an inside pocket and say, 'Well, ladies and gentlemen, that's all been very interesting; now, here is what we will decide.' And the troops lined up, the hands went up and the show moved on to the next business.

Chairs are, of course, not the only leaders. Most committees have alternative leaders who are accorded that role or arrogate it to themselves. They usually sit just off the line directly opposite the chair; they have the rule-book and standing orders by heart as well as precedents and, where possible, research findings. Few policy decisions in universities are backed by research. Many decisions affecting hundreds of lives are taken by staff, individually or collectively, with less background knowledge than is required for a final-year undergraduate project. Yet research has an esteem in the community outside committees such that its importation into that arena provokes a pause which, if not reverential, is at least, briefly, reflective. Subversives have their references handy. So alternative leaders get to the debate early to cap-ture the agenda; they bring new facts to the discussion to establish their authority and undermine the official line; and they make formal proposals within the frame of the committee's procedural protocols. Between them and the chair a virtual despatch box rises up.

The other alternative leader sits to the right of the chair with no formal voice, certainly no vote, officially no power, but lots of influence (Moodie and Eustace, 1974). Registrars do what research is done, prepare policy papers, define the options, slant the presentation to a favoured outcome and provide the official record of the debate, which is more selective than Hansard.

> I will set down what comes . . .
> to satisfy my remembrance the more strongly.
>
> (*Macbeth*, Act V, Scene 1)

Creative accounts can still be lodged by judicious reporting.

> 'Boy, you had a rough ride there,' said a member, commiserating with the chair. 'Not all all,' came the cheerful reply.
> 'But, you were attacked by four different people and the proposals came under heavy fire,' his sympathizer continued. 'You can't make progress now.'
> 'Wait,' said the chair, 'until you see the minutes.'

A good chair works with the committee secretary, but not to the extent of subordinating his or her formal role. The governing body of Derby College Wilmorton had a clerk who was paid on a casual basis with main employment in the firm where the chair also worked. The consequences were immense: five meetings were not minuted; members served illegally; meetings were called improperly; due process was not observed. The par-able told by Michael Shattock (FEFC, 1994) has lessons for us all.

Of course, Cardinal Wolsey saw himself as a leader and secretaries must learn too from his experience: the chair is always *primus inter pares*, even when you have your hand up his or her jacket manipulating the controls. He may be Bertie Wooster and not fit to be let out alone, but you are Jeeves, discreet, polite and almost invisible.

In one newish university, the planning committee had reached an impasse. It would need to meet again, soon, because the matter was urgent. 'It can't be for the next ten days,' said the registrar, 'because I'm out of the country.' 'But registrar,' said the vice chancellor, '*I* shall be here.'

Never develop, in Charles Steward's words, 'feelings of competence' (Fielden, 1975), even when the chair falls asleep in the middle of a meeting of the academic staff promotions committee. (A real example. The solution? Call for a 'comfort break' for the whole committee, creating a diversion and an impetus by getting to your feet as you dig the chair in the ribs.)

All is confirm'd, my lord, which was reported.

(Macbeth, Act V, Scene 3)

Context

When shall we ... where the place?

(Macbeth, Act I, Scene 1)

When a special meeting of a college governing body is called for a Sunday morning, at 24 hours' notice, even though a normal meeting is scheduled in the annual calendar for the Tuesday following, and when one of the 'alternative leaders' or dissenting voices is known to be out of the country, even someone with a blocked sinus could detect not only 'the faint aroma of performing seals' but the smell of their fishy titbits. Equally, when a meeting of the governing council of one partner in a federal university is due to be held in the offices of a firm of solicitors, some game is afoot.

The first was Derby College Wilmorton, again; the second, one campus of the University of Western Sydney contemplating bidding for independent status. The point is that arrangements such as those give messages. Do negotiating committees meet on neutral ground? Do working groups in someone's office get messages from interaction with interruptions and other symbols of status? Do mature students (and staff) get child care allowances paid to cover participation in meetings that drag on through the late afternoon? Does the table layout predispose to a particular form of interaction; a top table and 'the rest', for example? At Bristol Polytechnic in the 1970s, the academic board met in the shape of a tuning fork. At one meeting members arrived to a novel layout: tables for five set in a circle like covered wagons in the wild west. The whole process took on a new culture and a new dynamic. Groups of cognate interests were formed: the NATFHE table in the alternative leadership position; the 'key influentials' among the heads of department in a crucial third angle of a triangle with NATFHE and the chair; pro directors separated from the 'top table'; a 'blind spot' where those from art and design could hide quietly; and so on. Everyone could see everyone else, which helped towards a self-controlled process, and the layout led to a greater equalization of contributions, in contrast to the previous hierarchy.

The importance of layout is demonstrated by a second example, from elsewhere: here the board sat in a large rectangle, the long sides three times the length of the short; chaired from the middle of a long side. In one incident a member at one end of a long side made a pantomime of mopping up spilled water with, eventually, his sock, while a boring speaker at the other end of that same side apparently drew more laughs than ever before. When a new vice chancellor arrived, they moved to chair from the short side, allowing the main alternative leadership group to line up like a phalanx of knights along the opposite 'edge', with a clear boundary to the group at the corners. Again, the group dynamics changed ... to a more adversarial mode. King Arthur and Merlin (the registrar) were usually the only two on the 'top edge'; they kept control most of the time, but the fellowship of the previous arrangement was lost as Mordred and his cronies confronted them. Senate rooms in older universities often have officers on a raised platform facing members sitting in conference style: the implications for the dominant direction of any dialogue are clear.

Contributors

What beast was't, then?

(*Macbeth*, Act I, Scene 7)

All members are, of course, difficult, but some are more difficult than others. A bestiary guide developed with husbandry instructions by a number of staff developers includes:

- The *budgie*. A constant chatterer, distracting to neighbours and to the business of the meeting. Shame them into shutting up (Order! Order!) or ask for a contribution to follow what they were not listening to. Don't let them think they are clever boys.
- The *starling* interrupts. Reciprocate, and go formal so that he or she waits until called.
- The *kookaburra* jokes, which can be useful to help group process but needs to be limited, especially in international committees where humour differs across cultures. Train kookaburras by a quiet word outside.
- The *bullfrog* speaks loud, long and often, but without substance most of the time. The Open University senate has a three-minute rule in its standing orders and time flies for bullfrogs when they are enjoying themselves, until choked off.
- The *bulldog*. An aggressive growler, somewhat slow, who needs to be given useful tasks to perform for the master and praised for performance if he or she isn't to become ...
- The *wolf*, who may get personal in attacks and may attract a pack if not controlled.
- The *white rabbit* is constantly late. Don't make white rabbits comfortable when they arrive.

- The *hedgehog*: prickly, reserved but with some wisdom. Prime hedgehogs before the meeting that you will seek advice and show respect for it.
- The *cat*: a loner, not interested in others' views or the business of the meeting. Decide how far the cat's self-alienation is infectious: one can be left alone without harm.
- The *monkey* thinks he or she knows all the answers and leaps to conclusions. Accept the monkey's ideas as proposals to return to, which gives others time for more mature reflection.
- The *ferret*, known as Gradgrind since he or she always wants more facts and is often suspicious of concepts, ideas or anything less than concrete. Useful in the secondary stages of policy decisions: make the ferret a sub-group member with the remit to uncover the facts.
- The *fox* is there to trap the chair. Try a role reversal by asking him or her to make positive proposals, not to snipe at others.
- The *rook* is a lawyer from the barrack room, full of points of order and challenges to the chair. Use the democracy to establish process norms within the group: few will want formality.
- The *horse* is a keen, intelligent, hard worker. Public according of esteem is often a motivation stimulus, so give credit and praise, but don't overload.

All these underline the points made by two researchers on group work. Belbin (1992) emphasizes the need for group membership to have a balance of roles: the coordinator needs the implementer to put the plant's ideas into practice, the monitor-evaluator to help in the decision process, the company worker for support and so on. Adair (1986) stresses the need for balance in process among caring for:

- the needs of the *task* to be performed;
- the needs of the *group* to interact and cohere to be maintained as a collective;
- the needs of the *individual* for identity, recognition and useful purpose.

Conclusion

The committee's purpose may change or end. To the four stages referred to earlier, of forming, storming, norming and performing, need to be added two beyond that apex: transforming and mourning. Course committees in the Open University are exciting at the design and development stages; few want to be involved in delivery. This underlines Belbin's findings on Apollo groups, where creativity is strong but so is conflict; continuity and completion are bad. Composition and process for committees may, then, need regular review and some may need killing off. In several universities there are groups of people who encounter the same colleagues under different banners depending on which committee meets that day. Perhaps they need what the University of Northumbria at Newcastle has, an anti-bureaucracy committee. But, remember, that oxymoron, the good committee, does exist, if only for therapeutic reasons:

As I slowly improved, I contemplated going to my first committee meeting since falling ill. What my therapist helped me envisage were the likely negative possibilities: how bad would it be, for example, if I went and then had to leave? Would my colleagues be critical? I decided to go. Moreover, that afternoon I cycled for the first time in ages, to work. The committee meeting went well and marked a major stage in recovery.

(Wolpert, 1995)

10

Geographical Transitions

Michael Bradford

There have been major changes in secondary and higher education during the past decade, but few people working within either sector have been involved in, or are very aware of, the changes in the other. The transition for students from secondary to higher education, as a result of these changes and the lack of mutual awareness of them, has become a major gap which needs to be bridged. Some of the changes in the sectors have resulted from government's attempts to improve the competitive position of the UK within the changing global economy. Some have been influenced by the ideology of the New Right. Global and national economic changes have also transformed the transition from university to work, again making the lives of students more difficult than those of their predecessors. This chapter reviews these transitions with particular reference to the experience of students of geography, a subject that bridges the sciences and the arts.

In the context of the book, the chapter provides a case study of the processes of change affecting work in one discipline. It shows how the nature of work within higher education can only be understood by an appreciation of the broader context, especially the secondary education system and the employment sector to which HE students graduate. Thus the chapter itself provides a transition from 'The work' to 'The work context'.

An overview of change

There have been many fundamental changes in higher education in the UK during the past decade. Many of these reflect, directly or indirectly, responses to global economic change. One argument suggests that as governments have seen the UK's economic position in the world ever more threatened, they have sought to transform the higher education system to enable the nation to compete more effectively with traditional competitors in Western Europe, North America and Japan, and newer competitors in the rest of the Pacific Rim. The rapid move from an 'elite' towards a 'mass' system of higher education has been a major response to the attempt to achieve a more skilled and enterprising labour force. Thirty per cent of 19-year-olds now enter some form of higher education institution. The higher retention rates of British higher education mean that the percentage graduating is now more akin to its major European and North American competitors. A more cynical view of the sudden expansion and its timing during a major recession may suggest that an additional contributory factor was the political necessity of keeping unemployment figures down.

Simultaneously, governments have sought to transform primary and secondary education in order to achieve the same end, a more competitive state (Bradford, 1995). These attempts have been accompanied by other ideologies of the New Right: its neo-liberal wing introducing competition through open enrolment and the rhetoric of 'parental choice' on the assumption that competition improves standards; and its neo-conservative wing bringing in the National Curriculum, which reflects particular views of the self, very much social Darwinist ones, and a particular national identity, some would say a monoculture (evidenced, for example, by the impact of political interference with history and geography and the world; Graham and Tytler, 1993). These other policy initiatives, which were part of the 1988 Education Reform Act, incorporated other political agendas, such as the reduction in the powers of local government and teachers' unions, and an attack on 'progressive' and critical education in the classroom. In many ways, these other ideologies and agendas may have reduced the impact of attempts to produce a more competitive state through an improved labour force. For example, local authorities have had their economic development roles minimized and so cannot attempt to produce more competitive local states as has occurred in Australia; schools have been deflected into marketing in order to attract pupils, and therefore resources; and teachers have been engaged in implementing a new curriculum, with its accompanying bureaucracy and tests.

These major changes in schools during the past decade, whatever their effect on the future labour force, have concentrated much attention and teachers' time on the 5–16 age group, to whom the National Curriculum refers. At the same time that teachers were trying to introduce the National Curriculum, their support services at local authority level, namely subject advisors, were being drastically reduced. The new grant maintained schools were being ostracized by other schools in many local authorities and, because of competition for pupils through 'parental choice', there was little cooperation among the remaining schools and colleges. So instead of sharing ideas and experience, there were many cases where individual schools were reinventing the wheel. No wonder there was little opportunity to keep abreast of changes in higher education, and, in the absence of an advisor, no one to facilitate the process. The National Curriculum has also meant that less time has been available for considering and implementing change for the 16–19 age group, particularly in 11–18 schools. The lack of change at this level has widened the gap between secondary and higher education.

Even the expanding set of sixth form colleges, which might have been expected to be more able to concentrate on change in the 16–19 curriculum, experienced the distractions of removal of local authority control and marketing as a result of greater competition for students. Just as with the local management of schools in general, there has been less release of teachers' time to be involved in external INSET (in-service education and training) events. Certainly there has been less time for teachers to become aware of changes in their academic discipline in higher education, and perhaps, in some cases, because of being deprofessionalized by the onset of the National Curriculum, less motivation to find the time. For most teachers, their view of universities is based upon their own experiences, which means that many have little idea of the dramatic changes which have occurred in higher education.

The transition from elite to mass higher education was supposed to occur over a longer period of time, but other policy changes reflecting a neo-liberal move to introduce the market into the public sector and to reduce government expenditure resulted in higher education institutions competing for scarce funding by taking on more and more students. Government intervention in the market which it had itself created, in the form of a capping of student numbers, reflected its inability to fund such a sudden change. The sudden expansion in student numbers and a continually reducing funding per student, called an 'efficiency gain', peaking, one hopes, at an effective 7 per cent in the 1995 budget statement, has dramatically changed and will further worsen the student : staff ratio (SSR) in universities. Changes from 15 : 1 to over 22 : 1 in four years are not uncommon. Such a dramatic worsening of SSRs in the secondary or primary sector would have produced political uproar and media mayhem. University staff complain bitterly, but they have been distracted by the need to publish for the Research Assessment Exercise (RAE) and, for some subjects, preparation for the Teaching Quality Assessment (TQA) visits, where it is what is done within resource constraints that is important. Competition for research funds has become all important, yet the RAE is only about the redistribution of a pot of funds rather than a mechanism for expanding the pot (see also Johnston's analysis in Chapter 8).

The RAE rating, however, has become the major priority, because in many institutions it affects the amount of resources entering the department as well as the university. It affects the department's ability to attract and retain prestigious staff and young stars. In short, it affects the survival of departments in the same way that league table positions affect the survival of secondary schools. It is not surprising, therefore, that the longer running and resource-oriented RAE has received more attention and had greater effects on institutions than the TQA. Some argue that it has reinforced the tendency of older universities to prioritize research ahead of teaching and reversed the priority of the newer universities. Certainly it has focused academics' attention on their own sector. There has been less involvement in A level examining and less writing of texts, some of which used to bridge the secondary–higher education divide. In geography, there is lower membership and involvement in the Geographical Association, a professional body which used to attract both academics and teachers. The cohorts of academics who, as a matter of course, belonged to both the Geographical Association and the Institute of British Geographers or the Royal Geographical Society (recently merged to give greater political clout) had mostly retired by the late 1980s. Few present academic geographers know the structure of the National Curriculum and its geographical content, unless they have children at school. Still fewer know the structure of the subject core at A level and AS, to which all syllabuses in geography being taught from 1995 had to conform (other subjects had subject cores at or slightly before that time). Academics may have criticized some of their students for the poorer quality of their essay writing skills, without knowing that in some syllabuses the emphasis is on resource-based questions and structured essays, with very little open essay writing being required.

With all these changes within sectors, it is not surprising that they have grown apart and there is less knowledge about recent changes in the other sector which affect how students are prepared for university and treated when they arrive. It is worth examining some of the detailed changes in secondary education to show how the cohorts arriving at university straight from school are coming from very varied backgrounds: different types of learning environments, different syllabuses in geography and different combinations of subjects.

Changes in secondary education

Secondary education in the UK has been reorganized, producing a range of provision for 16–18-year-olds. In addition to 11–18 schools, there are sixth form and tertiary colleges. The private–state divide in educational provision, characteristic of the late 1970s, has become in some areas a continuum, with grant maintained schools and city technology colleges occupying the middle of the continuum and private schools with assisted places complicating the private end of the continuum (Bradford, 1993). So the types of establishment and contexts in which 16–18-year-olds study have diversified.

There has always been considerable variation within both the state and the private sectors, but these recent organizational and structural changes have further increased the differences in, among other things, class size, resources and the range of subjects available. In small schools students may be taught by the sole member of the geography department, who makes any selection of options within the syllabus for them; in large colleges they may have a range of specialist staff available who can offer the students a choice of options within their course and a choice of whether they follow a linear or modular route of assessment. Some students, therefore, begin to take greater responsibility for their own learning at an earlier stage. Students in 11–18 schools experience a considerable degree of continuity in their staff and fellow students between the ages of 16 and 18; others in sixth form and tertiary colleges face new staff and fellow students who have come from different educational contexts and varied backgrounds in geography. For some the school-to-college move helps the transition to higher education.

A view of geography in secondary education over the past 20 years suggests that it has been more concerned with pedagogy than with the content of the subject, at least until the National Curriculum, which was highly content-driven. The subject at the secondary level seems still to be strongly affected by the 'scientific revolution' which affected the discipline in the late 1950s and early 1960s in higher education geography. Hypothesis testing abounds, and in many cases it is the sole form of investigative work. Locational analysis and the use of models still prevail in many syllabuses, which perhaps as a result are highly economic in their view of human geography. Yet physical geography, where positivist approaches are more appropriate, was, until the National Curriculum, poorly represented in many GCSEs and some A level syllabuses. This became a focus of complaint for many in universities, some of whom decided to mount remedial classes for those having taken what became the most popular syllabus in the early 1990s. This syllabus was highly innovative, particularly in terms of pedagogy, incorporating an enquiry approach to learning and having a high coursework component. Until very recently, this was the 'new syllabus', yet it was devised and introduced in the late 1970s. Perhaps it should not be surprising that new teachers from university find that many of the A level syllabuses they are required to teach are as far removed from them as parts of a new Northern Examination and Assessment Board (NEAB)[1] A and AS geography syllabus (NEAB, 1995) seemed initially to teachers in their forties and fifties, who were educated during the 'scientific revolution'. The new NEAB syllabus included some aspects of social and political geography to give balance to economic and technological processes in its core human geography sections. This was meant to give those leaving school and geography a broader geographical preparation for life, as well as giving those continuing in geography a more complete background for their university courses. The NEAB syllabus's inclusion of crime and disease among its treatment of hazards seemed a major change to some, but both are inherently spatial and environmental. Disease, at least, has been taught in other contexts in school geography for decades; for example, sleeping sickness and tsetse fly in the study of some less developed countries. With so much change elsewhere in the curriculum imposed from above, some teachers have become, understandably, too set in their A level ways.

Unfortunately, holding or improving positions in league tables is not conducive to coping with the uncertainty of changing to more modern syllabuses. Informal league tables exist within schools among subjects and teachers are loath to change since it may threaten the consistently high percentage of good grades achieved. Yet many of the present A and AS syllabuses, recently recognized by the Schools Curriculum and Assessment Authority (SCAA) as satisfying the subject core, have too little relevance to the changing world and are by no means as good a preparation for life or future study as they could be. The introduction of the subject core was an obvious opportunity for change and updating. Superficially it seems strange that the opportunity has not been taken in many syllabuses. Geography, though, is a naturally dynamic subject and so the subject core was written to be sufficiently flexible to allow varying approaches and future change. Unfortunately, its very flexibility also made it difficult for SCAA advisors to exclude more dated geography syllabuses. The dated syllabuses did, after all, conform.

The competition among exam boards in a market conditioned by league tables and conservatism, produced by a surfeit of change elsewhere, meant that many A level boards made as little change to their syllabuses as was necessary to conform to the subject core, the new cap of 20 per cent on coursework and new rules for modular assessment. Indeed, it is the modular nature of the syllabuses that is the greatest change, since in many cases their content would not seem out of place in the late 1970s or early 1980s. The transition to university geography for those taking most syllabuses, though clearly not the NEAB one, is extremely difficult. The difference in approach and content presents more a chasm than a gap for many students.

The introduction of a subject core may be thought to have standardized the backgrounds of those studying geography entering higher education in 1997 onwards. However, as has been indicated above, the necessary flexibility of the subject core has allowed continued variation in approach and content. Each syllabus is set in its time, but collectively the syllabuses are set in varied times. The National Curriculum is set in a time well before it was formulated, because of the conservative tendency produced by the need to establish agreement and the political interference of the government, which removed anything that might threaten the societal status quo. The word 'critical' rarely appears. The word 'conflict' was removed. It is likely that a non-flexible subject core would have produced an equally poor, fossilized, stultifying structure.

In addition to these changes within geography itself, 1990s students approach geography at university with rather different combinations of subjects than they did over a decade earlier. Before the early 1980s, geography was traditionally accompanied by English and history, and to a lesser extent economics and biology, reflecting geography's bridging nature between the social and earth sciences. Now, while these subjects are still represented, there is a much greater variety of accompanying subjects. This reflects a generally greater flexibility of A level combinations, particularly permitted by the growth of large sixth form colleges. It partly concerns the bridging nature of the subject and partly relates to the growth of new subjects such as business studies at the expense of older subjects such as economics. The structure of the National Curriculum, in which the study of geography and history are statutory up to the end of Key Stage 3 (14-year-olds), and the early requirement (relaxed after the Dearing Report, Dearing, 1994) to take either one or half of each at Key Stage 4 (15–16), have meant that geography and history at GCSE have been timetabled as mutually exclusive alternatives in many more schools than in the past. So fewer students entering higher education can be expected to have that traditional combination in the future.

In a further break with tradition, those entering higher education are coming from increasingly varied educational backgrounds. While entry to the older universities, in particular, is generally still dominated by 18- or 19-year-olds coming straight from school/college or after a year out, there are many more mature students, some coming through Access courses and many more with non-A level qualifications such as General National Vocational Qualifications (GNVQs). The non-involvement of geographers in GNVQs does not increase the chances of geography in higher education attracting many with this new vocational qualification. The Dearing report on 16–19 education (Dearing, 1995a, 1996) will no doubt have an impact on the future backgrounds of student geographers.

In summary, students entering higher education to study geography have to adapt to very new learning environments and ways of study and, in many cases, to very new approaches and styles of geography. Universities receive students from increasingly varied backgrounds in terms of previous learning environments and still varied backgrounds in geography.

Changes in higher education

In higher education, in some ways diversity has been reduced. The abandonment of the binary divide, similar funding bases for teaching and the competition for research monies through the RAE have brought about some convergence. Differences may still exist in resource levels and perhaps in student : staff ratios, but older universities now share the newer universities' concern with teaching large classes. Many have moved to semesters and modular programmes, although it must be noted that the word 'modular' covers a multitude of sins or attributes, depending on your viewpoint. There seem to be many pressures, however, that are leading to the emergence of a hierarchy of universities, with levels distinguished by their emphasis on research. For some universities, research and postgraduate teaching may have much greater prominence, while there is a threat (or opportunity) that some others will become teaching-only institutions. The superficial unifying tendencies of recent years may simply be a prelude to further diversification.

At present though, students entering higher education still have a range of size and locations of institutions from which to choose, a range of size of geography departments and different types of programmes, with geography as the single, joint or part element. Some have more choice than others. Because the financial support of students is much worse than in the past, more feel restricted to universities accessible from the parental home. Finance and diet have become two areas which today's students have to learn to organize along with their time, in order to reduce the stress of university life. Some have more guidance over university entrance than others. Some can afford to visit many institutions before making their selection. Others have to choose, sight and site unseen. Wherever they finally go, they will usually find large first-year lecture classes, well beyond what they have experienced at secondary level. For some even their university small group teaching will be in groups larger than those experienced in the sixth form. In some institutions they will meet in small classes less than once a week or even less than once a fortnight. Some departments will balance intensive (small group) and extensive teaching throughout the three years. Others will leave the intensive work until the final year of the degree programme, when sometimes it is too late. Only a few will front-load the intensive work to act as a bridge from secondary to higher education.

Certainly the gap between universities and school/college, particularly school, must be recognized by both staff and students, and attempts must be made to bridge it. When arriving in higher education students can no longer rely on the study skills acquired at the secondary level. They have to learn new ways of studying and they can no longer rely on the level of access to HE staff that their school teachers enjoyed and perhaps prepared them for. The pressures of research and larger numbers mean that one of the major challenges facing university departments is to establish ways of devoting the necessary individual attention to all students, not just those who seek it, to ensure that they have sufficient opportunities to realize their potential.

In higher education in geography, the emphasis until recently, especially in the older universities, has been on the content of courses and perhaps the overall structure of the programme. Few thought in curriculum terms. Yet few subjects have the equivalent of the *Journal of Geography in Higher Education*, which has a strong, albeit no longer exclusive, orientation to improving teaching and learning. The small original core of staff, mainly from the old polytechnics, with an interest in innovation in teaching and learning has grown and widened. However, HE staff still take less interest in pedagogy than do geography teachers in secondary education, and HE staff still have little knowledge of secondary education.

Pressures for change affecting the transition from school to HE

There are some pressures for the establishment of a core curriculum in geography in the first year of higher education. These in part come from the earlier stages of education. After the National Curriculum, there are new national criteria governing GCSE syllabuses and the new subject core for

A and AS. Some call 16–18 education 'key stage 5' for short, and refer to the first year of higher education as 'key stage 6'. Language in itself can be a powerful motor for change. The proponents of such changes foresee a natural progression, the possibility of a 'seamless robe' of geographical education; however, they ignore the marked variation in the GCSE syllabuses which are first examined in 1998, as well as the great differences in approach and content among the new A levels, discussed above. They also ignore the increasing numbers of so-called 'non-standard' students, who will never be wearing the same robe, and the variety of more flexible structures in higher education which make it difficult to guarantee that any one student can follow the whole of a core programme in any one subject. In a separate and wider debate there are calls for a set of core, transferable skills which can underpin any degree programme. Here the issue is a subject-based core.

The other main pressures towards the establishment of such a core are the move for recognition of professional chartered status for geographers, reflecting the needs for employment in the European Union, and the technological potential of producing core material which may reduce the need for staff contact time. Chartered status does not have to be met by standardization; indeed, it is the professional bodies of other disciplines which are constraining much needed change and flexibility in those disciplines. It would be unwise to impose such constraints on a necessarily dynamic discipline such as geography, which has to respond to a changing world.

The technological imperative needs to be carefully examined. Investment by the Higher Education Funding Councils in the Teaching and Learning Technology Programme has stimulated much interesting and useful work and material. There will be much promotion of it to try to make the investment worthwhile, with encouragement for all departments to take up the materials. No doubt some will be of medium- rather than just short-term value. Much will be useful as learning material following or preceding rather than replacing staff contact time. Advocates of the large-scale production of core materials as a technological fix to solve the worsening student : staff ratios should, however, bear in mind the reducing shelf-life of much knowledge, a point that technologically oriented academics know so well. Thus, the switching of scarce resources from investment in people to investment in technological solutions, which are only cost-effective if used by many over a long period, must only be done with educational and economic eyes wide open. The technological 'can' should not become the educational 'will', in either sense of the word.

One of the present and future challenges in higher education is obtaining an appropriate educational balance of staff-intensive, staff-extensive and staff-free (in part, technology-intensive) learning and teaching strategies for each degree programme within the funds available. Whatever balance of strategies is reached, degree course directors need to consider the timing of the emphasis of the three elements so that the gap between school/college and higher education does not increase. Replacing large-scale lecture sessions (n.b. not traditional lectures) by impersonal interactions with machines may only widen the gap, when the lecture sessions have and realize the object-ives of stimulating thought, creating involvement, mapping future learning, conveying enthusiasm in the subject and showing interest in the students.

The balance of strategies is, however, not just a local decision. It is a system-wide decision too. It would be possible for higher education funding to be top-sliced in order to invest in technological solutions; for example, concentrated production for system-wide use of multimedia packages or whatever their equivalent is in the near future. Then, however, the context for local decisions will already have been made; that is, by enforcing a mix of even less staff and more investment in hardware.

It is to the advantage of commercial interests to encourage and facilit-ate such developments, knowing that they are guaranteeing a future market for their rapidly changing hardware. The enthusiasm of today's publishers for a core, so that they can produce textbooks to meet it, so repeating their experience with the National Curriculum, is mirrored by their hi-tech equivalents. Private–public partnerships may attract new investment with an overseas as well as national market in mind; indeed, there is con-siderable potential in the export of such knowledge-based materials. Such partnerships have their place, but they can often result in changed object-ives. Educational rather than technological and commercial priorities need to be uppermost.

There is a danger then that one response to less funding per student in higher education will be standardization of education with the establishment of subject cores. This may be a perfectly reasonable solution for subjects that necessitate ladder-based learning, but very stultifying for other subjects. The experience of designing the National Curriculum for schools showed how difficult it is to produce anything but a conservative, out-of-date view of a subject. Such processes are influenced by the views of a few and are open to much political manipulation. They are easily related to solutions for achieving common standards through national exams. League tables based on common assessment for higher education institutions would rapidly follow in order to inform resource allocations and student choice. The competitive framework of primary and secondary education would be repeated for higher education. The assumption that competition means improvement in stand-ards would underlie such a move. Yet there is already much tension in higher education between collaboration to share good practice and competition for students and resources. Intensifying competition would in many instances prevent improvement of standards. The establishment of subject cores with their prevention of innovation and their accompanying competitive processes are of debatable educational value at whatever level of education.

The transition from university to work

If present students face a more difficult transition from secondary to higher education, they also face a different and, some would argue, more

difficult transition to the world of work. In that there is much more overt concentration on the development of transferable skills and greater emphasis
on student profiling than in the past, it could be argued that the transition
is easier. But these educational changes have by no means penetrated all
university departments.

The transition itself, though, has changed. The increased number of
students entering the labour market coincided with much restructuring
as a result of global economic change and a major recession. In the recent
past it was common for students to be taken on by large organizations in
considerable numbers and to be trained together for a period of time. Now
there are many fewer large organizations because of downsizing. In 1993, the
top 1000 UK companies lost 1.5 million jobs. It is often higher education
institutions which, after their recent growth, are the largest organizations
in the local area. Small and medium-sized companies have been the key
growth sector for new graduate jobs. Between 1989 and 1991, over 90 per
cent of new jobs created in the economy were in firms with fewer than ten
employees. It is now common for students to be taken on by smaller organizations in ones and twos. Gone is the lengthy period of training. There is
no such tradition in small and medium-sized enterprises. Gone is the cama-
raderie and social safety of being part of a similarly aged group, something
that school-to-university students will have experienced for the whole of
their lives. Now they are expected to hit the job running.

While the recent greater incorporation into higher education of such
things as teamwork and report-writing skills may help our students, greater
experience of task-oriented education and tasks completed within a very limited time may help even more. Certainly students have to develop an ability to
make decisions with limited knowledge and a confidence to do so.

There seems to be a greater need for teaching departments to work
more closely with their institutions' careers services (HEFCE, 1995b). First
they need to be kept aware of changes in the graduate labour market.
Many will know about changing levels of demand. Fewer will be aware of the
changing structure of demand and the effects that has on the transition.
There is probably a need for closer integration of careers education programmes into the academic curriculum; that is, as credit rated course units.
There is a need for students and staff to be aware that 'a career' is for many
no longer a probable future. They are more likely to experience a number
of different 'careers'. 'What do you want to do when you leave?' no longer
means for life.

Staying in contact with past graduates and being more aware of their
employment positions five and ten years after graduation will allow a better
perspective on the university–work transition. Discovering which elements
of their undergraduate degree programme most helped in their work, and
which could have been amended in order to do so, offers ways of obtaining
constant feedback on one aspect of the efficacy of our programmes. We can
be better informed without committing the utilitarian heresy (Goodlad,
1995) in our approach to higher education.

Conclusions

There are many challenges ahead for higher education. It would help to meet these if the transition from school/college to university were better understood and if more work were done on bridging the gap in both secondary and higher education. To this end there is a need for greater interaction between staff in the sectors. Similarly, although not discussed here in such great depth, there is need for greater interaction between academics, careers staff and employers, and between departments and their graduates, to help bridge the university–work gap. Neither transition requires the intense involvement of many staff, provided that those who do get involved can cascade their understanding to others and affect the curriculum. In improving these transitions we would be helping to fulfil the educational, social and economic goals of individual students as well as assisting the social, cultural and economic development of the nation.

Note

1. A level and AS awards are made by a number of examining boards, which prescribe syllabuses and oversee arrangements to mark candidates' scripts or other work. The Northern Examination and Assessment Board is one of several such A level boards.

Part 3

The Work Context

11

Just Like the Novels?
Researching the Occupational
Culture(s) of Higher Education

Sara Delamont

If reality is multiple and contested, as post-structuralism would have us believe, then we must abandon the common sense assumption that novels reflect the real world: there is no uncomplicated real world to be reflected.

(Carter, 1990: 9)

Introduction

The title of this chapter is inspired by Ian Carter's (1990) monograph, *Ancient Cultures of Conceit: British University Fiction in the Post-War Years*. The purpose of the chapter is to outline some strategies for making the occupational culture(s) of higher education anthropologically strange. The need for such strategies is explained, then some possibilities are outlined and finally each strategy is used to explore an occupational culture in higher education.

The familiarity problem in social science and fiction

The chapter is written by an outsider to the higher education research community: a sociologist of education who has studied schools rather than higher education, except for a pair of projects on PhD students and their supervisors (Eggleston and Delamont, 1983; Parry *et al.*, 1994), and some historical research on women in universities (Delamont, 1989a). However, from reading the research in monographs on higher education (such as Clark, 1987a; Bourdieu, 1988; Holland and Eisenhart, 1990; Granfield, 1992) or in journals such as *Studies in Higher Education*, it is striking that:

1. The research is overwhelmingly about students and teaching faculty, not anyone else who works in higher education.
2. The research does not challenge the familiarity of higher education, but encapsulates an essentially taken-for-granted view of the sector.

The research on higher education suffers from a problem highlighted for studies of schooling by Howard Becker in 1971:

> We may have understated a little the difficulty of observing contemporary classrooms. It is not just the survey method of educational testing or any of those things that keeps people from seeing what is going on. I think, instead that it is first and foremost a matter of it all being so familiar that it becomes impossible to single out events that occur in the classroom as things that have occurred, even when they happen right in front of you. I have not had the experience of observing in elementary and high school classrooms myself, but I have in college classrooms and it takes a tremendous effort of will and imagination to stop seeing only the things that are conventionally 'there' to be seen. I have talked to a couple of teams of research people who have sat around in classrooms trying to observe and it is like pulling teeth to get them to see or write anything beyond what 'everyone' knows.
>
> (Becker, 1971: 10)

Becker's diagnosis of the chief failure of educational researchers appeared as a footnote to an article by Murray and Rosalie Wax (1971) in which they bemoaned the lack of a 'solid body of data on the ethnography of schools'. That lack has been remedied since 1971 (see Delamont and Atkinson, 1995), but there is, today, no solid body of data on the ethnography of higher education, and few attempts to study the occupational cultures of those who work in higher education, whether as students, faculty, technicians, secretaries, porters, cooks or administrators.

The familiarity problem as posed by Becker has also been diagnosed by Young (1971) and Wolcott (1981). Becker's comment and Wolcott's paper appeared in American 'anthropology of education' collections, while Young was writing for British sociologists, but they were in agreement about the familiarity problem. Researchers were taking too many features of education for granted. It is over 25 years since those diagnoses were first made. They have not been heeded sufficiently.

The central argument in Young's (1971) piece was that sociologists had focused so much on structures that they had neglected to study the *content* of education and who had power over it. Young did offer a solution: instead of taking the problems of teachers we should make our own research agenda. This has still to be achieved in research on higher education.

Researchers have not read widely enough, have consequently lacked vision and imagination, and have thus failed to make any substantial contribution to an anthropology or sociology of higher education. Six ways in which such a contribution could be made are examined, and their potential strength as means of making the occupational cultures of higher education *unfamiliar* is scrutinized.

Everyone in higher education research has been to university, many of them have been teachers in higher education, and thus higher education is 'so familiar'. When Becker says that getting researchers to see or write things which are insightful is like 'pulling teeth', he is expressing feelings familiar to many research supervisors and project directors. The very 'ordinariness', 'routineness' and 'everydayness' of life in higher education does indeed confound many researchers, who do complain that they are bored, they cannot find anything to write down and 'nothing happens'. All social science data collection is hard, but higher education does have a particular kind of familiarity, which makes it especially tough to make its occupational cultures anthropologically strange.

Becker does, therefore, have a point. However, it is not, or should not be, any kind of terminal diagnosis. Because higher education is familiar, this does not mean that the researcher passively accepts the difficulty. Rather, the task of the social scientist is *to make the familiar strange*. Blanche Geer (1964), Becker's colleague in two higher education research projects (Becker *et al.*, 1961, 1968) wrote the classic paper 'First days in the field' on the importance of fighting familiarity.

Just as there is a familiarity problem with the social science research on higher education, Carter (1990) reports a familiarity problem with British university fiction. Carter traced 204 fictional portrayals of British universities. He comments on three noteworthy features of those 204 treatments. First, there is an overwhelming preponderance of fiction about Oxford and Cambridge. There are 145 fictional depictions of Oxford and Cambridge among the 204 (of which 119 are portrayals of Oxford), four of any Scottish university, four of the University of Wales and only six of London. While fewer than 8 per cent of students go to Oxbridge, its presence in fiction is dominating.

Next, Carter highlights the complex relationship between the fictional universities and the realities of the higher education system in Britain. Carter points out that

> fiction constructs accounts of the world which it then seeks to pass off as real. Accounts are interested statements, assertions that this is to be admired, that challenged: they are not simple descriptions. A range of studies, from the UGC's research selectivity exercise through the *THES* peer reviews to A. H. Halsey's (1990) survey of donnish opinion, has shown that Oxford and Cambridge stand pre-eminent in British academic prestige. Just like the novels ... But novels conceal the fact that statements about academic prestige are essentially contested.
>
> (Carter 1990: 9)

Third, Carter (1990: 15) claims that there are only three plots in the British university novel:

1. How an undergraduate at Oxford (usually) or Cambridge came to wisdom.
2. How a don at Oxford (usually) or Cambridge was stabbed in the back physically or professionally, sometimes surviving to rule his college.
3. How rotten life was as a student or teacher outside Oxford and Cambridge.

He explores the messages conveyed by British university fiction, described in the next section, which are themselves thoroughly familiar ones.

Neither extant social science nor literature, therefore, gives us a position from which we can challenge the familiarity of our workplace, the familiarity of *our* occupational culture(s). In the next section, I examine the challenges to familiarity, first in the novels, and then those available to social scientists.

Challenges to familiarity in university fiction

In university fiction, the challenges to the status quo come from 'outsider' characters who disturb the placid taken-for-granted nature of the institution. Carter's (1990) analysis includes chapters on five types of besiegers attacking the Arnoldian academic citadel: Americans, foreigners, women, scientists and proletarians. Many of the stories feature dangerous barbarian outsiders who seek to enter or, far worse, destroy the real Oxford/university. These include: first, Americans (Morris Zapp in *Changing Places*, Browning the murderer in *When Scholars Fall*); then, comic or tragic foreigners (Mr Eborebelosa in *Eating People Is Wrong*); third, ball-crushing or pathetic women (Flora Beniform in *The History Man*, Alice Jago in *The Masters*, Margaret Peel in *Lucky Jim*); fourth, scientists who 'erode collegiality' and may even be communists, from working-class homes who work too hard (Donald Howard in *The Affair*, Rhys-Jones in *Death Is My Bridegroom*, Charles Blaine in *Vanderlyn's Kingdom*); fifth, and most serious of all, the boys from working-class backgrounds who are clever enough to be at university but lack cultural capital and social graces (Charles Luke in *The New Men*, Nick Junkin in *A Memorial Service*, Jack Butler in *Colonel Butler's Wolf*).

These five types of barbarian invader have their parallels in the strategies for making the social science research more challenging to the familiarity of higher education. We can parallel the American challenge in the fiction with adopting the methods of ethnomethodology (the most American of all approaches). The comic or tragic foreigner in the novels is paralleled in research by systematic attention to higher education in other cultures. The barbarian woman in the novels is methodologically equivalent to focusing on gender as a research strategy. The scientists, with their polluting 'industrial' values and adherence to laboratories rather than the common room, are paralleled by focusing on non-educational settings, and the working class of the fiction can be equated with a social science focus on occupational cultures in higher education other than lecturers or students.

The five types of barbarian catalogued by Carter can therefore be seen as paralleling five research strategies for challenging the complacency of over-familiar social science, as well as providing familiar plots for British campus fiction.

Social science challenges to familiarity

If we take higher education as our empirical area, there are the following five possibilities for action:

1. Adopt the manifesto of the ethnomethodologists. Given that the whole focus of ethnomethodology involves treating the 'regularities' of everyday life as problematic, the familiarity of higher education should be challenged by ethnomethodologically inspired fieldwork.
2. Study 'higher education' in other cultures, such as those of Orthodox Judaism, Islam, Confucianism or Buddhism, or totalitarian regimes or societies. This has been mainly the province of the anthropology of education, but there is no reason why it should not provide contrasts for all investigators.
3. Adopt *gender* as the main focus of the study. The researcher's attempt to focus on a neglected, taken-for-granted feature of life in higher education can highlight other aspects of it unrelated to gender per se.
4. Study non-educational settings chosen for their parallel features by theoretical sampling (Glaser and Strauss, 1967). Research on aspects of hospitals, prisons, factories, shops, street corners and TV studios (to take a few examples) gives a novel perspective to higher education research.
5. Focus on the occupational culture of any group *other* than lecturers or students: technicians, cleaners, porters, security guards, secretaries, administrators, gardeners or catering staff. The 'familiarity' of higher education is thus thrown into relief by contrast with the unfamiliar.

These five strategies are not mutually exclusive, but what is chiefly notable about higher education research in Britain (and in the USA and Canada) is that none of them has been adopted except by one or two 'eccentrics'. When we examine each strategy in turn, the most notable finding is that researchers have not tried it.

Adopt the ethnomethodological manifesto

Following Turner (1971), two important principles are involved in this strategy.

1. The researcher must recognize that every social scientist inevitably uses her member's knowledge when studying higher education. If she did not use her member's knowledge, she could not categorize 'universities', or recognize 'lecture theatres', 'lectures', 'laboratories', 'senate' or 'research'.

2. The researcher must pose the shared member's knowledge 'as problematic', and then she must 'explicate the resources' shared with participants *throughout* the research. Such procedures do, by their very nature,
make the 'all too familiar' university strange.

Study higher education in 'other cultures'

Educational anthropology is almost non-existent in Britain. Delamont and
Atkinson (1995) show how little cross-referencing there is between the
sociology and anthropology of education. Apart from one or two 'classic'
papers popularized by the Open University (e.g. Dumont and Wax, 1971),
the large body of work produced by applied anthropologists has been neglected by British scholars in education. The study of higher education has
neglected to draw insights from anthropology of education altogether. This
may be partly because there is relatively little anthropological work on
'higher' education in other cultures except that of Eickelman (1978, 1985)
on Islamic scholarly instruction.

Focus on gender

Several commentators have noted that much sociology of higher education has simply failed to use gender as an organizing principle at all (e.g.
Delamont, 1989b). Many 'invisible' features of education become problematic when gender divisions are scrutinized. This strategy is not mentioned
by Young, Becker or Wolcott. Young (1971) did not deal with gender: he did
not suggest that too much educational research took patriarchy and male
domination of structures, processes and content for granted. Becker (1971)
did not mention gender in his diagnosis of 'familiarity' in educational ethnography; an odd omission given the subsequent rise of feminist anthropology, and feminist sociology, with their debates on gender and research
methods (see Harding, 1987). Wolcott (1981), writing a decade later, still
did not propose making the 'malestream' nature of education problematic
as a way of forcing ourselves to 'see' what we otherwise take for granted. In
these three authors' work, educational research is criticized, but they do not
focus on gender issues as a cure for the 'staleness' of the discipline.

Gender is not the only cultural basis of difference that may help to render the familiar strange. Ethnicity may pose equally fundamental issues of
cultural dominance and definitions of the other. It is, however, in the context of gender that some of the methodological issues have become most
apparent. It is, for instance, among scholars advocating a 'feminist stand-
point' approach that gender is linked to phenomenological interest in
making everyday life 'strange'. As authors such as Stanley and Wise (1993)
argue, a thoroughgoing feminist stance should direct the researcher to
treat as problematic the taken-for-granted realities of everyday life. Gender,

therefore, presents itself as a methodological imperative for the educational investigator who seeks to render a chosen setting 'anthropologically strange'.

Study 'non-educational' settings

Sociologists of higher education in Britain are very bad at drawing contrasts using published material from other empirical areas of sociology. Research on teachers and teaching is detached from the sociology of work (see Delamont and Atkinson, 1995). Despite Goffman's insights and pioneering work, researchers have not used material on hospitals, factories or shops to draw parallels and contrasts with educational settings. Becker and Geer's educational work is cited, but that on other contexts for socialization into work (Geer, 1972) is not. Classic sociological work on non-educational settings in the interactionist tradition (e.g. by Anselm Strauss, Julius Roth and John Lofland) is ignored. An inspection of the bibliographies of published higher education research reveals that *only* educational studies are cited.

Yet there is enormous potential for data on non-educational settings to alert the researcher in higher education. Becker and his colleagues (1961) demonstrated this when they used ideas about 'gold-bricking' and 'level and direction of effort' from industrial settings in their work on student culture. Ideas from Strauss's work on psychiatric hospitals have been used to illuminate schools (Delamont, 1983) and the organization of bedside teaching in medical school science.teaching in schools to inform analyses of both settings (Delamont and Atkinson, 1995). The sociological work on teachers and teaching has suffered particularly from a failure to relate it to the research and theory on other occupations and professions (Delamont and Atkinson, 1995). People learn and teach in many settings which are not conventional schools and colleges, and studying such settings is always fruitful for educational researchers.

Focus on the unusual occupations in higher education

Casanova (1991) studied the working lives of secretaries in American elementary schools. The result is not just a fascinating insight into one occupational culture: it also forces the reader to refocus her thoughts on elementary schooling. The view from the secretary's office offers new insights into the social worlds of pupils and teachers. At present the only university secretary we 'know' about is Poppleton's Maureen (Taylor, 1994), and we need academic research on the real life Maureens. The occupational culture(s) of university faculty would be similarly illuminated by research on the other actors in the complex organization.

There are, then, five strategies for making higher education strange which have been neglected by investigators. The anthropologists Shirley and Edwin Ardener alerted us to the dangers of paying attention to the dominant group in any fieldwork setting and neglecting subordinate or, as they termed it, muted groups. Edwin Ardener (1972) first published this argument, later developed by Shirley Ardener (1975: 22), who explained: 'a society may be dominated or overdetermined by the model (or models) generated by one dominant group within the system. This dominant model may impede the free expression of alternative models of their world which subdominant groups may possess.'

At present the social science research on universities has focused too much on the dominant group and left out the many muted groups. In the next section of the chapter some ways in which each strategy can be used to produce novel insights are examined.

A sixth source of inspiration?

Alongside these five social science strategies we should also turn to the fictional sphere as a source of contrast and inspiration. As academic research faces up to the challenges posed by postmodernism (e.g. Lather, 1991), an analysis of university fiction is an excellent place to begin an exploration of the occupational culture(s) of higher education precisely because we *know* that, whatever these occupational cultures are like, they are not just like the novels.

The way forward

Ethnomethodology has been used to make maths and science problematic (e.g. Lynch, 1985; Livingston, 1986) but that work has not been mainstreamed into higher education research. The ethnomethodological work on talk in classrooms could usefully be extended to higher education settings. For example, Payne and Hustler (1980) commented on how teachers deploy the conventions of classroom talk to manage 'the class' as a cohort or collectively, while Payne (1982) similarly wrote about the incorporation of class members into the cohort. The ethnomethodologically informed approach, in common with discourse analysis, stresses the asymmetry in classroom speech exchanges, and views the characteristic pattern of events as the enactment of 'control' in the setting (see Atkinson 1981). Payne and Cuff (1982) and their contributors recommend the ethnomethodological approach to facilitate teachers' own analysis of their classroom practices. The analysis of turns at talk in school classrooms displays the elementary structural significance of interrogatory teacher–pupil exchanges. Further, it has drawn attention to the degree to which pupils have to work at the interpretation of teachers' questions if acceptable and appropriate answers are to be produced (Hammersley, 1977; French and MacLure, 1979, 1981; MacLure and French, 1980; Mercer and Edwards, 1981; Hargreaves, 1984). Conversation analytic and complementary perspectives again stress the interactional management of classroom knowledge.

An ethnomethodologically driven programme of research on talk in a variety of higher education settings would provide a whole new dimension to the field.

Higher education in other cultures

Eickelman's (1978) work on koranic scholarship is largely uncited by higher education researchers, yet that is an 'older' professorial culture than our own. Studies of Islamic 'higher' education make 'Western' higher education problematic in a number of ways.

Frances Trix (1993) studied for 15 years with an Albanian Bektashi religious sage in an Albanian Bektashi *tekke* (monastery) in Michigan, in the kitchen as often as the study-room. Learning and teaching took place at mealtimes, rather than in classes. Trix's account of learning in the Bektashi *tekke* serves to make many aspects of our taken-for-granted world problematic. She was a student/disciple for 15 years but had barely begun. We expect measurable gains in three or four years. Clearly our idea of academic *time* can be scrutinized more carefully. Trix had to initiate the topics for study, not the 84-year-old sage who headed the *tekke*; again a very different model of curriculum control from any in 'our' world. Third, Trix did not know, after 15 years, what she knew: there were no 'aims and objectives', no performance indicators. Yet this Bektashi scholarship goes back to the fourteenth century, and even if its *tekkes* would fail to get 'satisfactory' from a Teaching Quality Assessment, we have to recognize it as a place of higher education. Starting from Trix we could raise three very fundamental – currently unstudied – issues to make our higher education anthropologically strange.

Gender issues can make the researcher acutely conscious of the 'other' in higher education. For example, Coxon's (1983) study of a cookery class for men is a particularly intriguing one, insofar as the class *was* for men. It therefore provided an implicit challenge to taken-for-granted assumptions about gender and cookery. Coxon's participant observation of this class serves as a useful corrective to the stale familiarity of much observational research. The work of Aisenberg and Harrington (1988), who set out to compare 37 American women who had failed to gain tenure in university with 25 women who had become tenured, but found that all 62 felt marginal to their chosen profession, is a good starting point. Who feels as though he or she 'belongs'? Who never settles, and is always waiting for the tap on the shoulder telling him or her to leave the game? That would be a novel project in UK higher education.

Not least among the methodological consequences of gender as a 'strategy' as well as a 'topic' is the extent to which it focuses attention on 'difference'. Insofar as issues of gender are predicated on cultural definitions of contrast, such a focus will help the researcher to address local and generic issues of 'normality'. Insofar as definitions of gender may define the 'otherness' of particular categories of social actor, then the researcher is led to consider how 'the other' is socially constructed, and how otherness or difference is legitimated. Consequently, investigators may ask themselves quite fundamental questions: about knowledge and belief; about authority and control; about the everyday accomplishment of normal appearances. The social phenomena of difference and its constitution may help to make problematic the development and maintenance of careers and identities in educational settings.

Studying non-educational settings is a focus on learning which goes on in many places that are not labelled universities. Teaching comes in many guises, is a part of the occupational culture of many groups. Two 'exotic' examples from Brazil illustrate this. Brazilians who want to perform *capoeira* (a form of dance and martial art) may learn at an academy, but may study under a master 'in the streets and on the beaches' (Lewis, 1992: xxvi).

Leacock and Leacock (1975: 173–88) have provided a vivid account of teaching and learning in the *terreiros* of Belem in northern Brazil. *Terreiros* are centres of spirit possession, where mediums receive *encantados* (spirits), go into trances and may act as counsellors and curers. Leacock and Leacock show how mediums have to learn their role. Novices do not know how to behave when possessed by one particular spirit rather than another: 'The expression they use is "development". When a person is possessed for the first time, it is expected that he will fall on the floor, stagger about, and be unable to sing. As he "develops", however, the medium gains "control" and is able to dance, sing and speak as the *encantado*' (Leacock and Leacock, 1975: 173). Some *terreiros* run classes in which novices can practise going into a trance, and acquire the appropriate behaviours. The apprentice medium is told what spirit is possessing him or her, and is taught how to behave in the expected manner. A medium possessed by a dolphin spirit must learn a dance routine based on hopping. *Curupiras* are expected to bark like dogs, while mermaids have to grow long hair. One spirit, João da Mata, likes hats, so a medium expecting him must have a hat ready. All these behaviours and the use of props have to be *learnt*.

The occupational culture of university teaching is learnt, not on beaches or in *terreiros*, but at conferences and in common rooms, and research on teaching in non-formal contexts provides more insight than that on classroom instruction. The probationary lecturer learns how to 'develop' and gain 'control' under a spirit master: the process is more like spirit possession than we usually admit.

Instruction and learning go on in many non-university settings less exotic than *capoeira* academies and *terreiros*. The learning of the occupational cultures of prostitution, crime and sword swallowing in the USA and Britain also has higher education parallels. Heyl's (1979) informant (a 'madam') taught new recruits how to be high-earning prostitutes while they worked in her brothel. There are parallels with learning how to get research funds from sponsors. Hobbs (1988) discusses how young men in London's East End learn to be skilled at the locally recognized criminal activities. Mannix (1951) learnt to be a fire eater and a sword swallower. Systematic attention to learning in other settings will enrich higher educational research immeasurably.

The work of Howard Newby (1977) on deference and patriarchal authority structures could be used in educational settings to handle relations between ancillary staff and faculty, between faculty and students, and between lecturers and departmental heads. Work on factions and disputes in Cyprus (Loizos, 1975) and Sardinia (Schweizer, 1988) could illuminate the analysis of senior common room discussions and disputes. Every field of sociology and anthropology is replete with potentially valuable insights for making educational settings strange.

The *unusual occupations* offer their own potential for novel views of higher education. Scientific work depends on technicians: a study of how the laboratory looks from the technicians' room would reinvigorate the sociology of science. How do the cleaners, working in the offices at 4.00 in the morning, see the university? What is the world of the lecturer like when seen by a security guard or car park attendant? Do the canteen staff have a view on critical theory? Are the waitresses in the faculty dining club speculating on the next FRS elections? Starting from these 'outcaste' groups would provide real intellectual leverage on the occupational culture(s) of higher education.

The *fictional* world takes us into two new spheres, one theoretical, the other empirical. Theoretically it opens up postmodernism for us with its potentially liberating agenda. Patti Lather (1991: 21) summarizes postmodernism as follows: 'The essence of the postmodern argument is that the dualisms which continue to dominate Western thought are inadequate for understanding a world of multiple causes and effects interacting in complex and non-linear ways, all of which are rooted in a limitless array of historical and cultural specificities.' At its simplest, postmodernism is a challenge to the consensus, held among the educated classes in the Western capitalist nations since the Enlightenment at the end of the eighteenth century, that universal, objective scientific truths can be reached by scientific methods. (Such beliefs have never been held by the majority in Western societies, or by anyone in many other cultures.) Postmodernism argues that there are no universal truths to be discovered, because all human investigators are grounded in human society and can only produce partial locally and historically specific insights. While most scientists are totally untroubled by such claims – if they are even aware of them being advanced – and continue to 'do' science in the traditional way, the impact of postmodernism on the humanities and social sciences has been considerable and traumatic. Because postmodernism denies that there are any universal truths, it also destroys any scholarly work which tries to produce generalized, universalistic theories of anything.

Empirically, the fiction gives us three possible projects:

1. A reminder that folklore, urban legends, atrocity stories, jokes and myths are themselves worthy of study (see Delamont, 1991). While the most extreme examples live in the fiction, such as plagiarism (*Lucky Jim*), tradition versus modernity (*Porterhouse Blue*), abuses of power (*The History Man*) and ethnocentric misogyny (all of them), these *are* topics which can be studied through collections of the oral traditions that suffuse higher education.
2. An investigation of how far students and/or faculty derive expectations (and stereotypes of non-Oxbridge inferiority) of Oxbridge from the fiction.
3. A syllabus for a course on higher education which would be a reflexive basis for its participants to do their own investigations about project one.

Conclusions

The conclusion is simple: the multiple and contested realities of the occupation culture(s) of higher education need to be treated as problematic by researchers, who need to deploy a range of techniques to *develop* 'strangeness' in their investigations.

Acknowledgements

Karen Chivers word-processed this paper for me through multiple drafts with unflagging zeal, for which I am grateful. Gerald Bernbaum, Vice Chancellor of South Bank University, taught me all the important things I know about occupational cultures in higher education, but is not in any way responsible for the ideas in this chapter.

12

Which Academic Profession Are You In?

Oliver Fulton

The idea that there is a single, cohesive academic profession is both powerful and contested. Of course academia has long been stratified – into 'noble' and less noble disciplines, ancient and parvenu universities, professors (or their chairs) and lesser staff. But the notion of the collegium, the guild, united in the common purpose of the formation of youth and equal before the courts of pure reason and Popperian discovery, has deep roots.

There was an intriguing outbreak of debate in 1960s America. Talcott Parsons and Gerald Platt, while endorsing the by then undeniable description of US higher education as 'this highly differentiated system . . . [with an] exceptional . . . range of dispersion of quality', nevertheless purported to discover 'unity' in it – a unity sustained, in best Parsonian style, by the overriding value-orientation of cognitive rationality (Parsons and Platt, 1968: 497). Cognitive rationality in its turn implied (indeed functionally required) collegiality, autonomy and the synergy of teaching, training, research and consultancy. Perhaps untypically for Parsons, this was not just a functional inference: empirical evidence was offered – in the form of academic staff's attitudes and preferences, as measured by a questionnaire survey – to show that right across the USA's 'differentiated system', from the leading research university through to the most modest four-year college, there was a common interest in both teaching and research.

In a riposte pointedly entitled 'The structure of the academic profession*s*' (my emphasis), Donald Light (1974) firmly argued that the claim of unity has no merit. For one thing, he claims, if one takes any of the standard defining qualities of the professions, each discipline logically constitutes a separate profession: each has its own separate body of knowledge, each trains its own new members and each licenses, admits and regulates its own recruits, judging its members according to different norms and expectations. But in any case, Light argues that there is a second and even more crucial dimension: the real 'scholarly profession' is distinguished not by its espoused values or interests, but by active involvement in research and scholarship, and specifically by publication. He describes three occupational groups in the USA:

the scholarly profession(s) of producers of research and scholarship, a minority (he claims) of whose members work in universities and colleges; 'the faculty', i.e. the paid employees of higher education institutions; and a small subset where these two sets intersect, which he defines as the true 'academic professions'. As for the rest of the faculty, they are 'teachers' who do not advance knowledge, who might better be described as members of a 'semi-profession', whose status is low and who 'do not have democratic departments, though they say that they do' (no evidence is offered for this last claim). After all this, it is a trifle ironic to find Light describing *Parsons's* theory as 'elitist'.

As a debate, this one looks, in retrospect, just a little simplistic (though the arguments were of course both subtler and more balanced than these brief summaries allow). But it has the merit of allowing us to ask some simple questions. Theoretically speaking, these are of two kinds. The first concerns what constitutes or defines a profession. For Parsons, it is the values internal to the occupation; for Light, it is primarily the occupation's practices; for others, such as A. H. Halsey and Martin Trow (e.g. Halsey and Trow, 1971; Halsey, 1992) it would be both of these, but also structures, working conditions and what some would call social construction and others, more modestly, public perception.

The second question concerns the lineaments of the occupational group. There are four possible axes of differentiation, only two of which were referred to in this debate. If we think, worldwide, about the occupational group which Light calls the 'faculty' – people with academic positions in universities and colleges – we need to add to discipline and 'sector' (to use the pre-1992 English phrase) the two other dimensions of rank and nationality. These four dimensions are the main analytic focus of the first (so far as I am aware) international study of the academic profession [*sic*], funded by the Carnegie Foundation for the Advancement of Teaching in 1992, from which this chapter draws the empirical data which are described below.[1] I now briefly discuss each of these dimensions in turn.

Academic discipline

As far as disciplines are concerned, after Tony Becher's (1989) dissection of 'academic tribes and territories' it would be hard to deny the existence, *in research universities of the kind which he studied,* if not of all the structured differences which Light described, at any rate of a cultural diversity, stretching over both values and practices, which Becher convincingly links with the different intellectual projects and epistemological assumptions of the various disciplines.[2] Clark Kerr's well known description of 'the modern [research] university ... [as] a series of individual faculty entrepreneurs held together by a common grievance over parking' (Kerr, 1966: 20) may be a deliberate exaggeration: but substitute departments for individuals and you will be expressing a commonly held belief. And as Burton Clark has often demonstrated (e.g. Clark, 1983), the accelerating process of knowledge specialization leads to constant disciplinary fission and hence, presumably, to a steadily increasing fragmentation of academia.

Nevertheless, in formal terms Light's statement is at best only half true. Of course, each discipline has its own body of knowledge, and the only people who can make fully informed judgements that depend on that knowledge, whether these concern training and licensing, recruitment and promotion or the quality of academic 'output', are other members of the same discipline. But 'the faculty' of any institution, across the disciplines, are fellow-employees, subject to common working conditions (including recruitment, assessment and promotion procedures and pay scales); they and their departments are managed (and judged) by committees and other structures which – in almost all institutions – draw in representatives of both neighbouring and remoter disciplines; and in state-controlled or state-financed systems there are regulations and structures which relate to the occupation of higher education teaching as a whole, and are mirrored by trans-disciplinary unions and associations. Even from the viewpoint of the general public, there can be little doubt that the single profession has a perceived reality. It is a moot point whether a professor of biology, let us say, is seen primarily as a 'professor' or a 'scientist', but there can be little doubt that to be a professor carries a certain public weight, independent of the subject professed.

Institutions and sectors

On the institutional or sectoral dimension it is easy enough to construct a case for differentiation. It was probably the work of David Riesman which first illuminated the full diversity of American higher education, that most diversified of systems (see, for example, Jencks and Riesman, 1968): a diversity which is expressed in practices, structural conditions and, if institutional missions are any guide, in values as well. In the US case, there is room for debate over how far this diversity arose in response to market pressures, and how far to government regulation and prescription (as in the 'master plans' of California and other states). In the emerging mass systems of Europe, on the other hand, sectoral differentiation has normally been imposed, as in Germany's or the Netherlands' binary structures or the British pre-1992 binary 'system', and it is only recently, if at all, that the market (generally well regulated) has been permitted to play a substantial part in diversification. And as Martin Trow has often pointed out, while the market may give (some) institutions some leeway to position themselves on the basis of their own characteristics and strategic choices, external imposition and regulation inevitably problematize the relationship between structures (which the state dictates), practices (which it aims to control) and cultures (which are the property of the organization, and have a life of their own).

For our present purposes, this can best be illustrated by a consideration of the implications for academic staff. Binary systems aim to control sectoral functions, in other words to constrain institutions' missions, through forms of regulation, governance and funding which have been seen, in most analyses, as working mainly as constraints on the aspirations of the non-university sector; that is, as barriers to 'academic drift'. This analysis, implicitly if not explicitly, points the finger at the academics, since while the mission may be the institution's, the aspirations are surely carried by the staff. Certainly one of the most common means of specifying sectoral missions is to regulate staff working conditions in such a way as to restrict their role expectations, notably by limiting or eliminating their time and resources for research and scholarship.

But this implies that if they were unregulated, all members of 'the profession' would wish to engage in research and publication, would aspire to teach postgraduates or better qualified undergraduates and so on. An alternative approach, which parallels Huber's approach to disciplinary differences, is to take seriously the idea of different missions, and to ask what discriminates between the staff in different sectors. One could ask about their social and educational background and qualifications, as to some extent does Halsey (1992), for example – and he provides evidence for the UK to suggest that the staff of the former polytechnics are less well qualified than those of the 'old' universities, which are themselves hierarchically structured.[3] But one could also ask whether there may not be features of the non-university sector which are viewed positively by recruits to these institutions: if this is the case, career choices across the academic profession(s) might have a larger element of positive self-selection than is generally assumed by those who work in, and write from the perspective of, the traditional university sector. The Carnegie surveys do not permit us to answer this question; but in analysing the various sectoral differences which do and do not exist, it would be as well to bear the possibility in mind.

Academic rank

The two dimensions just discussed – discipline and sector – are the classic components in the literature on the academic profession or professions: the two main axes, for example, of Clark's 'master matrix'. However, if there is one respect in which it could be most legitimately argued that academia is not a classic profession at all, it must be its internal ranking system; that is, its management and career structure and its conditions of work. As with other 'guilds', the idea of the collegium implies partnership on terms of formal equality – if not equality of earnings or of the authority of experience, certainly the equality of status as a member of a self-governing and self-regulating occupation. There may well be, indeed there are, relics of this pattern in the relatively democratic and participative governance structures of traditional universities – at least as regards academic decision-making – but the rank structure is far from egalitarian. With few exceptions, modern academia abandoned the collegiate model a long time ago and replaced it with a hierarchy of appointments which command different material rewards, different status and different power. In some systems – notably those based on the German tradition – it could be claimed that, symbolically at least, the professor (who is, however, a civil servant and not simply an appointee of the guild itself) is the only true member of the profession, while, all other ranks represent at best apprenticeships for that position. But, as we shall see, the tension between this symbolic interpretation and the reality of rank in the German university seems to make this view less than convincing to the non-professors.

In fact, rank and career structures are under pressure in most European systems (Kogan *et al.*, 1994: Chapter 4). The process of massification, which has resulted in big increases in the number of academic staff and hence in the salary costs which they represent – by far the biggest single cost in university budgets – has led not only to pressure on salary levels and conditions of work (such as student : staff ratios), but also to attempts to change staffing structures, either as explicit national policy (as in Sweden or the Netherlands) or inexplicitly (as in the UK, where the incidence of short-term contracts and part-time employment has increased dramatically). In recent years a number of authors have begun to deploy terms such as 'proletarianization' or 'deprofessionalization'. For some writers this is ascribed to the consequences of managerialism, which may be seen as pursuing a state economic agenda (Miller, 1995), or as taking advantage of changes in the curriculum, as a result of the commodification of knowledge (Winter, 1995). In Halsey's (1992) study it also refers to a process in which academics themselves have connived – notably, in the British context, through the decision of the Association of University Teachers to affiliate to the trade union movement. In other words, the process of deprofessionalization, if such it is, may be not just an imposed degradation of working conditions, but a defensive and subjective response to (the fear of) degradation.

The debate about deprofessionalization is dealt with elsewhere in this book. For the present purpose, my question is whether any such process has affected – objectively or subjectively – the whole range of academic staff, or whether it has been more selective. There have been suggestions in the UK by present and former academic managers that the status of academics could best be preserved – or even restored – by 'paying twice as much to half as many people' (in the words of a current vice chancellor citing Hague, 1991). In other words, an elite group of staff would be singled out for good working conditions – presumably professors and professors-in-waiting – while the bulk of routine work would be carried on by a force of proletarianized assistants. By some interpretations, this might be a reasonable description of the present situation: but that is a question for empirical testing.

National systems

The concept of the 'invisible college' of leading researchers in a discipline knows no state boundaries. In the 'small world' of academic fiction, or in

Burton Clark's research communities, leading academics not only read and write for international journals, but move easily from country to country, whether for conferences or for career moves. Anxieties about the 'brain drain' – from Europe to the USA, from Eastern Europe to the West, from South to North and from developing to developed nations – are a symptom, and a clear indicator, of the globalization of academic work.

We know, of course, that this is not the whole truth. Incompatibilities of language and national culture certainly interact with disciplinary characteristics. In some disciplines there may well be a global network centred on multinational laboratories, disciplinary associations or journals, but in others (and not only in the modern languages and the disciplines with a traditional nation state orientation, such as history or law), there are persistent national differences which make globalization less straightforward. Even so, a functional analyst might argue that – disciplines aside – the nature of academic work should require a similar pattern of practices and values, at least in all those systems at roughly the same stage of development. But it is also possible to construct a counter-hypothesis, namely that the historic variety of national structures (notably in the approach to sectors and ranks) could well outweigh the homogenizing force of globalization.

A note on the survey

The Carnegie survey, carried out in 1992, included academic staff in both universities and other institutions of higher education in four European countries: universities, polytechnics and colleges of higher education in England; universities and *Fachhochschulen* in the former West Germany; universities and *Hogescholen/Hoger-Beroefsonderwijs* (HBOs) in the Netherlands; and both research and non-research universities and institutes in Sweden.[4] In each country the samples were designed in order to include, as far as possible, both permanent and non-permanent staff, and those in research posts as well as conventional academic positions. The number of usable responses ranged, in round numbers, from 1100 in Sweden through 2000 in England and the Netherlands to 2800 in Germany. Inevitably, this study can only give limited and indirect purchase on the inner life of higher education. Like any questionnaire-based survey it emphasized the measurable and the quantifiable – inputs, outputs and fairly crude expressions of opinion – at the expense of the subtleties of process – whether cognitive or affective. The main elements which can help us here are three sets of questions. The first of these is concerned with working conditions (including hours of work on different activities, notably teaching and research, both in and out of teaching terms), salaries, whether the respondent's work is appraised or evaluated and a set of opinions including both satisfaction with different aspects of the job (including the resources provided for it) and commitment to the discipline, department and institution. The second group contains questions about professional activity, including values (for example, preferences for teaching or research), responsibilities (undergraduate and postgraduate teaching duties, number of courses and students, research involvement and research grants) and outputs (publications). A third section concerns institutional governance, including perceptions of where decisions are taken, personal involvement in or influence on decision-making and opinions of institutional governance. But in a brief chapter of this kind only a few highlights of the results can be given.

Disciplinary differences

In the four Western European countries, there is (as far as our work has so far revealed) little evidence to support a Kerr-like description of autonomous or independent disciplines loosely coupled into an institutional structure. The strongest evidence in *favour* of such an interpretation comes, in fact, not from any analysis of disciplinary differences as such, but from answers to a single direct question about respondents' 'commitment' to their discipline, department or institution. In all four countries and in each sector, 'the discipline' evokes extremely high positive responses (90 per cent rating it 'very important' or 'important'), followed by 'the department', with 'the institution' in third place. This is consistent with a number of earlier surveys, which have found that when academics are asked to choose in this way, most are indeed inclined to emphasize their disciplinary loyalties: in Gouldner's terms, they evidently see themselves primarily as 'cosmopolitans' and only to a lesser extent as 'locals'.[5] These statements are a fairly good indication that academic women and men identify themselves with and through the discipline which they practise, and in which they have been trained. Insofar as they describe their departments and institutions as of lesser salience (and as we shall see later, this varies), one could argue that the hypothesis of disciplinary primacy is confirmed. But to say that people identify with their discipline more than with the immediate organizational context is not the same as saying that they are primarily shaped by it.

In a survey of this kind there are difficulties of analysis and interpretation. It would be impossibly unwieldy to analyse each of some hundred disciplines separately, even if the number of respondents permitted it. So the subjects have been grouped into five main areas: natural sciences, applied sciences, medicine and health sciences, social and behavioural sciences and humanities. Combining them in this way is rough justice within any one context, and much rougher across national systems and sectoral divisions, in which cultural traditions differ and the balance of numbers varies considerably. But with all due caution, the main disciplinary differences which can be identified seem to be related to differences in practice which are well known, and to differences in opportunity which are easily understood. In research in the university sector, for example, there are quite substantial variations, but broadly of a kind that would be expected: in input, i.e. in access to research grants; in process, i.e. in norms of collaboration versus lone scholarship; and in output, i.e. in publication rates and types of publication (e.g. books versus articles). And there are, also, differences in patterns of work. In England, for example, staff in the library-based disciplines (the humanities and to a lesser extent the social sciences) have quite polarized work patterns, with heavy teaching loads during term-time balanced by a sharp switch to research in vacations, while the laboratory subjects are rather more evenly balanced across the academic year.

But these are differences of practice around common norms. For example, although the balance of work may differ from discipline to discipline across the year, there are no consistent or substantial differences between the disciplines in the total number of weekly hours which their members work, either during term or in the vacations. Overriding the internal dynamics of the discipline, which undoubtedly determine how the working week is spent, there seems to be a strong and shared norm which determines the length of that working week.

Equally striking are the results of what was the key question for Parsons and Platt: whether academics' primary interests lie in teaching or research. As in their survey, and in many others since then, the clearest result is simply this, that the overriding norm for academic staff across disciplines (and taking academic rank, sector and country into consideration) is that *both* teaching and research are of subjective importance. Taking all four characteristics into account, there were only two groups, both in natural sciences, in which significantly fewer than half of all respondents answered 'both'; the proportion for almost every other group ranged between two-thirds and three-quarters. This is not to deny that within the groups answering 'both' there are disciplinary differences, with the natural sciences in universities 'leaning towards' research and the humanities towards teaching. Moreover, the same pattern can be discerned at the extremes, with some sub-groups of natural scientists – but by no means all – more likely to declare their interests as 'primarily' in research, and some of the humanities staff in teaching; and the social sciences generally tend to follow the humanities, and applied science and health the natural sciences. But any differences in preferences are considerably more marked with respect to the other characteristics to which I turn below. The general conclusion must be that, whether or not we choose like Parsons to ascribe the unity of teaching and research to the functional imperative of cognitive rationality, this unity is one which is shared across the academic disciplines in the European systems surveyed by the Carnegie questionnaires.

Sectoral differences

At the theoretical level it is quite possible to discuss sectoral differentiation in its own right. In the brief discussion above, for example, I suggested, first, that there have been common motivations for governments to structure and regulate the different sectors of higher education systems in similar ways; and, second, that there may be common value patterns motivating academic staff, either to aspire to 'university-like' status and working conditions from within the non-university sector or, perhaps, to select the non-university sector as their place of work. In practice, however, when we turn from discipline to sector, we inevitably turn from first-order to multivariate relationships. This is because the nature of sectoral differentiation varies from one country to the next.

There are common features of the four national systems. In all four countries, the teaching load of non-university[6] staff is considerably higher than that of the universities; outside the traditional universities, research is either not supported by central funds or is funded only to a very modest extent; and a different pattern of qualifications is offered, with the bulk, if not all, of postgraduate education provided in the university sector. However, the detail varies from country to country. Germany and the Netherlands are more sharply and formally differentiated than Sweden and, especially, England; in Germany, for example, the two sectors provide, by law, completely different qualifications in sharply different subjects, while at the opposite extreme the English polytechnics were able to base their academic case for university status in large part on the increasing convergence of degree courses and subjects of study.

However, the Carnegie survey clearly showed the persistence of very sharp differences in teaching loads between the sectors in each country, with teaching hours up to double in the non-university sector. Intriguingly, this difference in working conditions seemed to be slightly mitigated by somewhat smaller average class sizes in the non-university sector in each country. In Germany and the Netherlands in particular, university class sizes are far higher – no doubt in part because of the different subject mix, providing greater opportunity to run large lecture courses in university subjects. Another difference in the non-university sector's favour in each country is total working time. There is little difference between the sectors during the teaching term, but in each country, while the hours of work for university staff do not change during the vacations, those of non-university staff drop off by a factor of more than 25 per cent. Although the time that non-university academics spend on research goes up substantially in the vacations, it does not fully replace the time they save on teaching.

If we turn to orientations, the previous section has already described how the majority of staff in virtually every combination of discipline, sector, rank and country described their preferences as being for *both* teaching and research. If we simply compare the two sectors in each country, there is no doubt that this is the case. However, as before there are considerable differences. First, within the group that answered 'both', university staff – not surprisingly in light of their pattern of activity – are much more likely to 'lean towards' research than are non-university staff, who predominantly 'lean towards' teaching; and virtually no non-university staff in any of the four countries describe their preferences as primarily in research. Moreover, there is a substantial but variable proportion of non-university staff in each country whose preferences are primarily in teaching: just under 25 per cent in England and Sweden, 30 per cent in Germany and just under 50 per cent in the Netherlands. Here we can see that a real difference in the structures in each country is reflected in the cultural norms that staff will own up to: in the Netherlands, and to a lesser extent in Germany, it looks as if many staff have accepted the reality of the constraints on what they can do; whereas in Sweden and England – where the constraints are less severe – non-university staff seem to be adopting much the same values as their university counterparts. Does this tell us that Sweden and England have one profession, while the Netherlands has two?

It is clear that this difference in values is reflected in, or reflects, role attributions. In all four countries, university staff with few exceptions agreed with the statement that 'in my academic position at this institution, regular research activity is expected'. In England, a majority of non-university staff also agreed,[7] followed by Sweden with a little fewer than half. The proportions in Germany and the Netherlands were far lower. A similar pattern can be seen in research involvement: once again, there were sharp national differences to be found in non-university staff's replies to a question on whether they were currently engaged in a research project. But this national pattern does not show up to the same extent in publication output. Certainly HBO staff in the Netherlands have the lowest publication rates (standardizing for discipline); but in this respect there is little to distinguish the non-university staff in the other three countries, all of whose publication rates are far lower than their university counterparts.

Academic rank differences

If there were difficulties in comparing the sectors across four countries, comparing ranks presents an even harder problem. Each country has its own rank structure – indeed, in each case except Sweden there are quite distinct structures for the university and non-university sectors. In Germany, the Netherlands and Sweden, the university ranks have quite recently been reformed, in the latter two countries with a view to creating separate teaching and research positions in the lower or middle grades. Thus the survey results – which have only been fully analysed, as far as academic rank is concerned, for the university sector – reveal a varied and complex picture, which can only be discussed in general terms across all four countries.

However, it should be no surprise by now that the general value-preference for a combination of teaching and research holds true right across the members of different ranks in universities, with the only substantial exceptions being staff in explicitly defined research posts in each country on one hand, and on the other hand those Dutch and Swedish staff who are in explicit teaching posts. As far as the traditional core of the profession is concerned, the dual value orientation survives at all levels. And – leaving aside the kind of appointments just mentioned – the occupants of most ranks also achieve some kind of balance in their working time between research and teaching. But here there is far more variability between countries.

In England, the ranks are fairly close together and there is relatively little internal differentiation. In particular, a similar amount of research activity, by any measure, is the norm for all grades of university staff, with the only exception (apart from those on research contracts) being readers, whose research time is somewhat higher than those of other ranks. But teaching and administration vary quite substantially. Lecturers (the main career grade) have the highest teaching hours and professors much the lowest – but this is explained by the fact that English professors have the highest time commitment to 'administration' of any groups across the sample. This is almost the exact opposite of the situation in German universities, where professors have strikingly low administrative loads, but make up for this with larger teaching commitments than any other rank. On the whole, in Germany junior staff are more heavily involved in research and less in teaching than their seniors. In the Dutch universities, teaching hours are comparatively high across the board, but the pattern is more like England than Germany, with the lower ranks more involved in teaching and the senior more involved in administration – though not to the extent of English professors. In Sweden, however, yet another pattern prevails. Here, the more senior the rank, the more research is emphasized: Swedish professors spend far more of their time on research than any other rank except for the contract researchers.

Conclusion: national differences

This brief account of variations in two key elements of the academic role – value orientations and research and teaching involvement – has increasingly emphasized the persistence of national differences, whether in sectoral differentiation or in the structure of ranks. Indeed, one of the main purposes of the Carnegie survey, as originally planned, was precisely to examine national differences in what was at first called 'the condition of the professoriate' (Boyer *et al.*, 1994). Some of the cruder comparisons between countries – for example, in satisfaction and morale – seemed to differentiate the four European countries very sharply, with high levels of satisfaction in Germany and the Netherlands and much lower levels in Sweden and, especially, England. Multivariate analysis of the kind briefly illustrated here can help both to qualify these comparisons and to explain them. Thus, for example, we should note that German professors are (or were) exceptionally contented – to the indignation, incidentally, of the German public when these results were first released to the press – but that there is a very sharp polarization between the professors at one end of the spectrum and the junior staff, whose apprenticeship is longer than in any other European country and whose conditions of employment are particularly insecure.

I referred earlier to academics' notable commitment to their discipline in all four countries. It is shared across all of the ranks in the university sector in each country, although there is a modest tendency for staff in higher ranks to be increasingly identified with both their institution and their department. But the picture as regards commitment to the department and the institution is more complex. In England and Sweden we find similar patterns, whereby, in each case, the department scores nearly as highly as the discipline, and the institution, though in third place, is still regarded very positively by most academics. In the Netherlands and Germany, on the other hand, the ordering is still the same, but the levels of identification with department and, especially, institution are far lower, particularly in the case of Germany. This seems to tell us something important about the culture of academic life: if we combine this lack of commitment to the institution with the relative lack of involvement of senior German staff in administration, we may understand why the German public seems to regard university professors as irresponsible and smug. It may also suggest that English and Swedish academics have larger reserves of collegiality to call on in the hard times which they both see themselves as facing.

Earlier in this chapter I asked slightly frivolously whether we want to describe English and Swedish academics as belonging to a single profession, whereas the Netherlands – and Germany too if we take rank into account – may have two or more. This would be a gross over-simplification of a set of issues whose complexity I have done no more than illustrate. Nevertheless, in an analysis of the English system alone (Fulton, 1996), I suggested that, whatever the considerable evidence of discontent and even of deprofessionalization, English academics retain a set of attitudes and values which could be benevolently described as both professional and collegial. In particular, many of the differentials – whether by discipline, by sector or by rank – were smaller than, I felt, most observers might have predicted. In terms of the sectors, of course, this could be seen as evidence of the very well developed aspirations of the polytechnics, shortly to be fulfilled, to join the university club. A less benevolent interpretation (and one which I also permitted myself) would describe this apparent convergence more negatively: not so much 'academic drift', a pejorative term which does little credit to alternative missions and indeed belittles alternative clienteles, but more a hankering after a long-lost collegial culture and style. There is an element of nostalgia for a lost golden age, presumably destroyed by brutal economic and managerial realities. But more sharply still, I suspect that British academics have adopted the *principle* of mass higher education – as they clearly have – without fully accepting or understanding the *consequences* that will follow. How long can the single profession survive?

Notes

1. I should like to thank the Carnegie Foundation and the Andrew W. Mellon Foundation for their generous support for, respectively, data collection and analysis;

and my colleagues Juergen Enders, Peter Geurtz, Peter Maassen and Ulrich Teichler for their collaboration.

2. There is, however, a debate about the origins of these differences: see, for example, the debate between Becher (1990), who places a higher weight on internalist explanations, and Huber (1990).

3. The Carnegie surveys did not collect data which would make this kind of analysis possible on a comparative basis.

4. Technically, all the Swedish institutions surveyed were universities or university institutes. There is, however, a clear distinction between those 'with' and 'without' research. The English polytechnics and some of the larger colleges became ('new') universities later in 1992, after the survey was completed. For the comparative purposes of this chapter, both the Swedish universities without research and the English polytechnics and colleges are classified in the non-university sector.

5. Gouldner suggested that in the single college which he studied, 'cosmopolitanism' and 'localism' were polar opposites on a single dimension. In other contexts they appear to be independent attributes (see Halsey and Trow, 1971: 526–32).

6. See note 4 above.

7. The strength of the English response must undoubtedly be related to the pressures of the Research Assessment Exercises, in which polytechnic departments were allowed for the first time to compete alongside the universities in 1992, the year of the survey.

13

Autonomy, Bureaucracy and Competition: the ABC of Control in Higher Education

Marie Thorne and Rob Cuthbert

Introduction

Higher education in the UK has changed dramatically in the 1980s and 1990s, and in some respects these changes reflect a worldwide shift in how HE institutions are governed, managed and controlled. Many of these changes are part of a wider change in the conduct of public services, which has been extensively analysed and interpreted by people who work in higher education. However, the new academic understandings of context in public services have not yet been systematically applied to the changes in higher education. As the first generation of 'Thatcher's children' begin to make their initial choices of higher education it is timely to examine the impact of Thatcherite public service reform on the British higher education system.

This chapter aims to interpret HE change by looking at forces for change, the clash of ideologies and values, and changes in how order is maintained and control is achieved in HE. In doing so the chapter explores the appropriateness of market mechanisms and the utility of managerialism in highly professionalized organizations, key HE issues which are mirrored in other public services. Conflicting pressures for academic autonomy, bureaucratic efficiency and market competition underlie the changing patterns of control in the context of HE work.

The first part of the chapter summarizes recent legislative and structural changes in higher education in the UK, especially England. To structure the interpretation of these changes, we draw on a model developed by Mintzberg (1991) to interpret change processes and relations between organizations and their environments. His model identifies various forces for change in organizations, whose interplay determines the dynamic stability or instability of the organization. If any one force predominates then Mintzberg argues that a corresponding organizational form emerges in what he labels a 'configuration' – a relatively stable and persistent pattern.

Mintzberg's model identifies seven forces and corresponding organizational forms as follows:

Force	*Organizational form*
efficiency	machine bureaucracy
concentration	diversified
direction	entrepreneurial
proficiency	professional
innovation	adhocracy
cooperation	ideological
competition	political

Perhaps the most powerful force for HE change has been the government drive for *efficiency* and the associated use of bureaucratic, externally imposed forms of control, especially over the allocation and use of funds. This contrasts with the introduction of markets or quasi-markets, where control is exercised through empowering customers, inducing organizations to *concentrate* their efforts and thus promoting diversification in the HE sector. The changes in funding and the decentralization in the new market created the drive for the third force – control through *direction* – where the mission and strategy of the organization take on new significance as organizations become more diverse in response to market forces. What Mintzberg calls the drive for *proficiency* is stimulated by professionals working within the organization. Professionals prefer to exercise 'self-control' or autonomy, and work within a system of peer review, resisting hierarchical bureaucratic control. Institutions may also need to *innovate* to respond flexibly and swiftly to a rapidly changing environment. In HE notions of professionalism, academic autonomy and innovation come together in discussions of academic culture and changing academic roles, as Fulton's analysis in Chapter 12 shows.

For Mintzberg, these five forces are crucial to an understanding of the organization's relation with its environment. If one force predominates then the corresponding organizational form is predicted in a stable 'configuration'. However, it is more helpful in a complex environment to think of these as ideal types or tendencies, present to varying degrees at different times. Hence our treatment below considers these forces in turn as they manifest themselves in HE.

Mintzberg also identifies two further forces important in understanding organizational change. Where *cooperation* is the dominant force then the organization is in Mintzberg's terms 'ideological'. On the other hand, there will be forces for *competition* within the organization, which if dominant will make organizational politics a crucial issue in change.

Using Mintzberg's framework in this way helps us to identify the competing forms of control that exist and the different values that underpin them. Understanding the dynamic interplay between differing forces enables us to identify trends and patterns of control.

Recent constitutional changes in higher education

The late 1980s and early 1990s was a period of intense and rapid change in the legislative framework for and structure of the British HE system. The seeds of this change had been planted earlier with the creation and rapid growth in the 1970s and 1980s of polytechnics and colleges of HE, described by Sharp (1987). This expansion went hand in hand with the success of the Council for National Academic Awards (CNAA) in ensuring quality and credibility for the sector as a whole (Silver, 1990). This growth and credibility meant that the University Grants Committee's (UGC's) 1981 selective cuts, aimed at restricting access so as to preserve levels of funding in the face of government spending cuts, had worked only to accelerate the development of the 'non-university sector', as it was then described. The UGC universities were thus defeated in an attempt to assert control over how much HE there should be, and at what level of funding.

By the mid-1980s the polytechnics and colleges were chafing at detailed local authority control, even though their funding was in effect determined by recommendations of the National Advisory Body for Public Sector Higher Education (NAB). NAB was a forum where government, local authorities and institutions could in theory come together. Recognizing the pressure for institutional independence, NAB commissioned a series of Studies of Good Management Practice. The Studies led to a final report, *Management for a Purpose* (NAB, 1987), which recommended independent corporate status for HE institutions within a continuing framework of local authority control. This was overtaken by the government's wider aim to restrict local authority influence and the resistance of the institutions to anything less than full independence. The 1987 White Paper, *Higher Education: Meeting the Challenge* proposed to remove the polytechnics and colleges from local authority control and was enacted in the 1988 Education Reform Act.

The 1988 Act transferred staff and assets from the polytechnics and colleges into the new 'higher education corporations' (HECs) (see Cuthbert, 1988, for a detailed account of the changes and their implications for institutions). The HECs became funded by the Polytechnics and Colleges Funding Council (PCFC), a new agency also established by the Act. The universities, formerly funded by the UGC, became funded by another new agency, the Universities Funding Council (UFC). These arrangements, with PCFC and UFC assigned virtually identical powers, heralded the end of the binary policy. Within four years the Further and Higher Education Act 1992 unified control of the universities, polytechnics and colleges within each country, by creating Higher Education Funding Councils for England, Scotland and Wales.

The legislation also reconstituted the governing bodies of the new HE corporations, ensuring a majority of 'independent' governors with knowledge of 'industry, commerce, the professions and employment', and reducing the scale of and scope for membership by locally elected politicians and institutions' staff.

New legislation thus created major changes in both structure and control in the HE sector. An explicit aim of the reforms was to support the broad government drive for increased use of market forces to regulate the public service (Metcalfe and Richards, 1990). The creation of newly independent institutions in HE alongside the 'old' universities and the ending of the binary line ostensibly created a 'level playing field' in which competition would benefit consumers, however defined.

These HE reforms can be contextualized as part of a broader change in the public services, driven by government policies aiming to increase efficiency in service delivery and limit professional autonomy, by strengthening market forces and promoting managerial control. To examine this in more detail we turn first to the drive for efficiency.

The drive for efficiency and bureaucratic control

The creation of the Cabinet Office Efficiency Unit under Sir Derek Rayner, a businessman from Marks & Spencer, signalled 1980s government intentions to introduce more 'businesslike' approaches in public services. In HE the ideological intent of government was spelt out in the 1985 Green Paper (DES, 1985), *The Development of Higher Education into the 1990s*, which emphasized narrower utilitarian purposes for HE as a servant of the national economy. Managerial approaches in HE were encouraged by the Jarratt Report (CVCP, 1985), which argued that it was necessary for institutional leaders to see themselves as chief executives of major enterprises and adopt new approaches to strategic institutional management.

Trow (1994) describes the changes in British HE as a 'revolution' involving 'the emergence of "managerialism" in the governance and direction of British universities' (Trow, 1994: 11). He describes managerialism, as opposed to management, as not just a concern for the effectiveness of an organization, but an ideology, and goes on to differentiate between 'soft' and 'hard' forms of managerialism:

> The soft concept sees managerial effectiveness as an important element in the provision of HE of quality at its lowest cost; it is focused around the idea of improving the 'efficiency' of the existing institutions. The hard conception elevates institutional and system management to a dominant position in HE; its advocates argue that HE must be reshaped and reformed by the introduction of management systems which then become a continuing force ensuring the steady improvement in the provision of higher education.
>
> (Trow, 1994: 11)

Whereas soft managerialists retain a belief in HE as an autonomous activity, hard managerialism promotes a Taylorist philosophy (Taylor, 1947), which sees the route to efficiency as standardization, measurement and bureaucratic control. Managerial measures of performance become linked to funding; the solution to poor performance or inefficiency is more or better management. Trow argues that hard managerialism is a substitute for government's former trust in the ability of universities to govern themselves. In other words, managerialism becomes a weapon to assert government control over institutional autonomy.

Standardization can in principle be achieved by controlling inputs, processes or the designers and deliverers of the service themselves. Maximizing throughput while retaining quality depends on breaking down tasks and limiting their complexity, so that an organization can develop well rehearsed routines and predictable processes to cope with high volume. This language and thinking may seem alien to the higher education process, but such trends may be discerned in, for example, the differentiation of tasks exemplified by Corrall and Lester in Chapter 7, and in Winter's analysis of modularization and competencies in Chapter 6. Indeed, the idea of standardization is inherent in the metaphor of 'mass higher education', with its overtones of mass production on industrial lines.

However, the move towards standardization raises issues which defy such easy characterization, owing to the nature and fundamental purposes of education itself. It is only training, and not education, which has standardized outcomes. Although the process may be standardized to some extent, education still fundamentally involves individual learning and development with different meanings and impacts for different individuals. However HE institutions facing the drive for efficiency choose to aggregate students in classes, standardized modules and semesters, degree awards remain marks of individual achievement.

Carter (1989) argues that despite their differences most of the public services are characterized by having several input measures, but no or very few output or outcome measures, whereby to assess the impact of the service on the consumer. The lack of outcome measures makes it difficult to measure effectiveness and efficiency. However, this apparent difficulty has not prevented the introduction of a whole host of 'performance indicators' (see, for example, Johnes and Taylor, 1990; Cave *et al.*, 1991). Performance measurement was both officially sponsored by funding councils and unofficially promoted in such forms as *The Times Good University Guide* (O'Leary and Cannon, 1994).

'League tables' of performance can often be a measure of the management of the indicators rather than a measure of the value and impact of the service or process itself. Bureaucratic control is thus deflected in what can become a process of 'strategic compliance' (Lacey, 1977), as organizations produce statistics for external consumption rather than internalizing them as a legitimated form of control. In these circumstances the one apparently unambiguous form of control is control over funding.

Certainly, funding pressures and mechanisms played a large part in the rapid development of the sector. PCFC's funding method encouraged rapid expansion, by offering a core of institutional funding implying steadily reducing funding for the same student numbers, but inviting bids for marginal funding delivered in return for expansion. The consequence was a rapid expansion in overall student numbers and an even more rapid decline in levels of funding per student. The UFC, while preserving more continuity with previous UGC practice, also presided over declining real levels of funding per student. The creation of the HEFCs united the binary system under one funding agency, but also led to the formal division of HE funding into two elements, for teaching and research, separately assessed. Johnes and Cave (1994) analyse the workings of the teaching funding methods and their consequences.

Research funding was also subject to new measurement in the periodic Research Assessment Exercises described in detail by Johnston in Chapter 8. These accentuated the competitive pressures which already characterized academic grant-getting research, by importing competition and hierarchy into what had once been conceived of as a stable 'dual floor' of funding council research support. This was a natural concomitant of the expansion and diversification of the HE sector, which had made it clear that there was more than one kind of university, with more than one kind of mission and focus. The old assumption of mission equivalence (a fiction at least as far as funding was concerned, as Williams's (1991) analysis demonstrated) was a casualty of the new order, in which institutions jockeyed for position in the market, and which led to informally created alliances such as the 'Russell Group' of self-styled elite universities, so called because their representatives met in the Russell Hotel in London.

However, institutions continued to receive funds from the HEFCs as one block grant, without restriction on their use. The funding councils also relaxed controls on most capital funds, developing a common formula-based approach to their distribution and relaxing requirements to account separately for its use. These shifts in the nature of control can be seen as attempts to enable institutions to operate as freely as possible in the new HE market place.

The sheer weight of managerial processes imposed upon the institutions by the funding councils (Trow, 1994) illustrates the paradox in using 'managerialist' forms of bureaucratic control to achieve greater efficiency. It is hardly surprising that under such pressure some central management teams and senior staff adopted managerialist values antithetical to the values embodied in the educational mission of the institutions (Kogan, 1988; Pratt, 1990). In former polytechnics this debate became centred on the new constitution of the boards of governors, with their statutory majority of 'independent' members seen by some staff members as a managerialist vanguard. In the 'pre-1992' universities the effect was to accelerate the rise of central management groups seeking to take decisive and coordinated action at corporate level (Shattock, 1981), as a response to the changing institutional environment. Such groups sat uneasily with the loosely coupled, relatively autonomous small departments which inhabited the organized anarchy (Cohen and March, 1974); their rise equally fuelled fears of managerialism. Trow (1994) argues that the external control familiar to polytechnics came to be applied to all universities as the binary system was ended. The new funding agency was an important device to limit the autonomy universities had previously enjoyed. A further constraint on autonomy was the introduction of new market forces, which we consider in the next section.

Competition, markets and consumer control

There has always been competition in HE: for students (Higgins, 1991), for research funds (Ziman, 1991) and for reputation. So what is new? Johnes and Cave (1994: 95) argue that 'discussions about quasi-markets in the field of HE ... usually focus on new methods designed to introduce competition specifically for financial resources, taking competition for prestige for granted.' Government reforms have aimed to extend the scope of market forces to promote 'a more efficient and responsive system and fairer sharing of its costs' (Howarth, 1991: 5) and this is a worldwide HE phenomenon. However, Neave's (1991) comparative analysis concludes that: 'the path which Britain has hewn for its higher education system is far more radical in the undiluted application of ideologically driven policy than any of its major European neighbours' (Neave, 1991: 39).

The use of market forces aims to change producer behaviour by empowering the consumer or customer. There are obvious conceptual difficulties in defining the 'customer' in an HE context, since there are multiple stakeholders – government, society, funding councils, students, parents, employers – all of whom may in some sense be 'customers'. We will focus on two sets of stakeholders – students and funding agencies – to illustrate the effects of increased competition and market forces on control of HE work.

The fashion for consumerism in the public sector reflects the growing need for organizations 'to pay more attention to consumers' wishes, offer wider choice and develop techniques for marketing their services' (Pollitt, 1987: 43). HE, like other public services in the UK, has a government-imposed charter setting out the rights of the student as customer. The genie of consumerism, once out of the bottle, can be hard to contain. Hill (1995) has shown how institutions need to research and manage student expectations in managing service quality. Zemsky (1993) argues that consumerism is now dominating the development of US colleges and universities, through the demands of a new generation of students who want credentials and practical knowledge in an easily consumed package. Such students choose HE in a very different way from their predecessors; they purchase HE as a commodity rather than seek apprenticeship in the community of scholars. However, Shumar (1995) argues that it is unhelpful to see the rise of market forces simply in terms of a dialectic between collegiality and corporate bureaucracy. For Shumar the changes in the idea of the university are better explained as a process of 'commoditization'. He argues that when non-profit institutions respond to market forces by reframing their services as commodities, there is a steady change in their structure and ideology, involving, in HE, the erosion of the democratic and participatory ideal. Let us explore this argument by analysing in more detail how HE markets work and what they imply for control over work and workers in HE.

Markets can be seen as a form of organization which is efficient when certain conditions prevail (Williamson, 1975). A transactions cost perspective suggests that markets are efficient when there is relatively little ambiguity about performance (Ouchi, 1980; Cuthbert, 1987). For example, in an exchange of cash for a tin of baked beans, both buyer and seller can readily evaluate what they receive, and whether the exchange represents value for money. However, exchanges in HE are more ambiguous. Zemsky's new HE consumers offer cash and participation and demand credentials and easy routes, but they may be offered personal growth and expected to supply their own motivation to do hard intellectual work. The recognition of this problem of performance ambiguity in many public services has led to the development of the concept of 'quasi-market', a system 'set up in such a way that the provision of services remains free at the point of delivery' (Propper *et al.*, 1994) and in which Le Grand (1991) suggests that often professionals may act as purchasers on behalf of the otherwise insufficiently informed lay consumer.

In the higher education quasi-market the funding councils act as purchasers. However, Sizer's (1992) analysis concluded that funding councils could not serve as an effective proxy for price competition in a competitive market. Johnes and Cave (1994) note that existing methods of funding teaching in the UK tend to distort the quasi-market by overemphasizing uniform prices, and thus promoting cost equalization and quality regulation. They argue for the possibility of a true market driven by student buying power, which would eliminate the funding councils' role as purchasers.

However, markets, and quasi-markets, can also fail. Witzel (1991) analyses the failure of the UFC bidding system in 1989–90 to develop internal competition among UFC universities. He argues that 'A functioning market requires not only active and informed providers and purchasers, but an adequate flow of resources and an adequate capacity for growth in order to stimulate and maintain competition' (Witzel, 1991: 46). In the late 1990s it is debatable whether either of the latter conditions are satisfied in HE. Furthermore, the assumption underlying the development of markets is that strategy and policy making can be rigidly separated from the delivery of public services, as Walsh (1994) observes. Walsh argues that this affects the extent of malleability in the contracting process at particular points in time. For example, in transactions with a funding or research council, institutional freedom is largely confined to the period before a 'contract' is determined. Thereafter institutions are committed to a volume and pattern of provision and spending that acts as a major constraint. In HE, as in many other public services, institutions delivering services also expect to contribute to shaping strategy and policy – an expectation which market structures may inhibit or deny.

Witzel concludes that the inappropriate introduction of an internal market may simply replace large monolithic public services with smaller but equally monolithic institutions 'who, having gained control of their own budgets, will have increased their autonomy at the expense of government and consumer alike' (Witzel, 1991: 47). The 'Russell Group' of universities might be seen as aspiring to exactly such a position of monolithic institutional autonomy.

Potter's (1988) analysis of the power gap between providers and consumers holds that five factors underpin the principle of consumerism: access, choice, information, redress and representation. This provides a framework for evaluating the extent of consumer control in HE.

Access has in theory been guaranteed by the Robbins principle that 'courses of higher education should be available to all who are qualified by ability and attainment to pursue them and wish to do so' (Fulton, 1981: 5). The relatively generous British system of student support led to a market in which students could choose institutions, empowered by the 'voucher' of a grant. Paradoxically, the rapid expansion of access to HE in the 1980s led to the devaluation of the voucher as grants gave way to loans, weakening student power in the HE market at just the point when government policy aimed to strengthen market forces. The widespread problem of student poverty in the late 1990s increasingly limits access to those with sufficient financial means, while perhaps conferring increased power on those still able to afford access.

Only where individuals have genuine *choice* are services likely to respond to consumer demand. Against Zemsky's (1993) picture of dominant consumer power we might set the opposite view of students with inadequate *information* struggling to make complex choices in a bewilderingly varied market place where institutional efforts to communicate remain inadequate (Higgins, 1991). The rise of performance indicators and league tables is an explicit attempt to solve this problem, but too often may oversimplify or trivialize the choice process. In such circumstances choice becomes more stressful and may actually disempower the consumer (Barnes and Prior, 1995). If the level of ambiguity about the service is such that choice and information are unavoidably flawed, then *redress* for the consumer may need greater emphasis. Charters have stimulated the development of explicit complaints procedures, for example, and the once rare phenomena of student complaints and academic appeals against assessment and other decisions have become commonplace.

The contradictions inherent in government policy are again evident in consideration of the issue of *representation*. The ability of students' unions to represent the consumer of HE services has been restricted by legislation, notably the Education Act 1994, which has in effect defined for students and unions what should be the proper scope for their consumer power, by outlawing certain kinds of union activity and tightening institutional control over union activities. This exemplifies government control over the market, through definition of the services which consumers may legitimately demand. The instrumentalism of government policy defines HE as an economic investment rather than as a consumer good, and regulates the market accordingly.

How, then, do market forces and competition affect control of HE? The HE market is regulated by government and its agents, the funding councils. Within this constrained quasi-market, students as consumers have imperfect information, which limits their ability to make effective choices, and their rights of redress and representation have been developed in ways which stress individual rather than collective action. This might imply weak consumerist forces in the face of institutional providers' superior knowledge of products and services. The role of funding councils as purchasers provides some collective, if unrepresentative, redress. These kaleidoscopic shifts in control allow different interpretations. Langer's (1992) analysis of parallel changes in Austrian HE led him to discern a shift from ministerial to market control. Mackintosh *et al.* (1994) argue that HE institutions are subject to market forces in only part of their operations, and must therefore be managed as 'hybrids' which are both tax- and consumer-supported. Hybrids, they argue, inevitably have some degrees of freedom, within which they are in effect making public policy for HE. It follows that, 'Where providers are caught between users' pressure for good services and purchasers' cost-cutting objectives, efficient quasi-markets may require attachment to public service values' (Mackintosh *et al.*, 1994: 339). Whittington *et al.* (1994) suggest that market-driven change is highly complex and in particular runs the risk that change occurs at different rates at different levels. In particular, change at the top strategic levels is likely to lag changes at other levels. To understand this process better, it is necessary to turn to consider strategic management and direction.

Strategic planning and control through direction

Following Mintzberg, we might expect that where the force for direction predominates we would find HE institutions adopting an entrepreneurial style, constantly seeking new opportunities and adjusting organizational direction accordingly. In higher education there has been a growing emphasis on strategic planning by institutions; this might be seen as reflecting the central agencies' shift from a planning to a funding role, relocating some responsibilities for planning to institutional level and encouraging entrepreneurialism. However, it is too simplistic to infer that there has thus been a transfer of control to the institutions.

The funding councils require each institution to develop a strategic plan and annually to update and submit its five-year plan and a more detailed

12-month statement of immediate objectives. The conduct of each institution is subject to a financial memorandum setting out general rules of institutional conduct, and each year there is a funding agreement detailing the funds to be provided, the outcomes in terms of student numbers which are required in return and the financial penalties for failure. In practice it is student number projections and financial forecasts that most concern the funding council, but the requirement for plans can be seen as a managerialist control over institutions, a check that they are being 'properly managed'. Does this add up to control *over* institutions? Woollard (1996) describes his experience of working as a civil servant in the Department for Education thus:

> The department was still part of a command-and-control system, in which senior officials, rather than being managers of a system and partners in a vision, could easily come to feel like overworked hacks – 'hired guns' in the telling phrase of one of my ex-colleagues – finding new ways of enforcing (often against their own ideals and better judgment) the will of an 'elective dictatorship' on those stakeholders who were seen as the obstacle to that will.
>
> (Woollard, 1996)

However, the intermediation of the funding councils and the institutions' authorship of their plans does also create some institutional discretion over strategic direction. The question of who determines strategic direction, and how, thus admits of a range of answers, and strategic planning serves a range of purposes.

Defining strategic objectives may clarify the scope and nature of the institution. For Thomas (1990), a 'well directed' university is one which can both forecast and act to accommodate or benefit from changes which are outside its control. Strategic planning can help institutions retain a sense of independence and insulation from adversity, both by defining a focus for the organization and through identifying strengths, weaknesses, opportunities and threats, and responding accordingly. Even during a period of discontinuous change, where prediction and planning may be impossible, a well honed strategic process can be a useful organizational defence routine (Argyris, 1990) to handle problems and crises.

Strategic management enables each institution to determine its own profile in an increasingly diverse university sector, through the establishment of 'mission' and objectives. These provide a guide or focus in setting priorities and making decisions; for, example in determining the balance of effort between research and teaching, the nature of the provision offered and the range of subjects provided.

The binary system was a top-down imposition of strategic direction for the two distinct sectors: universities, and polytechnics and colleges. The ending of the binary line and the creation of a unified and enlarged HE sector allowed each institution more scope to determine its role in a more diverse HE system. Exploiting this scope came more naturally to some than to others. The new universities and colleges had been accustomed to what might be termed corporatist or managerial approaches to institutional direction. Many old universities, in contrast, remained loosely coupled organized anarchies which empowered the academic entrepreneur. In such institutions a sense of direction *emerges* from the activities and 'stream of decisions' (Mintzberg and Waters, 1989) of the key actors – the academics – whose ability to obtain research grants and funding directs the overall strategy of the university. This 'producer-led' approach, while it encourages the creation of new markets through entrepreneurial activity, can also lead to problems if the 'producers' fall out of alignment either with the rest of the organization or with the demands of 'customers' in the market, whether these are students, research councils or funding councils.

However, some universities, like some private sector companies, may perceive themselves not simply as entrepreneurs but as market makers. Consider, at the opposite pole to the managerialist ideal of strategic direction, McNay's (1995) account of Cambridge University's approach to research, derived by a group studying 'the entrepreneurial and adaptive university':

> They asked about the research committee – 'we haven't got one'; research policy? – 'it's a Good Thing'; control of quality? – 'we appoint top class staff and let them get on with it'; allocation of funds? – 'there is little held centrally for regular distribution.' As one Cambridge don summed up: 'Cambridge works in practice but not in theory.'
>
> (McNay, 1995: 108)

More precisely, Cambridge works in practice as an entrepreneurial adhocracy, not according to a managerialist theory of efficient bureaucracy.

This contrasts sharply with the drive for strategic planning in many universities, where articulating purpose, mission and direction is seen as the primary role of the board of governors, vice chancellor and corporate management group. Within the corporate framework, deans of faculties or heads of departments develop strategic plans for their own units which are aligned with and fill out the corporate vision. There is nothing new in 'the idea of the university'; Newman (1976) articulated an influential nineteenth-century vision of the university's mission and purposes, and there have been successive waves of re-visioning; for example, by Daiches (1964) for Sussex in the 1960s. What is new is the overlaying of such visions with the managerial apparatus of strategic plans and processes. Dill (1996) argues that this new drive for strategic choice is a natural consequence of environmental change. Organized anarchy depends on a 'munificent' environment which provides 'strategic certainty' for institutions. As resources become scarce, strategic uncertainty becomes the prevailing institutional condition and requires explicit attention to strategic choice.

In the new terminology, 'corporate strategy' defines what business, or businesses, the university is in. The key choices include the balance between teaching, research, consultancy, public service and other activities, and the disciplines or fields in which the university operates. Faculty and departmental plans then determine the 'competitive strategy': which markets are targeted, and how the institution competes in those markets, whether on reputation, price (e.g. in terms of entry qualifications) or otherwise. These different types of strategy may be closely linked or may operate in parallel (McLellan and Kelly's, 1989, framework sets out the possibilities), depending upon the level and type of control exercised from the centre.

As Whittington *et al.* (1994) point out, there is also a risk of time lags in change at different levels. In market-driven change the centre may lag behind the departments: the university may still be corporately priding itself on its reputation while departments drop entry standards to compete for students. In efficiency-driven change the departments may lag: the university articulation of a strategy to expand student numbers via stronger links with FE colleges in the area may not be taken up by departments accustomed to competing nationally for new entrants.

In the entrepreneurial organization control is achieved in the match between entrepreneurs' ambitions and sponsors' willingness to provide financial support; small atomistic flexible units each pursue their own direction. However, as these units come together in an increasingly resource-stretched institutional framework the departments and faculties become interdependent, tied more closely to a corporate whole. Control through entrepreneurially determined direction may give way to financial control or strategic control through planning, as the need for resource rationing and monitoring of effective performance increases.

It is ironic that HE reached the stage where strategic planning was deemed a prerequisite for determining priorities just as private sector organizations became increasingly aware of its limitations. Mintzberg (1994) recognizes the tendency of strategic planning both to reduce managers' power in strategy making and to emphasize analysis rather than synthesis: 'strategic planning often spoils strategic thinking, causing managers to confuse real vision with the manipulation of numbers' (Mintzberg, 1994: 107). Perhaps the most fundamental question for strategic planning in HE is the extent to which it involves, and the extent to which it controls, the professionals – academics and others who believe they have a right to participate in setting strategic direction.

Where professionals are controlled rather than controlling, it is meaningful to speak of clearer organizational focus – in Mintzberg's terms, *concentration* on particular kinds of activity, leading to *diversification* of the sector. Where professionals remain in control, then we may instead speak either of entrepreneurialism, as above, or of *professional organization* and *innovation*, to which our analysis now turns.

Professional self-control or academic autonomy?

Are academics professionals? Being a member of a profession normally involves: the possession of a systematic body of knowledge; a commitment to the client; the existence of an occupational association which grants the right to practise; and exclusive entry based upon credentials (Moore, 1970). Academics' claim to professional status is evident: consider, for example, such definitive sociological works as Clark's (1987b) *The Academic Profession.* However, there is, for example, no professional body to license and control entry to the 'academic profession'. This is an important and significant difference, as many of the occupational freedoms granted to professions are regulated through their own professional control systems.

A closer look at the ranks of the 'academics' reveals an important differentiation of roles, as Fulton has shown in Chapter 12. Clark (1994) surveys the growing tensions between teaching and research worldwide, and between different levels of teaching, and concludes that in most university systems there are two distinct tiers: the teacher, who spends most of his or her time teaching; and the lecturer or professor charged with doing research and given sufficient time and resources to do so. Trow (1994) offers a fourfold typology of orientations towards teaching, which extends Clark's teacher–professor distinction. Clark's teachers are in Trow's terms those who *transmit* knowledge, who might be oriented towards either their subject or their students. The former are the scholars, whose love of the subject is paramount, and who presume the same commitment in their students. The latter take student motivation as more problematic and admit a broader responsibility to promoting student learning. Research scholars (Clark's 'professors'), in contrast aim to *create* knowledge, but may equally display orientation towards either their subject or their (research) students. Some 'teachers' will of course also occupy the role of research student.

We would add that teaching and research roles are further complicated, on the one hand by changing relationships with other quasi-professionals such as librarians – as Corrall and Lester show in Chapter 7 – and on the other by the development of such roles as instructor, demonstrator and research or teaching assistant – which occupy a large grey area between quasi-professional academics and other staff. Universities and colleges also contain staff in support services who are clearly professionals: accountants, personnel officers, surveyors and so on. Here space compels us to focus on core teaching and research activities.

Professionals value autonomy and expect high degrees of personal discretion in defining the nature of their role. Peer review is important for professionals as it validates reputation, success and achievement. Professionals, unlike managers, do not recognize hierarchical authority, preferring a socially constructed pecking order based upon expertise, not position. Consequently professionals are motivated intrinsically and prefer to exercise self-control that stems from legitimated expertise. Professionals expect to be led, not managed, and led by one of their peers (Handy, 1979) in a relationship based upon trust.

Clearly academics, or at least 'professors', resemble professionals in many if not all these respects. Professors, for example, are cosmopolitans (Gouldner, 1957) who gain their identity from their academic discipline and peers rather than the institution they inhabit. Middlehurst and Elton (1992) argue that academics expect to operate in a climate of collegiality, where there is 'involvement of all academic members of the organization in committees, working groups and task forces, through consultation, as both leaders and led' (Middlehurst and Elton, 1992: 256).

However, Middlehurst and Elton (1992) also criticize universities' response to resource restriction on the grounds that there has been too much management and not enough leadership – in other words, a failure of professionalism. This alleged failure is all the more surprising, since HE institutions, unlike some other public services such as health, have not seen reforms import a new group of people from outside the service explicitly for their managerial skills. Nevertheless, Welch (1995) speaks for many academics when he bemoans 'The Rise of the Managerial Cadre' in universities, by what must in effect be the separation of some senior staff from their academic roots, through the adoption of a new set of values.

Middlehurst and Elton (1992: 261–2) also draw a sharp distinction between old and new universities: 'Polytechnics . . . embedded the kind of collegiality that stems from team work in their otherwise hierarchical structures. Thus, within universities, the new managerialism has clashed with the universities' culture and mission in a way that it has not done in the polytechnics.' However, in both old and new universities the law requires collective academic authority to be exercised through senates and academic boards. The clear definition of academic board constitution and powers for the new HE corporations, set out in the Education Reform Act 1988, can be seen as limiting the scope of academic power, but it also represents a guarantee of a significant role for academics in institutional governance.

Academic tenure has also long been seen in old universities as a crucial protection for academic freedom, and thus for an important dimension of professionalism, but the significance of tenure has been much circumscribed by legislation and case law, compounded by financial pressure which has prompted more than one institution to seek compulsory redundancies among its academic staff.

Academics, then, resemble professionals in many respects, but some academic roles are more professional than others. Changes in universities have made a major impact upon academic work, especially for Clark's teachers. Teachers may be professional accountants, engineers and so on, yet they see their role in the university as 'just employees in large institutions, with a job to do and a salary to earn at the end of the month' (Schwartzmann, 1994: 25). Schwartzmann (1994) identifies three types of academic: the 'liberal professional' or archetypal professor; the unionized skilled worker; and the academic civil servant, a modern version of the Chinese mandarin. Each type embodies a different relationship between the academic and the university. Increasingly, academic freedom and tenure are replaced by fixed-term contracts and performance-related pay to ensure the attainment of managerially defined objectives (Lewis, 1993). The drive for efficiency, increased student : staff ratios and greater managerial and government control have forced many staff to relinquish the professoriate model to become civil servants or employees.

The use of language reflects this shift: from professionalism to managerialism. In the past the term 'faculty' distinguished academics from other staff; now the term 'staff' may be used generically, to differentiate 'staff' from management, as Wasser (1994) observes. University staff are more often expected to be 'locals' rather than cosmopolitans (Gouldner, 1957), increasing the risk that academic and institutional loyalties conflict. If we accept Trow's (1994) conception of the teacher as concerned more with knowledge transfer than knowledge creation, then it becomes more likely that teaching work will be expressed in managerial terms and subject to performance measurement and bureaucratic control. In this vein, Tierney and Rhoads (1995) argue that the 'assessment movement' within HE overemphasizes facts rather than values, teachers as repositories of knowledge rather than learning guides and teaching products rather than learning processes. They conclude: 'Assessment, then, might be seen as a tool of control where managers exert more authority, and academic labour becomes deskilled and less powerful' (Tierney and Rhoads, 1995: 108).

The debate over values in teaching and learning has been particularly fierce in the growing attention paid to explicit assessment of quality in higher education. Concern for quality is a natural consequence of scarcity of resources; the resource providers want to know about quality and whether they are getting value for money. The deprecation of the 'quality industry' (see, for example, Finer, 1995) by HE staff may be in part a consequence of the same resource pressure, which makes staff time an ever more precious resource. However, staff resistance also reflects a conflict in values. Many staff see the new quality controls as an unnecessary diversion from core tasks: quality control which damages quality. This is consistent with the 'professional' view exemplified by the Cambridge anecdote above. Professionals know what they are doing and must be left to get on with both defining and achieving quality. Any other approach will weaken professionalism and thus damage quality. This clash of values and concern over control is reflected in the national debate over which form of quality assurance should predominate.

Government rhetoric espouses managerialist values and points to quality assessment as practised by the funding councils, in which external assessors examine teaching and learning processes at first hand before delivering judgements which carry the imprimatur of the government's funding agency. The universities' rhetoric promotes professional values of autonomy and self-determination, through the quality audit process which checks quality systems rather than teaching and learning itself. Auditors thus help institutions to regulate themselves, a value reinforced by the fact that it is the institutions that establish and control the auditing body, the Higher Education Quality Council.

Opinions differ widely over the significance of these distinctions. For Watson (1995: 338), 'In the spread of systematic external peer review, the argument for key elements of self-regulation, including assessment, has already been won.' Sharp (1995) also argues that both audit and assurance meet the necessary conditions for effective assessment of teaching and learning. However, Withers (1995) distinguishes between two traditions in quality assessment, of control and enhancement respectively, and sees HEFCE quality assurance, at least, as embodying the control paradigm. For Holmes (1993: 4) the excessively narrow '"managerialistic" striving for quality' has been counterproductive since it has actually weakened the fundamental interaction of teacher and student.

As the process of adjustment to managerialist reforms unfolds it also reframes earlier debates about control. The 'classic' account of control in academe centred on academic freedom, a concept itself susceptible to interpretation as part of a historical process of development of institutional independence. Searle (1972) identified the progression from the 'special' theory of academic freedom, in which the Humboldtian academy asserted its special rights to free expression in an illiberal environment, to the 'general' theory, in which academic freedom came to resemble closely the general societal freedoms of a liberal democracy. As individuals' freedom became less contentious, so the academic debate turned its attention to institutional freedoms. The role of the University Grants Committee as a buffer between state and institution was much examined and the appropriate balance between autonomy and accountability was explored (Berdahl, 1983).

These debates shaped understanding of the binary system in the UK, as, for example, in Brosan's (1971) distinction between 'matching' economic needs and 'monitoring' societal phenomena as institutional purposes. Implicit in the concept of 'matching' was a justification for tighter social control and perhaps less academic freedom than would be appropriate for a 'monitoring' institution. The enduring legacy of binarism was an assumed distinction between academic and vocational purposes, which coexisted uneasily with parallel assumptions that academic freedom was indivisible, and that higher education necessarily involved the simultaneous pursuit of teaching and research.

The tensions in these assumptions have been exposed by the processes of expansion, sectoral unification and institutional diversification in the HE sector. The differentiation between staff roles within institutions, and between institutional roles themselves, have shown that different patterns of control are possible for different kinds of HE work. For the professors the classic accounts of academic freedom and liberal professionalism may continue to be valid. However, for some – the unionized teachers, the academic mandarins – new forms of engagement with and control by institutions may become the norm. The appropriateness of new forms of control is contingent on institutional purpose. The danger is that managerialist controls will predominate in a system whose success still depends on the quasi-professional autonomy needed to deliver the unpredictable outcomes of higher learning, whether in teaching or research. This leads us to consider briefly the extent to which innovation should be a central feature of higher education.

Traditional accounts of academic work assert a necessary connection between individual academic autonomy and successful innovative practice in research and teaching. However, the increasing organizational differentiation between teaching and research, and the managerialist tendencies of government reforms, have led to new approaches to control innovation in HE.

Research, an inherently innovative activity, has resisted many attempts to bring it 'under control', although the customer–contractor principle has long been established. However, the research councils, as agencies for channelling public funds for research, have developed new approaches, such as defining research themes, and new vehicles, such as interdisciplinary centres, which might be construed as closer forms of control over the research enterprise. The research councils themselves have also been restructured and realigned with the government's Technology Foresight exercise, which also aims to control the direction of research activity rather more closely. Whether these changes will in fact change the nature of control over research remains uncertain; the timescale for assessing such reforms is necessarily very long. The funding councils also explored ways to tighten control over their own funding for research. However, a Coopers and Lybrand study led only to a requirement for institutions to account in rather more detail for how research funds were allocated, not for the outcomes from that allocation process (HEFCE, 1994).

The most significant change in control over research has been the Research Assessment Exercise (RAE) initiated in 1986, and subsequently extended to cover the whole of the expanded HE sector. The RAE, described by Johnston in Chapter 8, can be seen as an attempt at bureaucratic measurement of innovation and its outcomes. It was, however imperfectly, an operationally realized means of relating research quality to research funding. As such it symbolized the Thatcherite reforms of the public services to increase accountability and reduce professional control. Whether it actually improved research outcomes continues to be hotly debated. However, it certainly expanded the volume of academic publication, and no doubt tightened the recording of research effort.

Innovation in teaching has been a marked feature of HE development in the 1980s and 1990s. Institutions have developed new approaches to managing student learning, through such changes as semesterization and modularization, and have developed new 'products', such as courses in environmental science, cultural and media studies and so on. There have been sector-wide attempts at innovation, notably the funding council-sponsored Teaching and Learning Technology Programmes, but these are as yet unproven. There have been successful innovations at institutional level: witness the Open University and the University of Buckingham. However, it remains questionable whether innovation can be managed at a level higher, in many cases, than the staff group. If most innovation, even in teaching, remains a very localized process, then the effectiveness of bureaucratic control is severely circumscribed, and academic adhocracy must continue to play a major role in HE development.

Conclusions

In this chapter we have reviewed different forms of control in HE, and the values that underpin them. To conclude we will draw the various strands of the argument together in two frameworks, dealing respectively with conflict between values and with the distribution of power and control between multiple stakeholders.

Values are fundamental in any educational enterprise. They convey a sense of what should be, what is correct or proper in the work context. Especially where there is ambiguity, uncertainty or conflict, values can and should guide decisions and actions. Values are held by individuals (Williams et *al.,* 1989) but they are the bridge between visible organizational action and artefacts and the underlying shared assumptions that make up the organization culture (Schein, 1985). During a period of change it can be important for organizations and individuals to determine 'what values should be shared and what objectives are worth striving for' (Fitzgerald, 1988). In Mintzberg's terms, shared values promote an organizational 'ideology' in which *cooperation* is the dominant force. Where there is value conflict (for example, between managerialists and professionals), *competition* may become the dominant force, with organizations tending to pull apart rather than pull together.

For an overview of value conflicts in HE we will use Quinn's (1988) 'competing values' model, as adapted by Hooijberg and Petrock (1993). Their framework suggests that organizations differ on two critical dimensions. One runs from flexibility and individuality to stability and control. The other ranges from internal focus to external focus. Organizations can be located in this two-dimensional space according to the emphases of their dominant values. Applying this model to the changes in HE illustrates the dynamic interplay of competing cultural value systems.

Where there is an internal focus and emphasis on stability and control, Hooijberg and Petrock speak of a 'hierarchy culture'. This is the home of managerialism. Rules and procedures are important; stability and predictability are the key to greater efficiency. Authority resides in position; the organization is controlled by the exercise of legitimate hierarchical authority. The hierarchy culture is well adapted to stable environments where efficiency is a key requirement.

Where stability and control accompany an external focus, the model identifies a 'market culture'. The market culture is controlled through external competition, the achievement of measurable goals and targets and institutional concentration on particular kinds of activity. This leads to diversification within relatively stable market structures which differentiate institutions in terms of niche, reputation, teaching or research emphasis, price and so on.

Where an emphasis on flexibility and individuality is accompanied by an internal focus there is a 'clan culture'. Work is individually determined and individuals have a high degree of personal autonomy, both within the organization and from outside pressures. The organization provides a congenial supportive environment where members have a voice in decisions and group cohesion and morale are highly valued. Here we can recognize the traditional account of collegial higher education. Authority resides with the individual, or with the internal group, in a pecking order which may be relatively stable. Control is achieved through a commitment to shared values alongside an insulation from external environmental pressures. The breakdown of collegiality in HE, where it has occurred, can be largely attributed to a breakdown of the insulation from outside pressures, as expansion of public support for HE brought with it irresistible demands for greater accountability for how resources were used.

Finally, there may be the same emphasis on flexibility and individuality accompanied by an external focus: the 'adhocracy culture', more open, not as incestuous as the professional clan, not as inflexible as the hierarchy. Here creativity, entrepreneurship, flexibility and risk-taking are rewarded. There is resonance with Cohen and March's (1974) concept of the organized anarchy in HE. Authority resides with individuals, but participation by different individuals at different times is highly fluid. Control is achieved by the summation of individual actions aimed at matching ambitions with external opportunities and problems with solutions. This enables the adhocracy to adjust to rapidly changing environments. Adhocracy flourishes only where individuals can indeed identify sufficient external sponsorship to sustain the necessarily expensive loosely coupled organization.

Universities and colleges are unlikely to exhibit any one of these cultures in a pure form. The model should be seen as defining a set of ideal types. Moreover, it offers a framework not only for interpreting shifts in values and their effects over time (Ban, 1995), but also for explaining and predicting how and why change in organizational culture and cohesion occurs – by analysing the institution's relationship with its environment, and the clash of values between different internal groups. By looking at value conflict, the model also provides an insight into control. To reverse the perspective, we finally consider a framework which addresses the issue of control where there are multiple stakeholders, to offer some insight into how values come into conflict.

Stakeholder analysis recognizes and values different interests while providing a systemic framework to make sense of their dynamic interrelationship. Winstanley *et al.* (1995) combine a stakeholder perspective with a power matrix as a means of mapping key groups and determining how their power relationship may change over time. They differentiate between criteria power and operational power, using these as two dimensions on which to locate the various stakeholders. Criteria power is the ability of stakeholders to: define the aims and purpose of the service; design the overall system within which the system is provided; set or influence the performance criteria which guide public service activity; and evaluate the performance of public services on the basis of these criteria. Operational power is the ability to: provide the service and decide how to provide it; change the way the

Figure 13.1   Early 1980s: the binary system

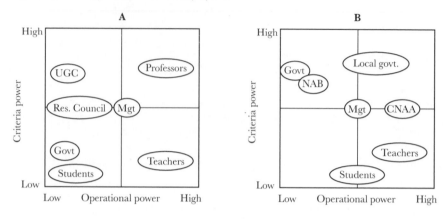

service is delivered operationally through the allocation of limited resources or by using knowledge and key skills.

Again, the combination of different positions on these two dimensions generates four broad possibilities or quadrants in which stakeholder groups may be located. High criteria power and low operational power leads to 'arm's length' power, while being high on both creates 'comprehensive power'. High operational and low criteria power is 'operational power', while those low on both are labelled 'disempowered'. We can use this simple matrix to interpret changes in HE, as Figures 13.1 and 13.2 illustrate. Inevitably any such illustration is partial; it cannot hope to include all the significant groups and actors. The figures should be seen as no more than an indication of how we can make sense of changes in the complex context of work in HE.

In Figure 13.1 we map the position of stakeholders in the binary system in the early 1980s, before the Thatcherite reforms of the 1980s and 1990s. Part A pictures the UGC institutions. The UGC operated at arm's length, but with considerable *dirigiste* powers, albeit seldom exercised; the same was true of the research councils, perhaps to a lesser extent. Government, buffered by UGC, was relatively disempowered. Professors were comprehensively powerful as collegiality prevailed; 'teachers' (junior academics, research assistants etc.) were relatively powerful in operational terms, but had little influence over criteria – what should be done and how it should be evaluated. Students could choose which courses to join, but their choices were constrained by a reputational structure which tended to assign the 'best' students to the 'best' institutions. Managers such as vice chancellors and deans had ill-defined authority but appreciable influence (Moodie and Eustace, 1974); registrars' authority was clearer and similarly significant.

In contrast, the pre-1988 Education Reform Act 'local authority' sector of HE shown at B had central government at arm's length; local government exercising a degree of operational power resented by the institutions;

Figure 13.2 Late 1990s: the changing pattern of HE

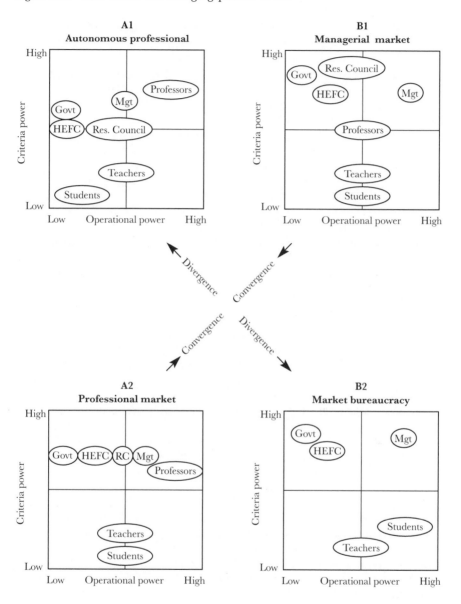

and NAB mediating between the two. Managers were much more influential, and CNAA wielded much of the academic criteria power which in universities was exercised by professors. Students were given more of a voice, not least because teaching loomed much larger in the institutional mission.

Figure 13.2 maps the changing picture after the HE reforms, in the late

1990s. It reflects the more overt diversity in the HE sector by differentiating between two kinds of institution in both A and B.

The first type, A1, we label the 'autonomous professional' university. Funding pressures and legislative changes have increased government's power, albeit still at arm's length, and reduced the funding council's similarly distanced authority. These institutions remain relatively insulated from the market place and student consumerism through entrepreneurship and a leading edge reputation with an emphasis on research. Research councils have become rather more operationally focused, while institutional managers have gained power to enable the university to respond more quickly to funding opportunities in the new and more competitive environment. Professorial power has been correspondingly reduced, but the institution continues to enjoy an extremely powerful competitive position in both teaching and research. Students in such institutions remain largely disempowered; 'teachers' have become even more constrained.

Type A2 we call 'professional market' institutions. Unable to avoid significant degrees of market risk, such institutions must cede more control to funding agencies, and empower managers even more to achieve corporate solutions to problems insoluble by a collegial organization. The power of the professoriate is consequently further curtailed; students, however, gain power because of the significance of maintaining student numbers to secure institutional income.

Type B1 institutions define their mission in terms of both research and teaching. Central government and the central funding agency retain significant power; research councils have even more power in the research funding domain because of the reputational significance of their funds for institutional success. Local government power has vanished; this and the reconstitution of governance has significantly increased managerial power, towards comprehensive power. However, the disappearance of CNAA control has empowered a new professorial class, less distinct from teachers, while students remain influential without having made enormous gains. We label these institutions 'managerial market' universities.

Finally, B2 institutions, which we label 'market bureaucracies', are those most exposed to market forces. While they may define both teaching and research as primary activities, research councils are relatively irrelevant to their operation. Students are the lifeblood of what are primarily teaching institutions, and their scarcity in a competitive recruitment market means that their power over both what kinds of course are offered and how they are delivered is greatly increased. Teachers retain significant operational power, to ensure that the institution is able to respond to market changes, but teachers enjoy little criteria power, and there is less evidence of a professorial group with significant criteria power. Government and funding councils remain very powerful, largely at arm's length.

This set of diagrams illustrates how overall patterns of power and control in HE are changing. The four types might again be seen as ideal types rather than accurate descriptions of any particular institution. Universities and colleges have become more diverse and fragmented, demonstrating how the changes in the external environment have affected institutions differently. Fragmentation of the system is a reflection of increased government power combined with greater market pressures and increased competition.

In the dynamic and continuously changing pattern of national provision, the power stakeholder analysis suggests that there are important trends towards both convergence and divergence in the system. 'Professional market' and 'managerial market' institutions are becoming more alike. Why? Some new universities have responded to the opportunity and pressure of the research assessment exercise and have consciously increased and focused their research efforts in a bid to enhance their reputation. Simultaneously, some of the 'old' universities, especially those losing ground in the concentration of resources for research, are becoming increasingly subject to market forces, student consumerism, teaching quality exercises and funding pressures.

In contrast, a comparison of 'autonomous professional' and 'market bureaucratic' types reveals the growing divergence in the system. Autonomous professional institutions, perhaps exemplified by the Russell Group, are clearly driven by entirely different concerns and pressures than are market bureaucracies, among whom we might place some colleges, especially those which continue to offer a mix of further and higher education courses.

Finally what does this changing pattern of control in HE and of HE in the UK signify? Evidently, in the decade from the mid-1980s to the mid-1990s the HE system became increasingly diverse, with convergence between some old and new universities counterbalanced by the widening gulf between an elite 'Ivy League' and some of the newer HE institutions. The purpose of this chapter was primarily to articulate and describe the changes in values and control and the reasons for them, rather than to evaluate them and to offer alternative prescriptions. Questions about what society wants from its higher education system must be put alongside what society, in the form of government, its agencies or the consumers, is prepared to pay for it. The current trend of increasing student expectations through consumerism while reducing funding is producing a tension in some universities and colleges that is increasingly difficult to manage. In future, the pattern of HE may change even further as universities become more distinctively focused upon particular 'products' and 'markets' to meet a far more diverse group of student and research interests. Increased participation rates, lifelong learners and the need for more students to find paid employment during their degree programmes will influence the types of programmes, styles and modes of delivery that are offered. The experience of working in higher education will become increasingly diverse, as institutions adapt work contexts to meet the systemic pressures of convergence and divergence.

Conclusion

14

All Work and No Play?

Rob Cuthbert

Working in higher education is a serious business, but should we see it as all work and no play? For fun, I started to search the literature linking 'work' and 'play'. Drawing a blank, particularly as far as higher education is concerned, I tried 'humour' with little greater success, and then went looking for 'fun'. It transpired that, for example, there were only 29 occurrences of 'fun' anywhere in the British Educational Index,[1] with hardly any referring to higher education.

Is this lack of a sense of humour in the literature a serious problem? Surely 'everyone knows' that fun, humour and play are a major part of work? The general management literature recognizes this, but largely in its exhortatory 'tips for managers' mode. See, for example, Rogers *et al.* (1984), who translate Peters and Waterman's (1982) *In Search of Excellence: Lessons from America's Best-Run Companies* for an educational audience. They construe the lessons in seven categories, one of which is 'fun and excitement'.

Teachers recognize the importance of fun for effective teaching and learning, which is to say in *students'* work. Administrators, too, have fun; there are occasional glimpses of this in the 'an administrator remembers' corner of the literature. See, for example, Kennedy (1988), reflecting on 20 years as an admissions officer, Evitts (1994), arguing that having fun is one of the tricks of the trade for creative alumni directors, and Hunter and Kuh (1989) paying tribute to the work of Elizabeth Greenleaf in developing the student affairs profession: 'Having Some Fun Getting the Job Done'.

However, the importance of humour seems not yet to have penetrated mainstream literature about the staff experience of working in higher education. Its study would be another of the ways in which we can make higher education culture strange, as Delamont urges in Chapter 11. Indeed, anthropologists must be exempt from any criticism of ignoring the significance of humour. The anthropological study of 'joking relationships' has its echoes in studies of organizational culture. Linstead (1985) argues that humour in organizations depends for its effect on the appropriateness of the joke in the social structure. In particular a joke, whether spontaneous or 'canned', enables the reversal – within the humorous framework – of problematic social relations or patterns of control. Radcliffe-Brown's seminal anthropological study showed the function of joking as a device for handling the problematic 'mother's brother' relation in patriarchal cultures. Surely we may derive equal illumination by studying the role of humour in HE contexts which also embody problematic or ambiguous social relations. For example, consider: a university department which employs the vice chancellor's spouse as a research fellow; the relationships between staff governors and the vice chancellor or principal; and a faculty whose former dean(s) remain key members of staff under new management.

Humour, says Linstead, may be used either to create ambiguity or to promote closure. It is in effect a hypothetical exploration of alternative social structuring within the 'safe' framework of play: 'What humour does is to symbolically reverse and revalue myth' (Linstead, 1985: 762). Its subversive effect depends on the extent to which its hypotheses can be translated into organizational reality.

Yarwood (1995) conducted what he called 'a serious inquiry into unofficial organizational communication' and identified eight functions of humour: to alleviate boredom; to provide personal enjoyment (i.e. just for fun); a coping mechanism; to make difficult messages easier to convey; a medium for exploring latent hostility; to contribute to change because of its ambiguity; to contribute to socialization; and to sustain organizational culture. For our purposes I will divide these into three groups of functions: the individual or intrapersonal, the interpersonal and the organizational.

At the intrapersonal level, humour to alleviate boredom, or just for fun, is a very important part of working life, which every individual experiences. Its importance is shown, for example, by the frequency with which job advertisements and person specifications call for 'a good sense of humour'. However, at this level its meaning is also largely individual rather than collective – which is why we can speak of other people having a 'different sense of humour' or even lacking one altogether. Humour for intrapersonal purposes may be crucial in understanding the psychodynamics of organizational life (Hirschhorn, 1988), but here I will focus on the more shared, interpersonal and organizational, functions of humour.

As an interpersonal skill or device, humour, to use Yarwood's (1995) categories, can make difficult messages easier to convey, help to explore latent hostility or offer a mechanism for coping. To develop the argument, reflexively, let us tell a few jokes and stories and analyse their meaning.

The common experience of HE institutions in the 1990s is of continuing and rapid growth in workload and pressure. In such circumstances it is not surprising that the following joke became widely told:

I thought I saw the light at the end of the tunnel, but then I realized it was just somebody with a torch bringing more work.

Told in 'symmetrical joking' – that is, between persons of the same status (Yarwood, 1995: 83) – such a joke is a coping device to promote solidarity in the face of external pressures. In asymmetrical joking it might be a means for a manager introducing new work to make the difficult message easier to convey. Equally, it might help a staff member, responding to such new work, to broach the hostility which it engenders without making a direct attack on the manager. Choosing how and when to use humour in such circumstances is an interpersonal skill which can do much to facilitate communication about the most difficult issues at work. Jokes can be seriously useful.

At organizational level, Yarwood's categories of humour's functions cover contributing to change through ambiguity, contributing to socialization and sustaining organizational culture.

Humour can contribute to change through its ambiguity, or its reversal of accepted organizational values:

A large faculty faced a problem with three members of staff widely recognized as poor teachers. In private management group discussion of whether to establish a teaching and learning committee, a colleague joked that the committee should comprise the three problem staff. Everyone laughed and then moved on to examine more serious suggestions.

At the end of the next faculty board meeting the dean, under 'Any other business', proposed that a teaching methods committee should be established to investigate and report on effective teaching methods. Heads nodded; the need was well recognized, as was the dean's habit of springing important items on the board in this way. The dean proposed that he should chair the committee and that it should have a small membership. Heads nodded again; the dean was still running true to form. The dean then proposed that the committee's members should be ... the three problem teachers. Silence fell, a mixture of embarrassment and wonder – is he joking? With silence taken as assent, the committee was established forthwith.

Its members were enthused. They studied teaching methods in other faculties and other institutions, and produced long reports that no one, except perhaps the dean, read. The reports made no difference to the teaching of anyone in the faculty – except the three committee members. Two became significantly better, albeit no better than average, performers as teachers. The third did not, but left the teaching profession a year later.

The initial joke reversed the accepted values: committees should be constructed on the basis of knowledge and expertise, or of political constituency, but not on the basis of lack of competence. The dean was able to see beyond the joke, make the hypothesis real and use it to bring about change.

Humour can explore problematic organizational relationships, such as those where a powerful deputy chief executive who 'runs things' can make power relations ambiguous. In what circumstances does the department head take the risky course of pursuing with the chief executive a request rejected by the deputy? Jokes can help define respective roles and boundaries:

> The principal is the shepherd of his flock, and the vice principal is the crook on his staff.[2]

The joke tells us that the principal is the unsullied academic leader as hero, while the deputy does the 'dirty work'; it guides others in the organization in terms of which issues should be raised with which manager, and how. Thus it helps socialization and maintenance of culture: it explains 'how we do things around here'.

> A college adopted a matrix structure to replace the former structure of discipline-based departments. The new organization structure was the subject of much discussion, writing and philosophizing led by the social scientists and humanities staff. The engineers and natural scientists, while including among their number some enthusiasts for the new structure, were more critical of the proliferation of new roles and jobs in the new organization. A cartoon drawn by one of the engineers showed one person saying to another: 'This is a matrix organization. That's why there's so much post-multiplication.' The college principal, himself an engineer, had the framed cartoon hanging on his office wall.

To mathematicians, scientists and engineers, a matrix is familiar as an ordered array of elements, and post-multiplication is a familiar kind of manipulation of the array. The joke lies in the pun, with the displaced concept of 'matrix' still being meaningfully paired with the displaced term 'post-multiplication'. To those who understand it, this is at best mildly amusing, but there is some symmetry and elegance in the pun, of a kind which appeals to the mathematical mind. Others need to have the joke explained, as I have just done, and even then it will not raise so much as a smile. Understood in context, *this is the point of the joke*. It is a commentary on the predictable and ultimately trivial concerns of the social sciences, and their subordination to superior natural science disciplines, as seen by the latter. It depends on an understanding only available to the scientist, and its display in the principal's office implicitly asserts the superiority of the 'hard' sciences, and their disdain for the fleeting enthusiasms of their social science colleagues.

In this case humour is being used to subvert the (implied to be) temporary organizational triumphs of one group and reassert the 'natural order'. It is also being used by the principal to placate the technologists resisting the new order, by reminding them of what matters in the long run, and whose side he is on. Humour is used to mark, or to reframe, organizational relationships of superiority or subordination. Duncan (1985) has argued for a 'superiority theory of humour at work' based on his analysis of joking relationships in small task groups. Similarly, Yarwood (1995) says that the ultimate implication of Radcliffe-Brown's thesis is that joking relationships serve the function of maintaining the distance between leaders and the rank and file. The principal's cartoon is perhaps an illustration at organizational level of the role that joking relationships can play in indicating status and status patterns.

In any case, the joke helps us to interpret the context and the culture. It tells us what is important and how it has different meanings to different groups in the college. Its ambiguity is not exhausted by the foregoing analysis. For example, to some people it might mean no more than that the principal had a strange sense of humour – a different message, but no less powerful as a guide to dealing with him.

Yarwood (1995: 89) suggests that 'Much mirth in organizations results from the juxtaposition of the naturalness and common sense of traditional institutions with the forced mechanical nature of bureaucracies. Out of such comparisons came Parkinson's Law, the Peter Principle and Catch-22.' Academic life has in similar vein generated its own principles. F. M. Cornford's (1908) Principle of the Wedge (never do anything, however small – it will be the thin end of the wedge) and Principle of Unripe Time (it is never the right time to do anything for the first time) can perhaps be explained by invoking Yarwood's juxtaposition of the natural and the bureaucratic. However, the particular nature of academic work is also revealed by some particular academic jokes.

Clark Kerr's (1966) proposition that a university is a collection of disparate individuals united only by a common grievance over car parking (or, in colder climes, central heating) encapsulates in a joke the loosely coupled organized anarchy of the university (see Chapters 1 and 13). Henry Kissinger reputedly once remarked that the backbiting in academe is so vicious because the stakes are so low. This reflects in a joke the distinctiveness of academic values, by juxtaposing 'real world' values (consider the dictionary definition of 'academic' as meaning 'of no practical importance') with the values of higher education, where 'academic' debates are waged with passion.

Where the backbiting is perhaps too vicious to permit humour as a release, then humour may be displaced into fiction. Yarwood (1995: 89) argues, for public administration in general, that fiction can illuminate how the individual relates to the organization because 'The authors of popular literature showcase a more outrageous humour.' Tom Sharpe (1978) Malcolm Bradbury (1984), David Lodge (1985), Howard Jacobson (1993) and Laurie Taylor (1994) have all shown how outrageous humour can help us see more clearly the HE institutions we inhabit.

Sometimes humour may be the preserve of a licensed 'court jester', able to say the unsayable and offer the outrageous hypothesis that may contribute to change. Kets de Vries (1993, cited by Yarwood, 1995: 89) has argued that 'the power of the leader needs the folly of the fool. The interaction of the two keeps each – and the organization – in psychological equilibrium.' The argument also resonates with de Bono's (1970) arguments for the use of lateral thinking and novel linguistic devices to enable new approaches to be considered, and echoes Cohen and March's (1974) endorsement of 'sensible foolishness' as a means to effective decision making and choice in an organized anarchy.

Thus humour, fun and play are important in many ways, at many levels, in higher education. They help to maintain individual and organizational equilibrium. They are a vital part of interpersonal relationships. A joke can reassert the organizational order, or subvert it. Humour, creativity and organizational change are closely connected, if not inextricably linked. Thus, if we regard higher education as all work and no play we deny ourselves a full understanding of working in HE.

This prompts the question: why has research into HE neglected this important dimension of work experience? Part of the answer is the under-exploitation of anthropology, with its explicit interest in joking, as a perspective on HE contexts. Yet other disciplines might have, but in general have not, chosen to turn their attention to humour and play in HE work.

Jokes are perhaps particularly resistant to orthodox academic study, because they embody that antithesis of sound academic practice, the un-attributed quotation. The anthropologists might start to remedy their neglect of HE by exploring this phenomenon: the lack of a sense of humour in research into HE. Without such a study we run the risk of confining the study of work in HE to a humourless perspective. The argument reflects Tausky's (1992: 3) point that 'the sociology of work would benefit from greater sensitivity to preconceptions'. Tausky argues in particular that most sociologists of work align themselves with one or other of two perspectives he labels 'pessimistic' and 'optimistic'. The Freud-inspired pessimistic perspective sees work as an inherently unpleasant activity in which behaviour is shaped by extrinsic rewards – money, status, power. On the other hand, a Marx-inspired optimistic perspective sees work as inherently desirable rather than loathsome, with behaviour driven by intrinsic rewards of challenge, growth and accomplishment.

We know something about academics' orientations to work; whether those *other than* academic staff, whose experience is largely ignored in the literature, would incline to an optimistic or pessimistic view of work is an empirical question of considerable importance, not least for the issues raised in the first part of this book, 'The workers'. It would be ironic if academics, who would generally see the optimistic perspective as better capturing their own view of work, managed through their work to establish the dominance of the opposite, pessimistic view.

If you have taken the time to read all of this book, you probably began in the optimistic camp, and I trust that the book has not altered your view in this respect. I hope you have found the contributions in turns fun, enjoyable, playful and stimulating new perspectives on unduly familiar phenomena. Higher education is not all work and no play: perhaps in thinking about working in higher education we should take ourselves less seriously.

Notes

1. I would like to acknowledge the substantial help of Judith Stewart in conducting literature searches for this purpose.
2. Jokes are rarely politically correct. It is tempting to speculate that political correctness is anti-joking precisely because political correctness is an attempt at control, and humour is essentially subversive rather than conducive to control.

References

Abbott, A. (1993) The sociology of work and occupations, *Annual Review of Sociology*, 19, 187–209.

Abercrombie, N., Hill, S. and Turner, B. S. (1984) *The Penguin Dictionary of Sociology*. London: Penguin.

Acker, S. (1989) Rethinking teachers' careers, in S. Acker (ed.) *Teachers, Genders and Careers*. Lewes: Falmer Press.

Adair, J. (1986) *Effective Team Building*. Aldershot: Gower.

Aisenberg, N. and Harrington, M. (1988) *Women of Academe: Outsiders in the Sacred Grove*. Amherst, MA: University of Massachusetts Press.

Albo, G. (1994) 'Competitive austerity' and the impasse of capitalist employment policy, in R. Miliband and L. Panitch (eds) *Between Globalism and Nationalism*. London: Merlin Press.

Ardener, E. (1972) Belief and the problem of women, in J. La Fontaine (ed.) *The Interpretation of Ritual*. London: Tavistock.

Ardener, S. (1975) Introduction, in S. Ardener (ed.) *Perceiving Women*. London: Dent.

Argyris, C. (1990) *Overcoming Organizational Defenses: Facilitating Organizational Learning*. Hemel Hempstead: Allyn and Bacon.

Armstrong, M. and Murlis, H. (1994) *Reward Management: a Handbook of Remuneration Strategy and Practice*, 3rd edn. London: Kogan Page.

Arnot, M., David, M. and Weiner, G. (1996) *Educational Reforms and Gender Equality in Schools*. Manchester: Equal Opportunities Commission.

Ashworth, P. and Saxton, J. (1990) On competence, *Journal of Further and Higher Education*, 14(2), 3–25.

Aspden, P. (1994) Carp pool reflections, on the art of doubt, *Times Higher Education Supplement*, 22 April.

Association of Graduate Recruiters (1995) *Skills for Graduates in the 21st Century*. London: AGR.

Association of University Teachers (1993) *Part-Time, Poor Deal – a Survey of Part-time Staff in the Traditional Universities*. London: AUT.

Association of University Teachers (1994) *Promoting Professionalism*. London: AUT.

Atkinson, P. A. (1981) Inspecting classroom talk, in C. Adelman (ed.) *Uttering, Muttering*. London: Grant McIntyre.

Atkinson, P. A. (1988) Ethnomethodology: a critical review, *Annual Review of Sociology*, 14, 441–65.

Bagilhole, B. (1993) Survivors in a male preserve – a study of British women academics' experiences and perceptions of discrimination in a UK university, *Higher Education*, 26(4), 431–47.

Ball, S. J. and Goodson, I. F. (1985) Understanding teachers: concepts and contexts, in S. J. Ball and I. F. Goodson (eds) *Teachers' Lives and Careers*. Lewes: Falmer Press.

Ban, C. (1995) *How Do Public Managers Manage?* San Francisco: Jossey-Bass.

Barnes, M. and Prior, D. (1995) Spoilt for choice? How consumerism can disempower public service users, *Public Money and Management*, July–September 1995, 53–8.

Barnett, R. (1989) *How Shall We Assess Them?* London: Council for National Academic Awards.

Barnett, R. (1990) *The Idea of Higher Education*. Buckingham: SRHE and Open University Press.

Barnett, R. (ed.) (1992) *Learning to Effect*. Buckingham: SRHE and Open University Press.

Barnett, R. (1994) *The Limits of Competence*. Buckingham: SRHE and Open University Press.

Becher, T. (1981) Towards a definition of disciplinary cultures, *Studies in Higher Education*, 6(2), 109–22.

Becher, T. (1989) *Academic Tribes and Territories: Intellectual Enquiry and the Culture of Disciplines*. Milton Keynes: SRHE and Open University Press.

Becher, T. (1990) The counter-culture of specialisation, *European Journal of Education*, 25(3), 333–46.

Becher, T. (1994) The significance of disciplinary differences, *Studies in Higher Education*, 19(2), 151–61.

Becker, H. S. (1971) Footnote added to the paper by Wax, M. and Wax, R. (1971) Great tradition, little tradition and formal education, in M. Wax *et al.* (eds) *Anthropological Perspectives on Education*. New York: Basic Books.

Becker, H. S., Geer, B. and Hughes, E. (1968) *Making the Grade*. Chicago: The University of Chicago Press.

Becker, H. S., Geer, B., Strauss, A. L. and Hughes, E. (1961) *Boys in White*. Chicago: The University of Chicago Press.

Belbin, R. M. (1992) *Management Teams: Why They Succeed or Fail*. Oxford: Butterworth/ Heinemann.

Berdahl, R. (1983) Co-ordinating structures: the UGC and US state co-ordinating agencies, in M. L. Shattock (ed.) *The Structure and Governance of Higher Education*. Guildford: SRHE.

Berkowitz, L. (ed.) (1978) *Group Processes*. New York: Academic Press.

Berne, E. (1967) *Games People Play: the Psychology of Human Relationships*. Harmondsworth: Penguin.

Billing, D. (1996) Review of modular implementation in a university, *Higher Education Quarterly*, 50(1), 1–21.

Blau, P. M. (1973) *The Organization of Academic Work*. New York: Wiley.

Bourdieu, P. (1988) *Homo Academicus*. Cambridge: Polity.

Boyer, E., Altbach, P. and Whitelaw, M. J. (1994) *The Academic Profession: an International Perspective*. Princeton, NJ: Carnegie Foundation for the Advancement of Teaching.

Bradbury, M. (1984) *The History Man*. London: Arrow Books.

Bradford, M. G. (1993) Population change and education school rolls and rationalisation before and after the 1988 Education Reform Act, in T. Champion (ed.) *Population Matters: the Local Dimension*. London: Paul Chapman Publishing.

Bradford, M. G. (1995) Diversification and division in the English education system: towards a post-Fordist model?, *Environment and Planning*, A 27, 1595–1612.

Bradley, J. and Eachus, P. (1995) Occupational stress within a UK higher educational institution, *International Journal of Stress Management*, 2(3), 145–58.

Brennan, J., Kogan, M. and Teichler, U. (1995) *Higher Education and Work*. London: Jessica Kingsley Publishers.

Brew, A. (ed.) (1995) *Directions in Staff Development.* Buckingham: SRHE and Open University Press.

Brosan, G. (1971) An array of institutions, in G. Brosan, C. Carter, R. Layard, P. Venables and G. Williams (eds) *Patterns and Policies in Higher Education.* Harmondsworth: Penguin.

Carroll, D. and Cross, G. (1989) *University Stress Survey.* Research report, School of Psychology, University of Birmingham.

Carter, I. (1990) *Ancient Cultures of Conceit: British University Fiction in the Post-War Years.* London: Routledge.

Carter, N. (1989) Performance indicators: 'backseat driving' or 'hands off' control?, *Policy and Politics,* 17(2), 131–8.

Casanova, U. (1991) *Elementary School Secretaries, the Women in the Principal's Office.* Newbury Park, CA: Corwin.

Cave, M., Hanney, S. and Kogan, M. (1991) *The Use of Performance Indicators in Higher Education: a Critical Analysis of Developing Practice,* 2nd edn. London: Jessica Kingsley Publishers.

Clark, B. R. (1983) *The Higher Education System.* Berkeley: University of California Press.

Clark, B. R. (ed.) (1984) *Perspectives on Higher Education: Eight Disciplinary and Comparative Views.* Berkeley, Los Angeles: University of California Press.

Clark, B. R. (1987a) *The Academic Life: Small Worlds, Different Worlds.* Princeton, NJ: Carnegie Foundation for the Advancement of Teaching.

Clark, B. R. (1987b) *The Academic Profession: National, Disciplinary and Institutional Settings.* Berkeley, Los Angeles: University of California Press.

Clark, B. R. (1993) The research foundations of post-graduate education, *Higher Education Quarterly,* 47, 301–15.

Clark, B. R. (1994) The research–teaching–study nexus in modern systems of higher education, *Higher Education Policy,* 7(1), 11–17.

Clayton, M. (1993) Towards total quality management in higher education at Aston University: a case study, *Higher Education,* 25, 363–71.

Cohen, M. D. and March, J. G. (1974) *Leadership and Ambiguity: the American College President.* New York: McGraw-Hill.

Cohen, M. D., March, J. G. and Olsen, J. P. (1972) A garbage can model of organizational choice, *Administrative Science Quarterly,* 17(1), 1–25.

Commission on University Career Opportunity (1994) *A Report on Universities' Policies and Practices on Equal Opportunities in Employment.* London: CUCO.

Committee of Vice Chancellors and Principals (1985) *Report of the Steering Committee for Efficiency Studies in Universities.* The Jarratt Report. London: CVCP.

Committee of Vice Chancellors and Principals (1993) *Promoting People: a Strategic Framework for the Management and Development of Staff in UK Universities.* London: CVCP.

Committee of Vice Chancellors and Principals (1994) *Universities and Communities.* A Report by the Centre for Urban and Regional Development Studies. London: CVCP.

Committee of Vice Chancellors and Principals (1995) *Strategy Paper on Vocational Higher Education.* London: CVCP.

Confederation of British Industry (1995) *The CBI Response to the Department for Education Review of Higher Education.* London: CBI (mimeo).

Cornford, F. M. (1908) Microcosmographia academica, in G. Johnson (ed., 1994) *University Politics.* Cambridge: Cambridge University Press.

Corrall, S. (1993) The access model: managing the transformation at Aston University, *Inter-lending and Document Supply,* 21(4), 13–23.

Corrall, S. (1995) Academic libraries in the information society, *New Library World,* 96(1120), 35–42.

Cottrell, P. (1995) Time to take control – accreditation and university teaching, *AUT Bulletin,* 201, 8–9.

Council for Industry and Higher Education (1995) *A Wider Spectrum of Opportunities*. London: CIHE.

Coxon, A. P. M. (1983) A cookery class for men, in A. Murcott (ed.) *A Sociology of Food and Eating*. Aldershot: Gower.

Cuthbert, R. E. (1987) Efficiency and the market mechanism in further and higher education, in H. Thomas and T. Simkins (eds) *Economics and the Management of Education: Emerging Themes*. Lewes: Falmer Press.

Cuthbert, R. E. (ed.) (1988) *Going Corporate*. Blagdon, Bristol: Further Education Staff College.

Daiches, D. (1964) *The Idea of a New University: an Experiment in Sussex*. London: Deutsch.

Davies, H. (1995) Setting an industrial standard for higher education, *AUT Bulletin*, 201, 4–5.

Davies, R. (1988) *The Lyre of Orpheus*. Harmondsworth: Penguin Books.

Dearing, R. (1994) *The National Curriculum and its Assessment: a Final Report*. London: Schools Curriculum and Assessment Authority.

Dearing, R. (1995a) *Review of the 16–19 Qualification Framework: Summary of the Interim Report. The Issues for Consideration*. London: Central Office for Information.

Dearing, R. (1995b) The McKechnie Lecture, University of Liverpool, quoted in Association of Graduate Recruiters (1995) *Skills for Graduates in the 21st Century*. London: AGR.

Dearing, R. (1996) *Review of Qualifications for 16–19 Year Olds: Full Report*. Hayes, Middlesex: SCAA Publications.

de Bono, E. (1970) *Lateral Thinking: a Textbook of Creativity*. Harmondsworth: Penguin.

Delamont, S. (1983) *Interaction in the Classroom*, 2nd edn. London: Methuen.

Delamont, S. (1989a) *Knowledgeable Women*. London: Routledge.

Delamont, S. (1989b) Gender and British postgraduate funding policy, *Gender and Education*, 1(1), 51–7.

Delamont, S. (1991) The HIT LIST and other horror stories, *Sociological Review*, 39(2), 238–59.

Delamont, S. and Atkinson, P. (1995) *Fighting Familiarity*. Cresskill, NJ: Hampton.

Department of Education and Science (1985) *The Development of Higher Education into the 1990s*. Cmnd 9524. London: HMSO.

Department of Education and Science (1987) *Higher Education: Meeting the Challenge*. Cm 114. London: HMSO.

Department of Education and Science (1991) *Higher Education – a New Framework*. Cm 1541. London: HMSO.

Department for Education (1994) *Higher Education in the 1990s*. London: DFE.

Derrida, J. (1992) Mochlos; or the conflict of the faculties, in R. Rand (ed.) *Logomachia: the Conflict of the Faculties*. Lincoln: University of Nebraska Press.

Dill, D. D. (1996) Academic planning and organizational design: lessons from leading American universities, *Higher Education Quarterly*, 50(1), 35–53.

Doherty, G. D. (1993) Towards total quality management in higher education: a case study of the University of Wolverhampton, *Higher Education*, 25, 321–39.

Dumont, R. V. and Wax, M. L. (1971) Cherokee school society and the inter-cultural classroom, *Human Organisation*, 28, 217–26.

Duncan, W. J. (1985) The superiority theory of humour at work – joking relationships as indicators of formal and informal status patterns in small, task-oriented groups, *Small Group Behavior*, 16(4), 556–64.

Eggleston, J. F. and Delamont, S. (1983) *Supervision of Students for Research Degrees*. Kendal: Dixon Printing Company for BERA.

Eickelman, D. (1978) The art of memory, *Comparative Studies in Society and History*, 20(4), 485–516.

Eickelman, D. (1985) *Knowledge and Power in Morocco*. Princeton, NJ: Princeton University Press.

Eisenstadt, M. (1995) Overt strategy for global learning, *Times Higher Education Supplement (Multimedia Features)*, 7 April.

Elgqvist-Saltzman, I. (1992) Straight roads and winding tracks: Swedish educational policy from a gender equality perspective, *Gender and Education. Special Issue: Women's Education In Europe*, 1(2), 41–56.

Eurich, N. (1983) *Corporate Classrooms: the Learning Business*. Princeton, NJ: Carnegie Foundation for the Advancement of Learning.

Evans, C. (1988) *Language People: the Experience of Teaching and Learning Modern Languages in British Universities*. Milton Keynes: SRHE and Open University Press.

Evans, C. (1993) *English People*. Buckingham: SRHE and Open University Press.

Evitts, W. J. (1994) New tricks of the trade, *Currents*, 20(7), 40–4.

Farish, M., McPake, J., Powney, J. and Weiner, G. (1995) *Equal Opportunities in Colleges and Universities: towards Better Practices*. Buckingham: SRHE and Open University Press.

FEFC (1994) *Derby College Wilmorton*. A report of an enquiry by M. Shattock, OBE. Coventry: Further Education Funding Council.

Fielden, J. (1975) The decline of the professor and the rise of the registrar, in C. F. Page (ed.) *Power and Authority in Higher Education*. Guildford: Society for Research into Higher Education.

Fielden, J. and Lockwood, G. (1973) *Planning and Management in Universities: a Study of British Universities*. London: Chatto and Windus.

Finegold, D., Keep, E., Miliband, D., Robertson, D., Sisson, K. and Ziman, J. (1992) *Higher Education – Expansion and Reform*. London: Institute of Public Policy Research.

Finer, C. J. (1995) Teaching quality audit, *Social Policy and Administration*, 29(4), 365–70.

Fisher, S. (1994) *Stress in Academic Life: the Mental Assembly Line*. Buckingham: SRHE and Open University Press.

Fitzgerald, M. (1995) A challenge to some sacred cows, *Times Higher Education Supplement*, 6 January.

Fitzgerald, T. H. (1988) Can change in culture really be managed?, *Organizational Dynamics*, 17(2), 5–15.

Fowler, H. W. and Fowler, F. G. (eds) (1964) *The Concise Oxford Dictionary of Current English*. Oxford: Clarendon Press.

French, P. and MacLure, M. (eds) (1979) Getting the right answer and getting the answer right, *Research in Education*, 22(1), 1–23.

French, P. and MacLure, M. (eds) (1981) *Adult–Child Conversation*. London: Croom Helm.

Fulton, O. (1981) Principles and policies, in O. Fulton (ed.) *Access to Higher Education*. Guildford: SRHE.

Fulton, O. (1993) Paradox or professional closure? Criteria and procedures for recruitment to the academic profession, *Higher Education Management*, 5(2), 161–71.

Fulton, O. (1996) Mass access and the end of diversity? The academic profession in England on the eve of structural reform, in P. Altbach (ed.) *The International Academic Profession: Portraits from Fourteen Countries*. Princeton, NJ: Carnegie Foundation for the Advancement of Teaching.

Furniss, W. T. (1981) *Reshaping Faculty Careers*. One Dupont Circle. Washington, DC: American Council on Education.

Geddes, T. (1993) The total quality initiative at South Bank University, *Higher Education*, 25, 341–61.

Geer, B. (1964) First days in the field, in P. Hammond (ed.) *Sociologists at Work*. New York: Basic Books.

Geer, B. (ed.) (1972) *Learning to Work*. Beverly Hills, CA: Sage.

Gell, M. and Cochrane, P. (1995) Turbulence signals a lucrative experience, *Times Higher Education Supplement (Multimedia Features)*, 10 March.

Gellert, C. (1991) Review of main developments, in Organization for Economic Cooperation and Development, *Alternatives to Universities*. Paris: OECD.

Giddens, A. (1984) *The Constitution of Society: Outline of a Theory of Structuration.* Cambridge: Polity Press.

Glaser, B. and Strauss, A. (1967) *The Discovery of Grounded Theory.* Chicago: Aldine.

Goodlad, S. (1995) *The Quest for Quality: Sixteen Forms of Heresy in Higher Education.* Buckingham: SRHE and Open University Press.

Gouldner, A. (1957) Cosmopolitans and locals: toward an analysis of latent social roles, *Administrative Science Quarterly,* 2, 281–306.

Graham, D. with Tytler, D. (1993) *A Lesson for Us All: the Making of the National Curriculum.* London: Routledge.

Gramsci, A. (1971) The formation of the intellectuals, in *Selections from the Prison Notebooks.* London: Lawrence and Wishart.

Granfield, R. (1992) *Making Elite Lawyers.* New York: Routledge.

Greenberg, J. (1995) On the open highway in search of serious money, *Times Higher Education Supplement (Multimedia Features),* 7 April.

Greenhalgh, T. (1995) Virtual lab for robotics goes on net, *Times Higher Education Supplement,* 10 February.

Gronn, P. C. (1983) After T. B. Greenfield, whither educational administration? Paper for the British Educational Management and Administration Society Conference, Manchester, September.

Guest, D. (1995) Why do people work?, in IPD National Conference Proceedings.

Hague, D. (1991) *Beyond Universities – a New Republic of the Intellect.* Hobart Paper 115. London: Institute of Economic Affairs.

Halsey, A. H. (1982) The decline of donnish dominion, *Oxford Review of Education,* 8(3), 215–30.

Halsey, A. H. (1987) Who owns the curriculum of higher education?, *Journal of Education Policy,* 2(4), 341–5.

Halsey, A. H. (1992) *Decline of Donnish Dominion: the British Academic Profession in the Twentieth Century.* Oxford: Clarendon Press.

Halsey, A. H. and Trow, M. (1971) *The British Academics.* London: Faber and Faber.

Hammersley, M. (1977) School learning, in P. Woods and M. Hammersley (eds) *School Experience.* London: Croom Helm.

Hammond, C. (1992) Information and research support services: the reference librarian and the information paraprofessional, *Reference Librarian,* 37, 91–104.

Handy, C. (1979) *Gods of Management.* London: Pan.

Handy, C. (1991) *The Age of Unreason,* 2nd edn. London: Arrow Books.

Harding, S. (ed.) (1987) *Feminism and Methodology.* Bloomington, IN: Indiana University Press.

Hargreaves, D. H. (1984) Teacher's questions, *Educational Research,* 26(1), 46–52.

Harman, K. M. (1990) Culture and conflict in academic organisation, *Journal of Educational Administration,* 27(3), 30–54.

Hart, A. (1995) Going for careers – not just jobs, *NATFHE Journal,* Autumn, 16–17.

Hartle, F. (1995) *How to Re-engineer the Performance Management Process.* London: Kogan Page.

Haselgrove, S. (ed.) (1994) *The Student Experience.* Buckingham: SRHE and Open University Press.

Haslam, C., Bryman, A. and Webb, A. (1993) The impact of staff appraisal in universities, *Higher Education Management,* 5(2), 213–21.

Hayek, F. A. (1988) *The Fatal Conceit: the Errors of Socialism.* London: Routledge.

Heckscher, C. (1994) Defining the post-bureaucratic type, in C. Heckscher and A. Donnellon (eds) *The Post-Bureaucratic Organization.* London: Sage.

Herriot, P. (1992) *The Career Management Challenge: Balancing Individual and Organizational Needs.* London: Sage.

Heseltine, R. (1994) A critical appraisal of the role of global networks in the transformation of higher education, *Alexandria,* 6(3), 159–71.

Heseltine, R. (1995) The challenge of learning in cyberspace, *Library Association Record*, 97(8), 432–3.

Heward, C. and Taylor, P. (1993) Effective and ineffective equal opportunities policies in higher education, *Critical Social Policy*, 37, 75–94.

Heyl, B. (1979) *The Madam as Entrepreneur.* New Brunswick, NJ: Transaction Books.

Higgins, M. A. (1991) The student market, *Higher Education Quarterly*, 45(1), 14–24.

Higher Education Funding Council for England (1994) *Accountability for Research Funds.* Circular 4/94. Bristol: HEFCE.

Higher Education Funding Council for England (1995a) *Higher Education in Further Education Colleges: Funding the Relationship.* Bristol: HEFCE.

Higher Education Funding Council for England (1995b) *Quality Assessment of Geography 1994–5. Subject Overview.* Report QO 11/95. Bristol: HEFCE.

Higher Education Quality Council (1994) *Learning from Audit.* London: HEQC.

Higher Education Quality Council (1995) *Investors in People Network for Higher Education Institutions*, Issue 4, August (mimeo). London: HEQC.

Higher Education Statistics Agency (1995) *Data Report – Students in Higher Education Institutions.* Cheltenham: HESA.

Higher Education Statistics Agency (1996) *Resources in Higher Education.* Cheltenham: HESA.

Hill, F. M. (1995) Managing service quality in higher education: the role of the student as primary consumer, *Quality Assurance in Education*, 3(3), 10–21.

Hirschhorn, L. (1988) *The Workplace Within: Psychodynamics of Organizational Life.* Boston: MIT Press.

Hirst, P. (1994) *Associative Democracy.* Cambridge: Polity Press.

Hobbs, D. (1988) *Doing the Business.* Milton Keynes: Open University Press.

Hofstede, G. (1991) *Cultures and Organisations: Software of the Mind.* London: McGraw-Hill.

Holland, J. and Eisenhart, M. (1990) *Educated in Romance.* Chicago: The University of Chicago Press.

Holmes, G. (1993) Quality assurance in further and higher education: a sacrificial lamb on the altar of managerialism, *Quality Assurance in Education*, 1(1), 4–8.

Hooijberg, R. and Petrock, F. (1993) On cultural change: using the competing values framework to help leaders execute a transformational strategy, *Human Resources Management*, 31(1), 29–50.

Hoskin, K. and Macve, R. (1993) Accounting as discipline: the overlooked supplement, in E. Messer-Davidov *et al.* (eds) *Knowledges – Historical and Critical Studies in Disciplinarity.* Charlottesville: The University Press of Virginia.

House, D. and Watson, D. (1995) Managing change, in D. Warner and E. Crosthwaite (eds) *Human Resource Management in Higher and Further Education.* Buckingham: SRHE and Open University Press.

Howarth, A. (1991) Market forces in higher education, *Higher Education Quarterly*, 45(1), 5–13.

Huber, L. (1990) Disciplinary cultures and social reproduction, *European Journal of Education*, 25(3), 241–61.

Hughes, C. A. (1992) A comparison of perceptions of campus priorities – the logical library in an organised anarchy, *Journal of Academic Librarianship*, 18(3), 140–5.

Hunter, D. E. and Kuh, G. D. (1989) Elizabeth Adele Greenleaf: having some fun getting the job done, *Journal of Counseling and Development*, 67(6), 322–31.

Incomes Data Services (1996) *Pay in the Public Services: Review of 1995 and Prospects for 1996.* London: IDS.

Jacobson, H. (1993) *Coming From Behind.* Harmondsworth: Penguin.

Jencks, C. and Riesman, R. (1968) *The Academic Revolution.* New York: Doubleday.

Jenkins, A. (1995) The impact of research assessment exercises on teaching in selected geography departments in England and Wales, *Geography*, 80, 367–74.

Jessup, G. (1991) *Outcomes*. London: Falmer Press.

John Fielden Consultancy (1993) *Supporting Expansion: a Report on Human Resource Management in Academic Libraries, for the Joint Funding Councils Libraries Review Group*. Bristol: The Higher Education Funding Councils for England, Scotland and Wales.

Johnes, G. and Cave, M. (1994) The development of competition among higher education institutions, in W. Bartlett, C. Propper, D. Wilson and J. Le Grand (eds) *Quasi-Markets in the Welfare State: the Emerging Findings*. Bristol: SAUS Publications.

Johnes, J. and Taylor, J. (1990) *Performance Indicators in Higher Education*. Buckingham: SRHE and Open University Press.

Johnson, G. (1994) *University Politics*. Cambridge: Cambridge University Press.

Johnston, R. J. (1993) Funding research: an exploration of inter-discipline variations, *Higher Education Quarterly*, 47, 357–72.

Johnston, R. J. (1996) And was it worth all the effort now that it's over?, *Journal of Geography in Higher Education*, 19 (in press).

Johnston, R. J., Jones, K. and Gould, M. (1995) Department size and research in English universities: inter-university variations, *Quality in Higher Education*, 1, 41–7.

Joint Funding Councils Libraries Review Group (1993) *Report*, Chairman Professor Sir Brian Follett. Bristol: The Higher Education Funding Councils for England, Scotland and Wales.

Kant, I. (1979) *The Conflict of the Faculties*. New York: Arbaris Books (original publication date 1798).

Kanter, R. M. (1983) *The Change Masters*. London: Unwin.

Keep, E. and Mayhew, K. (1995) The economic demand for higher education and investing in people: two aspects of sustainable development in British higher education, in F. Coffield (ed.) *Higher Education in a Learning Society*. Durham: Durham University School of Education.

Keep, E. and Sisson, K. (1992) Owning the problem: personnel issues in higher education policy-making in the 1990s, *Oxford Review of Economic Policy*, 8(2), 67–78.

Kennedy, A. M. (1988) Twenty secrets of twenty years, *Journal of College Admissions*, 121, 28–30.

Kerr, C. (1966) *The Uses of the University*. New York: Harper and Row.

Kets de Vries, M. (1993) *Leaders, Fools and Impostors*. San Francisco: Jossey-Bass.

Klein, J. (1993) Blurring, cracking, and crossing: permeation and the fracturing of discipline, in E. Messer-Davidov *et al.* (eds) *Knowledges – Historical and Critical Studies in Disciplinarity*. Charlottesville: The University Press of Virginia.

Koestler, A. (1964) *The Act of Creation*. London: Hutchinson and Co.

Kogan, M. (1984) The political view, in B. R. Clark (ed.) *Perspectives on Higher Education: Eight Disciplinary and Comparative Views*. Berkeley, Los Angeles: University of California Press.

Kogan, M. (1988) *Educational Accountability: an Analytic Overview*, 2nd edn. London: Hutchinson.

Kogan, M., El-Khawas, E. and Moses I. (1994) *Staffing Higher Education: Meeting New Challenges*. London: Jessica Kingsley Publishers.

Kotter, J. (1988) *The Leadership Factor*. New York: Free Press.

Kuhn, T. S. (1962) *The Structure of Scientific Revolutions*. Chicago: University of Chicago Press.

Lacey, C. (1977) *The Socialization of Teachers*. London: Methuen.

Langer, J. (1992) Austrian universities in transition: from ministerial control to market co-ordination, *Higher Education Policy*, 5(3), 21–3.

Lather, P. (1991) *Getting Smart*. London: Routledge.

Lawn, M. and Ozga, J. (1981) The educational worker: a reassessment of teachers, in L. Barton and S. Walker (eds) *Schools, Teachers and Teaching*. Lewes: Falmer Press.

Le Grand, J. (1991) Quasi-markets and social policy, *Economic Journal*, 101, 1256–67.

Leacock, S. and Leacock, R. (1975) *Spirits of the Deep*. New York: Doubleday.

Lenoir, T. (1993) The discipline of nature and the nature of disciplines, in E. Messer-Davidov *et al.* (eds) *Knowledges – Historical and Critical Studies in Disciplinarity*. Charlottesville: The University Press of Virginia.

Lester, R. (1979) Why educate the library user?, *Aslib Proceedings*, 31(8), 366–80.

Lester, R. (1984) User education in the online age, *Aslib Proceedings*, 36(2), 96–112.

Levy, P., Fowell, S. and Worsfold, E. (1996) Networked learner support, *Library Association Record*, 98(1), 34–5.

Lewis, J. L. (1992) *Ring of Liberation*. Chicago: The University of Chicago Press.

Lewis, P. (1993) Performance related pay in higher education: nine lessons . . . but no songs of praise, *Education and Training*, 35(2), 11–15.

Light, D. (1974) Introduction: the structure of the academic professions, *Sociology of Education*, 47(1), 2–28.

Linstead, S. (1985) Jokers wild: the importance of humour in the maintenance of organizational culture, *Sociological Review*, 33, 741–67.

Livingston, E. (1986) *The Ethnomethodological Foundations of Mathematics*. London: Routledge.

Locke, M. (1978) *Traditions and Controls in the Making of a Polytechnic: Woolwich Polytechnic 1890–1970*. London: Thames Polytechnic.

Lodge, D. (1985) *Small Worlds*. Harmondsworth: Penguin.

Loizos, P. (1975) *The Greek Gift*. Oxford: Basil Blackwell.

Lynch, M. (1985) *Art and Artifact in Laboratory Science*. London: Routledge.

MacFarlane, A. (1993) Time to get teaching on board, *Times Higher Education Supplement*, 13 May.

McInnis, C. (1992) Changes in the nature of academic work, *Australian Universities Review*, 35(2), 9–12.

Mackintosh, M., Jarvis, R. and Heery, E. (1994) On managing hybrids: some dilemmas in higher education management, *Financial Accountability and Management*, 10(4), 339–53.

McLellan, R. and Kelly, G. (1989) Business policy formulation: understanding the process, in D. Asch and C. Bowman (eds) *Readings in Strategic Management*. London: Macmillan/Open University.

MacLure, M. and French, P. (1980) Routes to right answers, in P. Woods (ed.) *Pupil Strategies*. London: Croom Helm.

McNay, I. (1995) From the collegial academy to corporate enterprise: the changing cultures of universities, in T. Schuller (ed.) *The Changing University?* Buckingham: SRHE and Open University Press.

Mannix, D. (1951) *Memoirs of a Sword Swallower*. London: Hamish Hamilton.

Massey, D. and Allen, J. (1995) High-tech places: poverty in the midst of growth, in C. Philo (ed.) *Off the Map: the Social Geography of Poverty in the UK*. London: CPAG Ltd.

Massey-Burzio, V. (1992) Reference encounters of a different kind: a symposium, *Journal of Academic Librarianship*, 18(5), 276–86.

Mercer, N. and Edwards, D. (1981) Ground rules for mutual understanding, in N. Mercer (ed.) *Language in School and Community*. London: Edward Arnold.

Messer-Davidov, E., Shumnay, D. and Sylvan, D. (eds) (1993) *Knowledges – Historical and Critical Studies in Disciplinarity*. Charlottesville: The University Press of Virginia.

Metcalfe, L. and Richards, S. (1990) *Improving Public Management*, rev. edn. London: Sage.

Michels, R. (1959) Democracy and the iron law of oligarchy, in *Political Parties*. New York: Dover Publications (original publication date 1915).

Middlehurst, R. (1993) *Leading Academics*. Buckingham: SRHE and Open University Press.

Middlehurst, R. and Elton, L. (1992) Leadership and management in higher education, *Studies in Higher Education*, 17(3), 251–64.

Miller, H. (1995) States, economies and the changing labour process of academics:

Australia, Canada and the United Kingdom, in J. Smyth (ed.) *Academic Work.* Buckingham: SRHE and Open University Press.

Mintzberg, H. (1991) The effective organization: forces and forms, *Sloan Management Review,* Winter, 54–67.

Mintzberg, H. (1994) The fall and rise of strategic planning, *Harvard Business Review,* January/February, 107–14.

Mintzberg, H. and Waters, J. A. (1989) Of strategies, deliberate and emergent, in D. Asch and C. Bowman (eds) *Readings in Strategic Management.* London: Macmillan/Open University.

Moodie, G. C. and Eustace, R. (1974) *Power and Authority in British Universities.* London: George Allen and Unwin.

Moore, W. E. (1970) *The Professions: Roles and Rules.* New York: Russell Sage.

Mouffe, C. (1993) *The Return of the Political.* London: Verso.

National Advisory Body (1987) *Management for a Purpose.* Report of the Good Management Practice Working Group. London: NAB.

National Commission on Education (1993) *Learning to Succeed.* London: Heinemann.

National Commission on Education (1995) *Learning to Succeed: the Way Forward.* London: NCE.

Neave, G. (1991) On visions of the market place, *Higher Education Quarterly,* 45(1), 25–40.

Newby, H. (1977) *The Deferential Worker.* London: Allen Lane.

Newman, J. H. (1976) *The Idea of a University* (ed. I. T. Ker). Oxford: Oxford University Press (original publication date 1853).

Newman, J. H. (1982) *The Idea of a University.* Indiana: University of Notre Dame Press.

Newman, J. (1994) Marking schemes are for dullards, *Times Higher Education Supplement,* 8 July.

Nohria, N. and Berkley, J. (1994) The virtual organization: bureaucracy, technology, and the implosion of control, in C. Heckscher and A. Donnellon (eds) *The Post-Bureaucratic Organization.* London: Sage.

Norris, G. (1978) *The Effective University: a Management by Objectives Approach.* Farnborough: Saxon House, Teakfield.

Norris, N. (1991) The trouble with competences, *Cambridge Journal of Education,* 21(3), 331–41.

Northern Examination and Assessment Board (1995) *Geography A-Level Syllabus,* amended and modular version 1997. Manchester: NEAB.

O'Leary, J. and Cannon, T. (1994) *The Times Good University Guide 1995–96,* 2nd edn. London: Times Books.

Organization for Economic Co-operation and Development (1993) *Pay Flexibility in the Public Sector.* Paris: OECD.

Ouchi, W. G. (1980) Markets, bureaucracies and clans, *Administrative Science Quarterly,* 25(1), 129–41.

Palmer, R. (1989) A career in higher education – challenging or cul-de-sac?, *Personnel Management,* April.

Parry, O., Atkinson, P. and Delamont, S. (1994) Disciplinary identities and doctoral work, in R. G. Burgess (ed.), *Postgraduate Education and Training in the Social Sciences.* London: Jessica Kingsley.

Parsons, T. and Platt, G. M. (1968) Considerations on the American academic system, *Minerva,* 4(4), 497–523.

Partington, P. (1994) Human resources management and development in higher education. Paper for the Quinquennial Conference of the Conference of European Rectors, Budapest. Sheffield: Universities' and Colleges' Staff Development Agency.

Payne, G. (1982) Dealing with a latecomer, in G. Payne and E. Cuff (eds) *Doing Teaching.* London: Batsford.

214   References

Payne, G. and Cuff, E. (eds) (1982) *Doing Teaching*. London: Batsford.

Payne, G. and Hustler, D. (1980) Teaching the class, *British Journal of the Sociology of Education*, 1(1), 49–66.

Pedler, M., Burgoyne, J. and Boydell, T. (1991) *The Learning Company*. London: McGraw-Hill.

Peters, T. (1989) *Thriving on Chaos*. London: Pan Books.

Peters, T. J. and Waterman, R. H. (1982) *In Search of Excellence: Lessons from America's Best-Run Companies*. New York: Harper and Row.

Pollitt, C. (1987) *Performance Measurement and the Consumer*. London: National Consumer Council.

Portillo, M. (1995) Speech to Confederation of British Industry Conference, 5 June.

Potter, J. (1988) Consumerism and the public sector: how well does the coat fit?, *Public Administration*, 66, 149–64.

Powney, J. and Weiner, G. (1992) *Outside of the Norm: Equity and Management in Educational Institutions*. London: South Bank University.

Pratchett, T. (1987) *Equal Rites*. London: Corgi.

Pratt, J. (1987) The economics of post-compulsory education, in H. Thomas and T. Simkins (eds) *Economics and the Management of Education: Emerging Themes*. Lewes: Falmer Press.

Pratt, J. (1990) Corporatism, competition and collegiality, *Reflections*, 2(2), 33–7.

Prigogine, I. and Stengers, I. (1985) *Order out of Chaos – Man's New Dialogue with Nature*. London: Fontana.

Propper, C., Bartlett, W. and Wilson, D. (1994) Introduction, in W. Bartlett, C. Propper, D. Wilson and J. Le Grand (eds) *Quasi-Markets in the Welfare State*. Bristol: SAUS Publications.

Quinn, R. E. (1988) *Beyond Rational Management: Mastering the Paradoxes and Competing Demands of High Performance*. San Francisco: Jossey-Bass.

Rice, R. E. (1992) Toward a broader conception of scholarship: the American context, in T. G. Whiston and R. L. Geiger (eds) *Research and Higher Education*. Buckingham: SRHE and Open University Press.

Rinderknecht, D. (1992) New norms for reference desk staffing: a comparative study, *College and Research Libraries*, 53(5), 429–36.

Rogers, V. R. *et al.* (1984) Excellence: some lessons from America's best-run companies, *Educational Leadership*, 41(5), 39–41.

Rooker, J. (1993) Opportunity and achievement, *Times Higher Educational Supplement*, 12 November.

Rorty, R. (1979) *Philosophy and the Mirror of Nature*. Princeton, NJ: Princeton University Press.

Rorty, R. (1989) *Contingency, Irony and Solidarity*. Cambridge: Cambridge University Press.

Rourke, F. E. and Brooks, G. E. (1966) *The Managerial Revolution in Higher Education*. Baltimore, MD: Johns Hopkins Press.

Sayer, A. (1995) *Radical Political Economy: a Critique*. Oxford: Blackwell Publishers.

Schein, E. H. (1985) *Organisational Culture and Leadership*. San Francisco: Jossey-Bass.

Schon, D. (1983) *The Reflective Practitioner*. New York: Basic Books.

School Curriculum and Assessment Authority (1995) *Looking Forward: Careers Education and Guidance in the Curriculum*. London: SCAA.

Schwartz, C. A. (1994) Scholarly communication as a loosely-coupled system – reassessing prospects for structural reform, *College and Research Libraries*, 55(2), 101–17.

Schwartzmann, S. (1994) Academics as a profession: what does it mean? Does it matter?, *Higher Education Policy*, 7(2), 24–6.

Schweizer, P. (1988) *Shepherds, Workers, Intellectuals*. Stockholm: University of Stockholm Press.

Scott, P. (1983) Has the binary policy failed?, in M. Shattock (ed.) *The Structure and Governance of Higher Education*. Guildford: SRHE.

Searle, J. (1972) *The Campus War*. Harmondsworth: Penguin.

Senge, P. (1993) *The Fifth Discipline: the Art and Practice of the Learning Organization.* London: Century Business.

Shapin, S. (1994) *A Social History of Truth.* Chicago: University of Chicago Press.

Sharp, P. R. (1987) *The Creation of the Local Authority Sector of Higher Education.* Lewes: Falmer Press.

Sharp, S. (1995) The quality of teaching and learning in higher education: evaluating the evidence, *Higher Education Quarterly,* 49(4), 301–15.

Sharpe, T. (1978) *Wilt.* London: Pan Books in association with Martin Secker and Warburg.

Shattock, M. L. (1981) University resource allocation procedures: responses to constraint, *International Journal of Institutional Management in Higher Education,* 5(3), 199–205.

Shumar, W. (1995) Higher education and the state: the irony of Fordism in American universities, in J. Smyth (ed.) *Academic Work: the Changing Labour Process in Higher Education.* Buckingham: SRHE and Open University Press.

Silver, H. (1990) *A Higher Education: the Council for National Academic Awards and British Higher Education 1964–1989.* London: Falmer Press.

Simon, H. A. (1976) Theories of decision-making in economics and behavioural science, in F. G. Castles *et al.* (eds), *Decisions, Organizations and Society.* Harmondsworth: Penguin.

Sizer, J. (1992) Can a funding council be a proxy for price competition in a competitive market?, *Higher Education Policy,* 5(3), 27–9.

Smiley, J. (1995) *Moo.* London: HarperCollins.

Smircich, L. (1983) Concepts of culture and organizational analysis, *Administrative Science Quarterly,* 28(3), 339–58.

Smyth, J. (ed.) (1995) *Academic Work: the Changing Labour Process in Higher Education.* Buckingham: SRHE and Open University Press.

Stanley, L. and Wise, S. (1993) *Breaking out Again.* London: Routledge.

Stiver-Lie, S., Malik, L. and Harris, D. (eds) (1994) *World Yearbook of Education 1994: the Gender Gap in Higher Education.* London: Kogan Page.

Stoner, J. A. F. (1961) A comparison of individual and group decisions involving risk, quoted in R. Brown (1965) *Social Psychology.* London: Collier-Macmillan.

Storey, J. and Sisson, K. (1993) *Managing Human Resources and Industrial Relations.* Buckingham: Open University Press.

Swann, W. (1992) Hardening the hierarchies: the National Curriculum as a system of classification, in T. Booth *et al.* (eds) *Curricula for Diversity in Education.* London: Routledge and Open University Press.

Targett, S. (1995) Keys to the wired valley, *Times Higher Education Supplement (Multimedia Features),* 7 April.

Tausky, C. (1992) Work is desirable/loathsome: Marx versus Freud, *Work and Occupations,* 19(1), 3–17.

Taylor, F. W. (1947) *Scientific Management.* London: Harper and Row.

Taylor, L. (1994) *The Laurie Taylor Guide to Higher Education.* Oxford: Butterworth/Heinemann.

Taylor, P. (1990) The impact of institutions of higher education on local income and employment: the case of Bristol Polytechnic, *Higher Education Review,* 22(2), 39–58.

Thomas, R. (1990) Corporate planning in a university, *Best of Long Range Planning,* 7, 93–101.

Tierney, W. G. and Rhoads, R. A. (1995) The culture of assessment, in J. Smyth (ed.) *Academic Work: the Changing Labour Process in Higher Education.* Buckingham: SRHE and Open University Press.

Tiffin, J. and Rajasingham, L. (1995) *In Search of the Virtual Class: Education in an Information Society.* London: Routledge.

Triesman, D. (1994) The Association of University Teachers – the first 75 years, *Supplement to the AUT Bulletin,* October.

Trix, F. (1993) *Spiritual Discourse.* Philadelphia: University of Pennsylvania Press.

Trow, M. (1992) Uncertainties in Britain's transition from elite to mass higher education, in T. G. Whiston and R. L. Geiger (eds) *Research and Higher Education: the United Kingdom and the United States*. Buckingham: SRHE and Open University Press.

Trow, M. (1994) Managerialism and the academic profession: the case of England, *Higher Education Policy*, 7(2), 11–18.

Tuckman, B. W. (1965) Developing sequences in small groups, *Psychological Bulletin*, 63, 384–99.

Turner, R. (ed.) (1971) *Ethnomethodology*. Harmondsworth: Penguin.

University Grants Committee (1967) *Report of the Committee on Libraries*, Chairman Sir Thomas Parry. London: HMSO.

Vickers, P. and Martyn, J. (eds) (1994) *The Impact of Electronic Publishing on Library Services and Resources in the UK: Report of the British Library Working Party on Electronic Publishing*. Library and Information Research Report 102. London: British Library.

Wagner, P. (1994) *A Sociology of Modernity: Liberty and Discipline*. London: Routledge.

Wallach, M. A. and Kogan, N. (1965) The roles of information, discussion and consensus in group risk-taking, *Journal of Experimental Social Psychology*, 1, 1–19.

Walsh, K. (1994) Health in the marketplace, in E. Tam (ed.) *Marketing, Competition and the Public Sector*. Harlow: Longman.

Ward, R. (1995) Industrial relations strategy and tactics, in D. Warner and E. Crosthwaite (eds) *Human Resource Management in Higher and Further Education*. Buckingham: SRHE and Open University Press.

Warden, R. (1995) Metaphor made real with an open mind, *Times Higher Education Supplement*, 13 October.

Warner, D. and Crosthwaite, E. (eds) (1995) *Human Resource Management in Higher and Further Education*. Buckingham: SRHE and Open University Press.

Wasser, H. (1994) Editorial, *Higher Education Policy*, 7(2), 7–9.

Watson, D. (1995) Quality assessment and 'self-regulation': the English experience, *Higher Education Quarterly*, 49(4), 326–40.

Wax, M. and Wax, R. (1971) Great tradition, little tradition and formal education, in M. Wax *et al.* (eds) *Anthropological Perspectives on Education*. New York: Basic Books.

Weber, M. (1964) Characteristics of bureaucracy, in L. Coser and B. Rosenberg (eds) *Sociological Theory*. New York: Macmillan (original publication date 1922).

Weick, K. E. (1976) Educational organizations as loosely coupled systems, *Administrative Science Quarterly*, 21(1), 1–19.

Welch, R. (1995) Rise of the managerial cadre, *Times Higher Education Supplement*, 16 June.

Whittington, R., McNulty, T. and Whipp, R. (1994) Market-driven change in professional services – problems and processes, *Journal of Management Studies*, 31(6), 829–45.

Williams, A., Dobson, P. and Walters, M. (1989) *Changing Culture*. London: IPM.

Williams, B. (1991) *The Effects of the New Funding Mechanisms in Universities*. London: Centre for Higher Education Studies, Institute of Education, University of London.

Williams, G. (1984) The economic approach, in B. R. Clark (ed.) *Perspectives on Higher Education: Eight Disciplinary and Comparative Views*. Berkeley, Los Angeles: University of California Press.

Williams, P. (1993) Total quality: some thoughts, *Higher Education*, 25, 373–5.

Williamson, O. E. (1975) *Markets and Hierarchies: Analysis and Anti-Trust Implications*. New York: Free Press.

Winstanley, D., Sorabji, D. and Dawson, S. (1995) When the pieces don't fit: a stakeholder power matrix to analyse public sector restructuring, *Public Money and Management*, 15(2), 19–26.

Winter, R. (1993) The problem of educational levels (Part I), *Journal of Further and Higher Education*, 17(3), 90–104.

Winter, R. (1994a) The problem of educational levels (Part II), *Journal of Further and Higher Education*, 18(1), 92–106.

Winter, R. (1994b) Work-based learning and quality assurance in higher education, *Assessment and Evaluation in Higher Education*, 19(3), 247–58.

Winter, R. (1995) The University of Life, plc: the 'industrialization' of higher education?, in J. Smyth (ed.) *Academic Work*. Buckingham: SRHE and Open University Press.

Winter, R. and Maisch, M. (1996) *Professional Competence and Higher Education: the ASSET Programme*. London: Falmer Press.

Withers, R. (1995) Quality assessment: two traditions (a review article), *Quality Assurance in Education*, 3(2), 39–46.

Witzel, M. L. (1991) The failure of an internal market: the Universities Funding Council bid system, *Public Money and Management*, 11(2), 41–8.

Wolcott, H. F. (1981) Confessions of a 'trained' observer, in T. S. Popkewitz and B. R. Tabachnick (eds) *The Study of Schooling*. New York: Praeger.

Wolpert, L. (1995) Descent into darkness, *The Guardian*, 17 August.

Woodsworth, A., Maylone, T. and Sywak, M. (1992) The information job family: results of an exploratory study, *Library Trends*, 41(2), 250–68.

Woollard, A. (1996) Bureaucrat's dilemma, *Times Educational Supplement*, 23 February, 17.

Worley, J. and Follett, B. (1995) The man who gets things done, *Library Manager*, 12, 20–3.

Wright, A. (1994) The university in the community, in National Commission on Education, *Universities in the Twenty-First Century – a Lecture Series*. London: NCE and CIHE.

Yarwood, D. L. (1995) Humour and administration: a serious inquiry into unofficial organizational communication, *Public Administration Review*, 55(1), 81–90.

Yeomans, K. (1995) Access to a life-long college, *Times Higher Education Supplement (Multimedia Features)*, 12 May.

Yorke, M., Cooper, A., Fox, W., Haines, C., McHugh, P., Turner, D. and Woolf, H. (1996) Patterns of marks in modular schemes, and some implications, in S. Fallows *et al.* (eds) *Modularization and Semesters*. London: Kogan Page.

Young, M. F. D. (1971) Introduction, in M. F. D. Young (ed.) *Knowledge and Control*. London: Macmillan.

Zemsky, R. (1993) Consumer markets and higher education, *Liberal Education*, 79(3), 14–17.

Ziman, J. (1991) Academic science as a system of markets, *Higher Education Quarterly*, 45(1), 41–61.

Zuber-Skerritt, O. (1992) *Professional Development in Higher Education: a Theoretical Framework for Action Research*. London: Kogan Page.

Zuboff, S. (1988) *In The Age of the Smart Machine*. New York: Basic Books.

Index

The Society for Research into Higher Education

The Society for Research into Higher Education exists to stimulate and coordinate research into all aspects of higher education. It aims to improve the quality of higher education through the encouragement of debate and publication on issues of policy, on the organization and management of higher education institutions, and on the curriculum and teaching methods.

The Society's income is derived from subscriptions, sales of its books and journals, conference fees and grants. It receives no subsidies, and is wholly independent. Its individual members include teachers, researchers, managers and students. Its corporate members are institutions of higher education, research institutes, professional, industrial and governmental bodies. Members are not only from the UK, but from elsewhere in Europe, from America, Canada and Australasia, and it regards its international work as among its most important activities.

Under the imprint *SRHE & Open University Press*, the Society is a specialist publisher of research, having some 60 titles in print. The Editorial Board of the Society's Imprint seeks authoritative research or study in the above fields. It offers competitive royalties, a highly recognizable format in both hardback and paperback and the world-wide reputation of the Open University Press.

The Society also publishes *Studies in Higher Education* (three times a year), which is mainly concerned with academic issues, *Higher Education Quarterly* (formerly *Universities Quarterly*), mainly concerned with policy issues, *Research into Higher Education Abstracts* (three times a year), and *SRHE News* (four times a year).

The Society holds a major annual conference in December, jointly with an institution of higher education. In 1993, the topic was 'Governments and the Higher Education Curriculum: Evolving Partnerships' at the University of Sussex in Brighton. In 1994, it was 'The Student Experience' at the University of York and in 1995, 'The Changing University' at Heriot-Watt University in Edinburgh. Conferences in 1996 include 'Working in Higher Education' at Cardiff Institute of Higher Education.

The Society's committees, study groups and branches are run by the members. The groups at present include:

Teacher Education Study Group
Continuing Education Group
Staff Development Group
Excellence in Teaching and Learning

Benefits to members

Individual

Individual members receive:

- *SRHE News*, the Society's publications list, conference details and other material included in mailings.
- Greatly reduced rates for *Studies in Higher Education* and *Higher Education Quarterly*.
- A 35 per cent discount on all SRHE & Open University Press publications.
- Free copies of the Proceedings – commissioned papers on the theme of the Annual Conference.
- Free copies of *Research into Higher Education Abstracts*.
- Reduced rates for conferences.
- Extensive contacts and scope for facilitating initiatives.
- Reduced reciprocal memberships.
- Free copies of the *Register of Members' Research Interests*.

Corporate

Corporate members receive:

- All benefits of individual members, plus
- Free copies of *Studies in Higher Education*.
- Unlimited copies of the Society's publications at reduced rates.
- Special rates for its members, e.g. to the Annual Conference.
- The right to submit application for the Society's research grants.

Membership details: SRHE, 3 Devonshire Street, London WIN 2BA, UK. Tel: 0171 637 2766. Fax: 0171 637 2781 *Catalogue*: SRHE & Open University Press, Celtic Court, 22 Ballmoor, Buckingham MK18 1XW. Tel: (01280) 823388.

HUMAN RESOURCE MANAGEMENT IN HIGHER AND FURTHER EDUCATION

David Warner and Elaine Crosthwaite (eds)

The major element of the budget of all educational institutions is spent on people. Their management and motivation is a prime concern of educational managers. At a time of unprecedented changes, this book provides the first ever comprehensive coverage of the key aspects of human resource management – central to the success of every educational institution.

Human Resource Management in Higher and Further Education has been written by a team of senior educational managers, academics and external experts. They examine the current major issues and future challenges; reflect and explore the trend toward greater managerialism; and include helpful case studies as well as analytical accounts of the topics covered. This is an essential guide to all the important areas of human resource and personnel management as they relate to further and higher education institutions.

Contents
Setting the scene – Managing change – Developing a human resource strategy – Managing diversity – The learning organization – Effective communication – Managing and rewarding performance – Executive recruitment – Essential employment law – Making educational institutions safer and healthier – Developing managers – Industrial relations strategies and tactics – Managing information – Bibliography – Index.

Contributors
Jo Andrews, David Bright, Elaine Crosthwaite, Emily Crowley, Diana Ellis, David House, Peter Knight, Elizabeth Lanchbery, Patricia Leighton, John McManus, Geoffrey Mead, Rebecca Nestor, Jennifer Tann, Elizabeth Walker, Roger Ward, David Warner, David Watson, Bill Williamson.

224pp   0 335 19377 3 (Paperback)   0 335 19378 1 (Hardback)